THE MAGIC OF FORGIVENESS

THE MAGIC OF
FORGIVENESS

Emotional Freedom and Transformation at Midlife

TIAN DAYTON, Ph.D.
Author of the bestselling
Daily Affirmations for Forgiving & Moving On

Health Communications, Inc.
Deerfield Beach, Florida

www.hcibooks.com

Library of Congress Cataloging-in-Publication Data

Dayton, Tian.
    The magic of forgiveness : emotional freedom and transformation at midlife /
Tian Dayton.
        p. cm.
    Includes bibliographical references.
    ISBN-13: 978-0-7573-0086-8
    ISBN-10: 0-7573-0086-3
    1. Middle aged women—Psychology.   2. Middle age—Psychological aspects.
    3. Self-actualization (Psychology)   4. Forgiveness.   I. Title.

    HQ1059.4.D397 2003
    30.244—dc21

                                                                    200301710

HCI, its logos and marks are trademarks of Health Communications, Inc.

Publisher: Health Communications, Inc.
            3201 S.W. 15th Street
            Deerfield Beach, FL 33442-8190

R-02-06

Cover design by Lisa Camp
Cover illustration ©2003 Jean Douglas
Inside book design by Lawna Patterson Oldfield

To Mom,
With Love
and
Understanding

Ultimately, make it your goal to move on to forgiveness of yourself and those causing you pain in the past. Forgiveness doesn't mean that what happened to you was acceptable. It simply means that you are no longer willing to allow a past injury to keep you from living fully and healthfully in the present.

~CHRISTIANE NORTHRUP, M.D.
THE WISDOM OF MENOPAUSE

Contents

Acknowledgments

Okay, I admit it, I don't really love writing acknowledgment pages. I'm always afraid I'll leave someone out, and I will look, horrified at the finished book and it will be too late to fix it. The other reason is that I am painfully aware that a book passes through more hands and hearts than can ever fit on an acknowledgment page, no matter how carefully written—even if I say I'll try to remember the most important people, it's full of pitfalls. But here goes, my best attempt for this book, to say thank you to those who have been helpful in getting *The Magic of Forgiveness* to you, the reader.

This book was the idea of Peter Vegso, publisher of Health Communications. I got a call from him sometime after breakfast over a year ago. He asked me if I wanted to do another book on forgiveness, as a companion book to my bestseller to date, *Daily Affirmations for Forgiving & Moving On*, which I wrote in 1992. When I wrote that book, research showed that people didn't buy books with "forgiveness" in the title. Research was evidently wrong. Many people, it turned out, struggle with the issue of forgiveness. I think this is so, because deep down we intuit that it is in forgiveness that we will find our real emotional freedom. That is the spiritual, emotional and psychological intersection where we will find the truth that will set us free. That is where even our bodies will be able to let go of whatever we're holding onto that is pulling us down and robbing us of our joy. So I agreed to do it. It's a great subject and one in which I'm already obviously interested. One that I witness clients struggling with on a day-to-day basis. One on which I have received the most touching letters of my career. I will never forget the workshop I gave, after which a woman came up to me with a book that was literally in pieces, barely held together by a rubber band, and asked me to sign it. It was so used by her that I couldn't even read the cover, but it was *Daily Affirmations for Forgiving & Moving On*. She told me, "I never knew someone could understand how I felt from inside, it was like you were living in my skin." That's why I had to say "yes" to writing this book. I had to keep pursuing a subject that was important to so many people, and I was sure it would be good for me, too. After September 11, it also just seemed to be the right subject to explore.

Christine Belleris, my old friend and editor at Health Communications, and I traveled a journey with this book—from its being a book on forgiveness to a book on forgiveness for women to a book on forgiveness for women in midlife. Current brain research that I found convinced both of us that this book had to be designed for us, all of our friends and all the midlife women that we knew. This was the book that could explain what was going on with us emotionally, psychologically and physically, and point a path toward using this changing, shifting time of life to grow, to come alive spiritually and to understand the deeper nature of relationships. And we knew, women being what we are—keepers of the hearth and explorers of wisdom—that once we got the message, we would pass it along to those we loved. We would get it to pay forward. Lisa Drucker, this book's primary editor, was a constant creative companion and source of support on what felt like a very important journey, I hope to both of us. Thank you, Lisa, you have been wonderful.

I also need to acknowledge Jean Douglas, the artist who painted the image on the cover. No one could be more generous and pleasant to work with, and I truly appreciate her throwing herself into creating an image that worked graphically and that, as a painter of considerable sophistication, she could live with artistically. It felt like it told the story to me, and I am ever grateful.

I further need to acknowledge Kimberly Peck for all of her hard work in the preparation of the first manuscript, and enthusiasm for (a burgeoning midlifer herself) and interest in the subject. Thanks also to Lawna Patterson Oldfield for her exacting and creative typesetting of the insides of this book. A book can abound with good information, but if it isn't readable and attractive, the material feels too dense. Lawna did a wonderful job of presenting this material beautifully.

And the person I want forever to acknowledge as being the cornerstone upon which everything else in my life has been built, including forgiveness, is my husband, Brandt. Our partnership over the past thirty years has given us two wonderful people we are lucky enough to call our children, as well as each other and ourselves. No one could remain happily married or in a compatible family for a long time without learning and practicing forgiveness on a daily basis. William Blake says it best, "And throughout all eternity, I forgive you, you forgive me."

Author's Note

All the case studies and letters in this book are composites of real stories and from real people. In all cases, names have been changed to protect privacy and guarantee anonymity.

The generosity of those who have allowed their stories to be shared brings depth and life to these pages, and I hope honors their experiences.

Introduction: Making Peace with the Past to Live in the Present

Few of us on our deathbeds say, "I wish I'd held onto a little more resentment, taken a bit longer to let go of old pain or nursed a grudge more fervently." Relationships are what we remember. Did I love and was I loved? Did I let go of hate in time to enjoy the pleasure that could have been mine?

Mark Twain felt that we never really understand life until we face death, that we don't see the full picture until we live long enough to know what life is really all about. In fact, he suggested it might be helpful if we could "start out dead," and that way we could save a lot of time, getting to where we need to ultimately end up much sooner. With his trademark humor, he made a rather useful suggestion. If we project ourselves out a few decades, if we see life, the world and our relationships from the clarity of knowing we will one day lose them, will the thing we're obsessing about feel all that important? Is it worth what it is doing to our insides, the quality of our emotional and psychological lives, and the peace and comfort of our relationships to hang onto hurt, resentment and anger?

Forgiveness is a process, not an event. But simply because we think it would be a nice thing to do to forgive doesn't mean it's easily accomplished. We plow through layers on our way to forgiveness of ourselves or anyone else, predictable stages similar to the grief process. Forgiveness is really a verb; it requires us to *work*. But why would any rational, self-respecting person forgive a wrong done to them for any reason? After all, won't that open us up to more pain? Won't we be, in effect, saying it wasn't that bad, that what happened was somehow okay?

How can forgiveness be a self-respecting act when it clearly could put us in harm's way all over again? Here's how: Forgiveness allows us to take the power into our own hands, whether we're forgiving our own mistakes or another person's.

Our peace of mind is of more value than any particular act, forgivable or not, committed by another person. I drag my emotional state around wherever I go, and if what I'm dragging around is full of pain, anger, hurt or resentment, it's with me all the time. Period. Nowhere to go. It becomes who I am. So by hanging onto the inevitable resentment and rancor associated with not working through something and letting it go, I incorporate those feelings into my own self, my own thoughts, my own emotions. They become part of me, part of who I am. Because who I am is a brilliantly woven mosaic of genetics and the sum total of my experiences. And even more important than my experiences is the meaning that I make of my experiences, because that's the "how-to book" I write that drives my life.

If I'm the one who's holding onto resentments, then I'm the one who's causing myself continual pain. Forgiveness lets me take things into my own hands, rather than live at the other end of someone else's mistakes. I'm calling the hurtful issues what they are and deciding to do what I need to do to move on in spite of whether or not the other person is capable of acknowledging the situation. In this way, "forgiveness is the ultimate revenge," as Josh Billings says. I'm getting out whole and intact. I'm empowering myself to act in my own self-interest. Rather than waiting for another person to change so I can feel better, I'm letting myself feel better all on my own. If this seems to let someone else off the hook (or even lets me off the hook), then so be it. And if it's me that I'm forgiving, is that so wrong? So many of us just can't forgive ourselves. We hold things against ourselves to the extent that it literally undermines our health and our joy in living. Does it really benefit anyone—ourselves or those we love—if we lock ourselves into a cycle of self-blame and self-recrimination? There's a big difference between holding ourselves accountable for our actions in a mature way and tearing ourselves up inside. Owning up to our mistakes and taking responsibility for them is a good thing; condemning ourselves and beating ourselves up inside benfefits no one.

Forgiving requires deep emotional work, but this is precisely why it is so worthwhile. If we truly and sincerely wish to have a forgiving mind-set as a part of our lives, then we are setting the wheels in motion to do all the internal processing this will require, like working through resentments, and consciously looking for positive meaning through suffering. It is not the one-time act of forgiving that we are going for; it is the gain from the psychological and emotional work that will allow us to develop a fuller and deeper connection with self, others and a power greater than ourselves.

Forgiveness is the ultimate statement of self-love. If I love myself I don't want to do things to hurt myself or another person. Some things aren't within our control, but forgiveness is. We can't always make sure we don't get hurt, but we can have much to say about how we react to getting hurt and how we deal with it when we hurt another. The beauty of forgiveness as an overall goal in our lives and relationships is that it motivates us to confront and move beyond our own inner blocks.

THE MIDLIFE WOMAN

Beginning in perimenopause and throughout menopause, women's brains are being rewired in ways that will doubtless sound only too familiar to you. The parts of the brain that are being constantly stimulated are the ones having to do with the storage and processing of painful memories, including feelings of anger and sadness, *and* the pituitary gland often referred to as the "God Spot" (the part of the brain that we try to stimulate in meditation and which produces states of calm, serenity and self-reflection [more on this part II]). So if you find memories and feelings from hurtful episodes in childhood, that painful divorce or your turbulent adolescence wafting across your mind and heart—along with those few gray hairs and an extra wrinkle or two—you're right on schedule. Welcome to midlife.

Midlife woman finds herself at the crossroads of a strange and beautiful journey. Many women at this stage of life report an increased urge to "look within for answers," carve out more time for quiet and reflection, and take time just to "smell the roses." Having accomplished her biological mandate to create a home and bear and nurture children into adulthood, she is ready to spend some time nurturing herself. What better time to clean our emotional houses; to look inside and use the biological shifts that are encouraging us to feel and heal old wounds so that we can ready ourselves for and be present to the riches that await in the second half of our lives—which, thanks to thirty years recently (and unusually) being added to our lives, we can now look forward to. With the confidence, self-awareness and understanding that we can and have endured and thrived, we may be in the best position ever to reflect on those issues and situations that in the past may have felt overwhelming or like too much to get into. Besides, who had the time for self-reflection when there were lunches to be made, kids to chauffeur around, careers to build, partners to keep happy, and countless other details that consumed our lives and kept our focus ever elsewhere. Now, when the dust settles, here we are with ourselves, and all that that contains. Life is offering us a new and different challenge: to live more consciously, to use our newfound time and energy to resolve old issues and move into the next stage of living with greater freedom and awareness.

This is not to suggest for a moment that forgiveness is simple to do or that we can arrive at it easily. Not even saints can. Deep hurt requires deep forgiveness, and deep forgiveness requires soul-searching. This may include passing again and again through a cauldron of steaming feelings that arise out of a septic emotional wound, and examining and reexamining the thinking and feeling that wrapped themselves around our psychological and emotional development.

For the woman who decides to travel the path of working through these types of issues toward acceptance, integration and letting go, there will be lifelong rewards. She will be creating a reservoir of calm and caring within herself from which she can draw sustenance throughout all her days, gathering the tools and garnering the skills and wisdom she will need at every stage of the process. She'll free up the energy that's been tied up in holding down pain and resentment, and then she can reinvest that energy in whatever ways she chooses.

AN EVOLUTION OF THE PSYCHE

I have become convinced that we are evolving into more conscious beings, attaining increasingly higher states of consciousness, and that, for women, midlife transformation is part of the plan (probably with a parallel process for men). What was once the province of a few seems now to be the desired state of many. Young people today often have a level of emotional literacy that my generation had to work very hard to achieve. We raised them with greater awareness of their emotional needs and desires, and so this understanding has been slowly incorporated into them over time, and they are already improving on what we taught them.

Our current world presents some very unique challenges. Evolution during the Ice Ages was speeded up, as humans met the harsh and complicated challenges of survival in a world that made life difficult. Likewise, today's world is changing very rapidly. It simultaneously shrinks and expands through technology, bringing us together and pulling us apart, blasting us with more information than any time in history. It is a world pressing us toward change on every level. Survival of the fittest is rapidly transforming into "survival of the wisest" (or the most creative). The psychological, emotional and spiritual challenges we face are constantly demanding that we understand and incorporate new information and points of view. Cultures have collapsed into each other, and the distance between the races has shortened more in the last twenty years than in centuries. Women's roles have expanded to incorporate what was once thought to be male terrain, psychologically and emotionally, as well as physically. The workplace is transforming to include a feminine sensibility, while the homefront incorporates a male perspective. We find ourselves doing the complicated work of untangling centuries of cultural, social and gender issues so that we can live more peacefully and fruitfully in our evolving constellations of social and personal roles and relationships. Forgiveness can be culturally validated or invalidated as collective resentments get passed along from generation to generation and become ever more complicated to deconstruct. We see evidence of this every time we pick up a newspaper or turn on the TV.

In this book, we will focus on forgiveness in interpersonal relationships, primarily those with parents and/or spouses, the types of issues that tend to get restimulated in midlife. And these more intimate issues are what, as a psychologist, I primarily deal with in my practice. As women, we have such an important role to play, because "the hand that rocks the cradle" really does rule the world, or at least profoundly impact it. As the Hindus say, "the mother's lap is the child's first classroom."

THE SPLIT BETWEEN PSYCHOLOGY AND SOUL

Psychology has long ignored the soul. And forgiveness has been seen as belonging to the realm of religion. But when we divide ourselves up into neat, antiseptic little compartments, sending our body to a doctor, our minds to school, our emotions to a therapist and our souls to religious institutions, we invite internal disconnects. We tell ourselves that certain parts of us are only allowed to show up by themselves, that our mind and body are disconnected from one another and our souls are even further away. But, in truth, they are all connected and each affects the other. What we think and feel shows up in our bodies, and our spirituality (or lack of it) influences everything, from how we live to how we die. The human being is still one of the most exquisite creations in the universe, so complicated that we tend to divide ourselves up to better understand ourselves. But when we divide ourselves up, we understand ourselves in part only. The mind, body, emotions and spirit were meant to function together. And forgiveness is no exception; it, too, is meant to balance and counterbalance other internal states.

But forgiving to be some sort of a "goody-goody" just doesn't work. Forgiving to be better than the next guy, rather than serving to reconnect us, asks the relationship to hold a kind of falseness. It doesn't work either. Forgiving to get the power back in your camp is a temporary solution at best. People are smarter than that. Even if we don't say it, we smell a rat, and part of us waits for the truth to reveal itself. But the kind of forgiveness that comes from the heart, that taps into the wisdom and depth of unseen realms, that is born of a sincere wish to understand and grow, the kind that is humble and recognizes that none of us is perfect, is the kind that *does* work. It restores inner peace and grows soul.

Now, a few words explaining the structure of the book. Part I begins by showing the connection between forgiveness and relationships. How does a forgiving attitude contribute to living in our relationships in a more peaceful, happy way, and how does that benefit our physical, emotional and spiritual health: How, in other words, does it impact our biology? How does midlife open a biological, and thereby an emotional, door for women to reexamine and resolve past issues so that we can live and love more fully in the present? What are the predictable stages that we go through as we travel the path of forgiveness and what can we expect to encounter on our journey?

Read this book in order or flip to the stage that you're feeling stuck in for comfort and connection. Then, after you've explored where you are, dive into the rest of the material to find out how you got there and how you can get out. The breakdown into stages makes the process manageable and helps with that overwhelming "I don't know where to start" feeling. The exercises in part II give us a chance to really personalize the process and feel we're actively doing something with our thoughts and feelings around the issues we're dealing with. It's a modern version of the turn-of-the-century ladies' journal that was part of every woman's life in an era when they understood the power of the written word. Part II is where we have a chance to roll up our sleeves and sink our hands into the tools and techniques of forgiveness. It is divided up into sections that correspond to part I, so that you can read the book either from cover to cover, or flip from narrative to tools and exercises related to a specific stage or topic. This flexibility of format will be particularly important for you when you use the book as a sourcebook for addressing the variety of forgiveness issues throughout your life. Also in part II are affirmations (both ones created for this book and from my previous book, *Daily Affirmations for Forgiving & Moving On,* now a companion book to this one) to support and inspire you, as we walk together along the path of forgiveness, one day at a time.

PART ONE

THE PATH TO FORGIVENESS: UNDERSTANDING THE PROCESS

MYTHS ABOUT FORGIVENESS

If I forgive, my relationship with the person I'm forgiving will definitely improve.

If I forgive, I'll no longer feel angry at that person for what happened.

If I forgive, I forgo my right to hurt feelings.

If I forgive, it means I want to continue to have a relationship with the person I'm forgiving.

If I forgive, it means I'm condoning the behavior of the person I'm forgiving.

If I haven't forgotten, I haven't really forgiven.

I only need to forgive once.

I forgive for the sake of the other person.

Forgiving myself is selfish or wrong.

It isn't important to forgive myself.

ONE

Healing Our Relationships

In a way, forgiving is only for the brave. It is for those people who are willing to confront their pain, accept themselves as permanently changed, and make difficult choices. Countless individuals are satisfied to go on resenting and hating people who wrong them. They stew in their own inner poisons and even contaminate those around them. Forgivers, on the other hand, are not content to be stuck in a quagmire. They reject the possibility that the rest of their lives will be determined by the unjust and injurious acts of another person.

~BEVERLY FLANIGAN
FORGIVING THE UNFORGIVABLE: OVERCOMING THE LEGACY OF INTIMATE WOUNDS

No one is perfect. When we try to be perfect, we wind up feeling like a perennial failure; and when we insist on perfection in our relationships, we doom them from the start. Perfection is a fantasy, a flight from reality, a fairy tale, albeit a beautiful one at times. Forgiveness, of ourselves and others, allows us to embrace our own or other people's imperfections, so that we can release pain and feel pleasure—so that we don't undermine our experience of joy.

Forgiveness, on all levels, whether you're forgiving the person who nudged ahead of you in the grocery line or your mother for ignoring you as a child, is relational in nature; it is about either restoring a relationship connection in the real world or restoring the connection that lives inside the self. Relationships are core to the world in which we all operate.

Forgiveness forces us to deal with whatever issues are blocking our ability to relate or to be comfortable with our own insides, and that's where the healing is. If our motivation is to forgive another person, then we've set the bar very high. It means the internal work doesn't stop until we can stand thinking about or being in the presence of that person without wanting to wring his or her neck. Stopping the work when we get emotional distance isn't enough—though true forgiveness paradoxically gives us that distance. Nor is stopping the work at giving up the fantasy of ever getting what we wanted, or still want, from the relationship and taking responsibility for filling that gap ourselves and moving on with our lives. Though true forgiveness ultimately can take us there, too. Nor is it stopping the work at shoring up the self, feeling deserving of all the good life has to offer and going after it or accepting it when it comes. Forgiveness asks us to go all the way. All the way through the self toward the other and back again. That's why it's so powerful and healing. It goes full circle. It is often motivated by a growing awareness that the bitterness and rancor we may carry toward another person are doing more to harm us than them. We begin to question whether nursing a grudge or waiting in the wings for our moment of revenge is worth the calories we're burning by feeling the hate and hurt living inside us. Entertaining ideas of forgiving another person actually makes us more aware of ourselves. This may seem like a paradox because forgiveness appears to be aimed outside the self toward another person, but in truth, identity is fluid, not static, and incorporates, at least to some extent, pieces of those who raised us.

In our childhood developmental stages, we take in, at least in part, the personalities, points of view, morality and belief structures of those closest to us, and we incorporate them into our own character structure. They become a part of our internal world. Our self-image is, at least in part, formed by the reflected appraisals of others. We internalize the way those close to us *see* us or *are* with us, and that becomes incorporated into how we see or are within ourselves. Nature and nurture work together in a dynamic fashion to form a neural imprint that builds on our genetic structure, impacting the creation of "us." Our biology is not static. Each tiny interaction we have with our caretakers affects our neural wiring. They are the neural bricks that build the foundation of who we are. The *nature-versus-nurture* argument reflects a kind of black-and-white thinking that is anathema in nature. Nature is much deeper and wiser than that. We come into this world with a genetic predisposition, and from that point on, nature and nurture interact every step of the way to develop an ever-evolving work of art: us. Our limbic systems, which we will delve into in chapter 2, have carefully recorded our emotional interactions and ways of being with those close to us, causing us to go into the world with those attractors as our biological gravity, pulling toward us those with patterns that in some way correspond to ours. The story of who we are is recorded on our corpus, and continues to be recorded as we move through life. It has much to do with defining who we are and who we choose to be with, and it continues to be written as we live inside our intimate relationships.

This is where the line between self and relationship naturally blurs. Our wish to see the self as completely independent and having little to do with those around us is as unrealistic as our fantasy that we can fuse with others and become them. People exist in a context. To deny the impact that others have on *our* sense of basic security and neural wiring does not bring us strength; it only distorts our own picture of ourselves.

We can view our drive toward forgiveness as an attempt to restore equilibrium within the self and/or the system in which we live. This doesn't mean that we should encourage a premature, false sort of forgiveness. Nothing rings less true than people who force a sickeningly sweet smile and feign forgiveness. Even if they believe it themselves, others rarely do. We sense that their smile is hiding anger, or even contempt, and we instinctively don't trust it. If we deny our authentic feelings, be they wrong or right, we deny part of ourselves. We make those around us feel crazy—they hear one thing but sense another. We force the emotions we're not looking at into the basement of our psyches. They will inevitably find their way back upstairs. The more we have psychological constructs that disallow our own negative feelings, the more those negative feelings get played out in toxic ways. Forcing forgiveness is like forcing any other deep emotion, such as love. If it's not there, it's not there.

If we sincerely wish to forgive someone for a wrong we feel they have done us, we need to be willing to examine the ramifications of that wrong as it has impacted us. If we're angry and pretend we're not, then our mouths are saying one thing but the rest of us is carrying a different message. There is no short-cutting this process. Most of us have to flail around for a while, feeling angry, hurt and betrayed, explore our wish for revenge, and eventually recognize it's probably in our own best interest to work toward some kind of forgiveness so that we don't perpetuate negative feelings in our own homes, friendships or workplaces (to say nothing of our bodies, hearts and minds).

Forgiveness is hard work. We may need to nurse a grudge before we become willing to let it go. It may be critical for own sanity and sense of self to experience the full extent of our rancor for some time before we can consider getting past it. We may have to grieve what happened, or never had a chance to happen, before we can move along in our process and come to terms with the feelings we carry toward ourselves or whatever our part might have been in setting up a painful relationship dynamic. Even if we've been innocent victims, we may still carry a sense of irrational culpability and blame, imagining that, "if only we'd been stronger, wiser, sharper, tougher," we could have kept harm at bay; or if we'd played our part somehow differently, we wouldn't be where we are now. Many innocent victims carry these feelings of irrational guilt, and even though what happened may have in no way been their fault, they may have been left to make sense of it with only the developmental equipment available to them at the time the hurtful situation was happening. They may not only need to grieve the wrong, but also rediscover the wounded little person inside of them, who will have to come to terms with having been hurt in a way that can't be undone, per se. The undoing or reworking will come not from denying or rewriting the original set of wrongs, but from honestly exploring the effect they had on forming who we are today. So the forgiveness of both ourselves and another person will arrive, if it arrives, as a by-product of facing the painful issues that are blocking our ability to move forward in our lives. There is a broad continuum along which our individual forgiveness issues might fall. Getting past the pain resulting from serious situations will require deeper work for a longer period of time, while smaller hurts may require no time at all to let go of. It all depends on where our individual issues fall within the continuum, on how serious the offense was or is.

Forgiveness is a sort of umbrella organization for powerful emotions within the self or directed toward others. It is a way of living that keeps us honestly confronting the petty grievances or significant wounds that keep us in a state of emotional fight, flight or freeze. It is a motivator for examining ourselves and our relationships, inspiring us to keep them clean and up-to-date, so that we can live within them in an authentic and genuine way; it greases the wheels for overhauling our internal engines and getting emotional tune-ups.

Before my husband and I got married, we attended the wedding of an old friend. The bride's father gave a toast: "There are four little words that I've found very important in preserving peace and happiness in a long-term marriage," he said. "They are 'Thank you' and 'I'm sorry.'" My husband, then boyfriend, and I rolled our eyes. No humor, no poetry, no lifelong soul mate, just "thank you" and "I'm sorry"? What could be more dull?

After my husband and I had been married for five years, I found myself saying, "Remember that really boring toast that the father of the bride made at Nat's wedding? I mean it was so one-dimensional, I know, but you know the part about 'thank you' and 'I'm sorry' (self-conscious giggle here)? Well, maybe it wasn't so . . . stupid. I mean, maybe it wasn't altogether the dumbest thing you could possibly say." My husband said he had to agree. Maybe, after five years of marriage he could see a modicum of wisdom in it . . . somewhere.

When we had been married for ten years, my husband turned to me over dinner. "That guy, the 'thank you, I'm sorry' guy . . . well, I kind of think he might have been onto something. Simplistic, I know, but something not altogether off-base." I had to agree.

At about the eighteen-year mark, many wounds and slights later, seemingly at once we both blurted out, "I think that guy hit it on the head. Without 'thank you' and 'I'm sorry,' we wouldn't be sitting here today still loving each other. We would have separated in body or heart because it's impossible not to hurt and be hurt often in a committed relationship and family."

Now, coming up on thirty years of marriage, I imagine myself in the not-so-distant future standing up at one of my own children's weddings and saying, "There are four little words . . ."

It would be impossible to keep one's heart intact or love alive in a long-term relationship if there were no forgiveness. In order to stay connected to another person over a long period, we have to learn to forgive the constant slings and arrows that our flesh is heir to. We have to learn to forgive ourselves for our own inevitable inadequacies, and those we're in relationships with for theirs. Forgiveness in a long-term relationship is by no means confined to affairs or life-altering mistakes. It is an atmosphere, part of each and every day. How we react when our spouse steps on our foot without meaning to, uses up all the fresh towels or burns dinner is part of the climate we live in and create for our children.

Our children grow up in the space between their two parents. What that space contains, they contain. So when we're talking about the climate created by two people, we're talking about the emotional atmosphere lived in by a whole family because, even if parents aren't dictatorial, they are in charge; they set the tone, they teach by their own behavior, they model love and forgiveness, or the lack thereof. This is why the emotional and psychological wounds from childhood have such lifelong resonance. They live in our neural wiring and they get restimulated when, as adults, we reenter the adult arena of intimate relationships. What we don't resolve comes back to haunt us and our children. Confronting the issues that complicate our ability to have healthy, intimate relationships is the greatest gift we can give our children and grandchildren; it pays forward.

Once, my husband and I were sitting in a therapist's office, each of us recounting all the many things we did on behalf of the other and our family. Our lists were endless: "I do all the household stuff, the kids' lives, the toothpaste, the food, the cat . . . you name it, I do it all." "Well, I do all the money management, the bills AND the kids always come to me with their homework, and I walk the dogs . . ." Before we got into our "you never" lists, the therapist interrupted us, "Let me get this straight, so you feel you do about what percent, 40, 50, 60 percent?" "Sixty, definitely." "And how about you?" "Sixty sounds about right." "That *is* about right," replied the therapist, leaning way back in his swivel chair. "Most couples whose relationships work feel, in my experience, that they're each giving around 60 percent."

So maybe a deep, committed relationship isn't just 50–50. Maybe it's 60–60 and it adds up to 120 (a sort of "pregnant" 100), and that's about right.

Another story that always sticks in my mind is one from a friend whose relationship we have grown up alongside. They were talking with each other about some friends who were divorcing, and how many little losses their friends and their friends' children and their friends' relatives and their friends' friends were all feeling, when her husband, usually quite eloquent, was at a loss to find a sentence that could describe why he found it so hard to comprehend all the little things he would have to separate from if he lost his wife. He turned to her and said, "Yeah, but you're my, you're my . . . well . . . but . . . you're my . . . person." Actually, my breath caught in my throat when she told me. "My person." The person with whom I cast my fate to the wind so long ago, who held my future happiness in his hands, who meant more to me than anything, who I followed into what felt like nowhere and everywhere, who I've loved and hated, embraced and rejected. The father of my children, my father and brother and friend. My mother. My lover. The man who has listened to more laughter, silliness and tears than anyone. Who has sustained me and held me and loved me. My cheerleader. My foe who spurs me on and keeps me in perspective. The carrier of my personal history and the story of my life. The horse I bet on a long time ago and won. You're my person. You're the one. To leave you would be to leave big chunks of myself. Who I was, who I am, who I will be.

awesome

Relationships in today's world are increasingly under a microscope. If we aren't getting all our needs met from this one person we've chosen to spend our lives with, we can feel cheated, as if we're in the wrong place. But in my experience, it is not possible to meet most of our needs in one place. Relationships will ebb and flow. They don't need to be perfect in order to be good enough; in fact, wanting them to be perfect can have the inverse effect of making them feel worse than they are. Because we expect so much we set ourselves up for disappointment. This is not to say that we shouldn't want more and be willing to work for it; only to make the point that pop psychology may have created a myth of the perfect relationship that no one has. Coming to terms with what is or is not realistic to expect can free us up to relax and enjoy what we *can* have, and to set out to meet *some* of our needs elsewhere. With thirty years added to the average life span in this century, we're probably better off if we can take responsibility for our own happiness. <u>If we come to our relationship reasonably full inside, we'll tend to be less</u> demanding, which will result in our feeling like we're actually getting more. Another of life's little paradoxes.

❧

To forgive is to set a prisoner free and discover that the prisoner was you.

—Unknown

Lee's Story

*L*ee is a woman in midlife. She grew up in America, but her family is from Taiwan. She has spent her life straddling two cultures, constantly translating everything from dining customs to the role of women, mentally boomeranging back and forth between two ways of living life. A daughter in an Asian family, she felt different from the American girls with whom she grew up. The expectations of her family simply didn't match what she saw going on around her with other little girls. In some ways, she felt lucky, even better than her American counterparts, while in other ways she felt like an outsider looking in, her nose pressed up against the glass of a culture that seemed both foreign and familiar.

Lee was expected to work hard and make use of the opportunities that presented themselves in this land of plenty, to make her parents' constant sacrifices worthwhile and bring dignity and success to her family. Marriage, too, was critical. And to a man with good prospects, one who would maintain her cultural values, who would not encourage her to abandon her family responsibilities. Being a good daughter was paramount within her home and came with considerable expectations. And she tried hard to fulfill them: to be gentle (but tough); kind (but aggressive, when necessary); brilliant; pretty; and good potential-wife material, the kind of girl some lucky man could "take home to his mother." Lee had a busy life and tried hard not to disappoint her parents . . . how could she? They worked so hard and sacrificed so much. They loved her, and she loved them. Self-exploration was not exactly a luxury they had time for; they were busy making a life, and if they carried grief they didn't show it. They did seem to get angry a lot, and Lee's mother had a sort of glaze across her face, but sad things (what they left behind in Taiwan, for example) were only obliquely referred to, not cried about or talked over openly.

So Lee cried for them. She cried her mother's tears and dreamed her mother's dreams. While other little girls were climbing trees and "wasting time" playing after school, Lee was helping her mother, practicing piano and doing her lessons so she would get good grades. And she did. She got As in school, was in the chorus and got into a good college. She married early to a promising young man who was studying law and was from a family they knew. Lee got a job at an advertising firm and worked her way up to an executive position. She was a hard worker and was rewarded for it. At twenty-seven, Lee and her husband started to have children. Her mother helped her so that she could continue to work. After her second child, she worked part-time and then quit to stay home just before giving birth to her third. Everything seemed to be going along as planned, and Lee didn't really question it or think too hard about how happy she was or wasn't. When she felt emptiness between herself and her husband, she just got more involved with her children, and that seemed to fill the void nicely. Her children became everything to her. *Everything.* But as she entered her forties, and they grew up and needed her less, she found herself feeling like her life yawned before her. She feared that she wouldn't be able to fill her future happily. She tried to share these thoughts with her husband, but he couldn't really relate. This was just life, that's all, and she had to learn to accept it. Besides, he was very busy and still had a lot of years left to work at his career; he didn't mind the idea of life being a little less complicated and having his wife pay more attention to him. Couldn't she go back to advertising if she wanted to?

In the extra time created by her home emptying out, along with the biological changes accompanying perimenopause, memories of the hopeful, dutiful little girl she had been began to waft across Lee's mind. She felt a dull pain for that little girl who never got to know herself and the woman who never had her own dreams. When she looked in the mirror, she saw her mother's daughter, not herself. She wondered who she might have been, might have become, if things had been different, if she had been encouraged to have thoughts and feelings all her own, if she had a clue as to who she might be on the inside.

Correspondingly, Lee's husband was experiencing some panic attacks at work and was advised to get therapy. In the course of trying to get on top of these damn, disquieting attacks that were getting in the way of work, he began to discover a person he hardly knew—himself. This made it seem okay, even right, for Lee to consider therapy, too. She had a lot of trouble spending this kind of money on herself, but they had good insurance so she gave it a try. Lee didn't really know how to start talking about herself; she wasn't used to it, her focus had never been there, she'd always been so very busy living the life that was expected of her. When her therapist asked her how she felt about this or that, Lee was sort of dumbfounded. What was that supposed to be all about? Initially it annoyed her, and her therapist seemed nosey, even impolite; but gradually, it came to feel good, to trace the tiny threads, the wistful thoughts that passed across her mind back through time to a little girl named Lee. The words that were never attached to what went on in her inner world as a child could be attached now, and little Lee began to speak through her adult self. She talked on and on about how it felt to be Asian in a white world, to be Mommy's Little Girl in a sea of tomboys, to be practicing piano while other little girls her age were playing kick the can, and to feel the weight of her parents' sacrifices all around her when she longed to feel free. But did she long to feel free? She felt guilty even thinking about it because as the feeling arose, so did the visage of her ever-dutiful mother, doing without so many things, defining freedom so differently from what it had come to mean one short generation later. Wasn't she just being spoiled? Wanting more? Shouldn't she be careful of being ungrateful lest she invite an evil eye for her greed? But Lee's memories were part of her consciousness now, invading her otherwise well-organized mind with thoughts of what was, what could or should have been, if only she had known then what she knew now. It was scary, very scary, to go digging around in a past that was long over, turning up all sorts of thoughts that could breed dissatisfaction or make her want what she couldn't have, but here it was happening anyway, in spite of her, it seemed.

Slowly, over time, Lee came to know the language of her own heart and hear the music of her own soul. And when she felt strong enough to open her eyes and see and her mouth to speak, she met her husband . . . parts of him that she had never known before. Both she and the man she had lived her life with had thoughts and feelings that neither had ever shared.

But the real surprise to her was her children. All this time that she had been so focused on them, they had been observing everything about her. There was nothing much she told them that they didn't already know, hadn't already thought about, cried about, giggled about, and come to accept and understand. She had spent so much time loving her family that she hadn't really stopped to be loved herself, to let them love her, to let that feeling in. Knowing herself made her feel calmer inside, more vulnerable and less in need of controlling circumstances, so the love that her family gave her fell on an appreciative heart, a heart that knew its longing for love. She was grateful, so deeply grateful, to have these people in her life, so grateful to have herself back, or here, in some ways, for the first time. That place of fullness inside emptiness. And she hadn't gone anywhere outside herself to get something to fill up on. She had gone inside and met herself, created room and space so that she could feel what she already had.

Many women in midlife go on this sort of inner journey. At first, it can seem terrifying to question long-held values and beliefs, to rock the boat; but often, we find that the journey of self-discovery, though challenging and difficult at times, is the most exciting one of our lifetime, and leads toward greater understanding of ourselves, our relationships and our higher purpose.

In the next chapter, we will explore how our emotions affect our physical health, and why working through painful emotions to more positive ones is health-smart.

TWO

The Health Benefits of Forgiveness

The body remembers what the mind forgets.

~Jacob Levy Moreno

MIDLIFE BIOLOGY AND FORGIVENESS

If along with hot flashes, interrupted sleep and a thickening midsection you are finding your mind wandering back to images and feelings from your childhood or wishing for a few moments of stillness, you are *not* going crazy. You're beginning to experience some of the changes that accompany perimenopause and menopause. More than forty-nine hundred women enter menopause each day, the largest group, thanks to baby boomers, of any time in history. Midlife takes women on a strange and beautiful journey. It places us at a crossroads, sometimes called a "crisis," where we are being biologi-cally urged to assess the life we've lived and ready ourselves for what lies ahead. Like all crises, it holds opportunity, if we can use it as such. Whether it's stimulated by a song, a smell or an old familiar place or object, your memory bank at midlife is being opened by a hormonal key. You may find yourself wanting or needing quiet time to self-reflect, unwind or simply "be" for a little while. You may feel drawn from within or pulled toward inner transformation and spiritual thinking. Or you may feel an increased need to explore your inner depths and the deeper meaning of your life and relationships.

Says Christiane Northrup, M.D., author of *The Wisdom of Menopause:*

Until midlife, a woman characteristically focuses her energies on caring for others. She is encouraged to do so, in part, by the hormones that drive her menstrual cycle—the hormones that foster her instincts for nurturing, her devotion to cohesion and harmony within her world. But for two or three days each month, just before or during our periods, there is a hormonal inter-lude when the veil between our conscious and our unconscious selves is thin-ner and the voice of our souls beckons to us reminding us of our own passions, our own needs, which cannot and should not be subsumed to the needs of those we love. Each month we have the opportunity to tune into our inner-world; in midlife, that veil is lifted all the time.

Northrup goes on to explain how women's brains are "rewired" during perimenopause and menopause to make self-reflection and intuition a primary focus:

. . . for biological reasons, females of the human species are often easier to control intellectually, psychologically, and socially during their childbearing years than they are before puberty (from birth to age eleven) or after menopause. When we are creating a home and building a family, our primary concern is to maintain balance and peace. We seem to know instinctively that when raising a family it's better for all if we compromise and maintain whatever support we have, even if it's less than ideal, rather than risk going it alone. This may mean we lose sight of our individual goals. Our ability to go with the program is in fact protective.

But during menopause (and once a month for pre- and perimenopausal women) our hormones are all over the map. Beginning in perimenopause, GnRH (gonadotropin-releasing hormone), which is produced in the hypothalamus, stimulates FSH (follicle stimulating hormone) and LH (luteinizing hormone), which are produced in the pituitary and stimulate the rise of estrogen and progesterone during the monthly menstrual cycle. At midlife, our "kick switch" for these hormones is on all the time. What can this mean emotionally and psychologically? The hypothalamus is associated with the storage of painful memories. "Sadness consistently activates the ventromedial prefrontal cortex, hypothalamus and brain stem," says Antonio Damasio in *The Feeling of What Happens*. And the hypothalamus is also associated with feeling and expressing anger, according to Norman Rosenthal in *The Emotional Revolution*. The pituitary gland has long been associated with meditation, intuition and higher wisdom. Mystics focus on the pituitary gland during states of meditation. If in midlife both the hypothalamus and pituitary gland are being regularly stimulated, we can easily extrapolate the possible effect. Memories that are associated with feelings of anger and sadness may bubble up to the surface at this time of life. We may also feel a greater need for quiet time, and find that our ability to reflect on these memories and intuit their deeper meaning becomes part of our mental and emotional needs during this period. Exploring our internal world and making meaningful connections that help us understand who we are seems to be the work of midlife. This is how we develop wisdom. Spiritual renewal is happening naturally as our pituitary glands are being stimulated, thereby encouraging meditation and deep self-reflection.

It seems clear enough that nature's purpose for our lives as young women is to nurture offspring and raise families. Less clear is what nature intends for us to do after midlife. It would seem by the way our brains are rewiring themselves that we are being ushered into a place of wisdom and spiritual awareness, if we can process what may be coming to the surface. If you see nature as incorporating a divine plan, all of this makes perfect sense. In the same way that the world needed us to nurture children and keep the hearth as young women, nature may need us to become what George Valliant calls in his book *Aging Well*, "keepers of meaning" as we age.

EMBRACING THE GIFT OF MIDLIFE BRAIN CHEMISTRY

Erik Erikson talks of this period of life as wisdom versus despair. I think this sums up nicely what we're facing as we enter our second half of life. I would, however, reverse it: despair versus wisdom. What we're faced with is the opportunity to work through despair in order to gain wisdom as the fruit of our hard work. Without some sort of personal growth or spiritual program, life, at this stage, may feel confusing or at times lacking in meaning. Some may spend midlife quietly mourning either what happened or what never got a chance to happen, without shifting into their next and higher purpose. But if we step back and look at midlife changes as part of God's or nature's plan, our usefulness to ourselves and society can ripen as we age. In the same manner that society mandated us as young women to care for the young so they could thrive, as older women our communities may need us to guard our emotional and spiritual well-being, comforting and reassuring younger generations, pointing the way to the deeper meaning in life. This was what my grandmother did, and what so many grandmothers do naturally for their families. It nourished us, and it nourished her as well. Using this midlife change to clean out our emotional closets can set us up for a better, more conscious quality of life in ensuing decades.

As old memories rise to the surface of our minds, forgiveness becomes an essential part of moving into the later stages of life. We can imagine the torture of simply churning around in recollections of a painful past that the hypothalamus is naturally pushing forward without a spiritual way out. Forgiveness, or the transcendent function associated with the pituitary gland, offers us that path toward integration and wholeness. Just as with any other type of motivation toward growth, the desire to forgive and move on into a more spiritual time of life encourages us to confront the pain and anger that block it. [Further on in this chapter, we will discuss in detail the biological infrastructure of forgiveness.]

If we divide the question of forgiveness in two, it's easier to work with: One, is it good for me to let go of my negative feelings, toward myself or someone else, so that I can restore my own inner peace? And two, how should I act with the person I'm forgiving? The answer to part one is virtually always yes. The answer to part two varies according to circumstances. Even when we're innocent victims who did nothing to bring harm onto ourselves, we can still carry the irrational feeling that something we did or something we were brought harm to us. We may feel we should have known to get out of harm's way sooner or that we should have fought harder to protect ourselves. Or we may resent feeling victimized. All these feelings can get in the way of our ability to consider forgiveness as an option, or to grant ourselves the right not to forgive without feeling like we're somehow a bad person for not wanting to.

They also get in the way of our ability to forgive ourselves. How we choose to behave with a person we're forgiving needs to be carefully considered. If it's someone who is, because of his or her own problems, likely to continue to hurt us, we may forgive that person, but still wish to severely limit contact with him or her. Because we forgive does not mean we condone or necessarily wish to re-engage. It simply reflects a decision we've made not to live at the other end of a problem that we can get free of and move on.

At other times, we may have our own part in a conflict or hold ourselves irrationally responsible even if we weren't responsible, so forgiving *ourselves* is also important. Until we can do that, forgiveness of another may not hold. We may all live with the fantasy that if we stay mad enough for long enough, eventually, we'll get that person who hurt us to suffer. And this may be true to some extent. But *we* suffer more.

The task and gift of midlife is that we have another chance to let the emotional centers of our brains speak, and see what cognitive meaning we have made of the circumstances of our own lives, which we've been living by and with for the first half of life. It is the care and quality of this reflection that may well have a significant impact on the rest of our lives.

We've added three decades to the average life span in the last century, so some of this is uncharted territory; we're making it up as we go along. But one thing is clear: We're being given a second chance to resolve old wounds. Like it or not, what may lie in our unconscious as unfinished business or unresolved pain will likely bubble to the surface at this time of life.

The Buddhists say that life is a balance between pain and pleasure. If we spend too much time in either one, we get thrown off. Our happiness is impaired if we get stuck in either place, too much light burns and too much darkness destroys our will to live. The Christians put "forgive us our trespasses as we forgive those who trespass against us" immediately after praying to be given "our daily bread" in the Lord's Prayer. Can we infer from this that something about forgiveness of ourselves and others is as important to the life of the spirit as bread is to the body?

The Hindus call this season of life the spiritual one. After the primary tasks of our lives have been accomplished, we can loosen our grip on the life of the householder and move into a spiritual understanding of the deeper meaning of life.

When I was thirty-five, I was diagnosed with cancer. Within five days, I went from being a healthy, young wife and mother with an eight-year-old and a five-year-old to having no uterus at all, my childbearing years cut off and surgical menopause thrust upon me. There was not a lot known then about what the changes of surgical menopause meant. In retrospect, everything changed. Memories of my parents' divorce, my father's alcoholism and all that my family went through protruded themselves into my consciousness. Suddenly, I felt less endlessly patient with the little demands of motherhood, and I felt as if a fire had been lit under me driving me to put huge amounts of energy toward a life's work. My creativity and curiosity surged, along with my driving need to figure out who I was and what my life was supposed to be about. Nearly twenty years, two kids, a thirty-year marriage, twelve books and a whole career as a psychologist later, it's all making sense to me. At thirty-five, I went through what most women go through in their forties and fifties: menopause and all that goes with it. Retrieval, renewal, rewiring and recovering everything from my inner child to my ancient soul.

We will see how the thoughts we think and the emotions we feel directly affect our health. Our sympathetic and parasympathetic nervous systems set us up to respond to situations in our life. "Despite that we've learned a lot about healthy exercise practices, healthy diets, and good medical care, the bottom line is that the most significant way of contributing to our own good health is through the quality of our thought processes. This power is a valuable gift, in light of the lack of control we have over other aspects of life," explains Christiane Northup in *The Wisdom of Menopause.*

In the early 1970s, I went to India to study the relationship between Eastern and Western philosophy and psychology. I stayed, for a while, at a yoga institute on the banks of the Ganges River. Every morning at five, we woke up and began our day with hatha yoga. The various postures that we did were designed to stretch our muscles and balance our sympathetic and parasympathetic nervous systems. After the physical exercises were over, we began breathing exercises, alternating the flow of air into our bodies through our left and right nostrils, the goal being to bring these two systems into balance. Once we had brought our body and mind into balance, we were ready to meditate. The yogis sought attainment of this balance as a means of meeting the challenges of living with internal calm.

The bottom line, according to Northrup, "is that what goes on in your mind boosts either parasympathetic or sympathetic nervous system activity. Every thought and every perception you have changes the homeostasis of your body. Will it be the brakes or the accelerator, a health account deposit or a health account withdrawal?" She goes on:

. . . this, in a nutshell, is how your autonomic nervous system translates how your view of your world impacts the state of your health. The language spoken by the autonomic nervous system is translated to the rest of your body by hormones. The primary messengers of the sympathetic nervous system are hormones called norepinephrine and epinephrine, which are often referred to together as adrenaline. They are produced in the brain and in the adrenal glands. Every time adrenaline levels go up, levels of another adrenal hormone, cortisol, also go up. While cortisol provides a much-needed boost in the short run, helping you get through an occasional crisis, it has its dark side. If you live in the SNS's "fast lane" for a long time, prolonged elevation of cortisol can cause a number of problems. Initially cortisol sparks up your immune system, but if stress keeps the body in a constant state of flight or fight readiness, cortisol's effects on the immune system quickly become a liability. White blood cells get pumped into the bloodstream, flooding the system with germ fighting warriors. Over time, the immune system and the

bone marrow become depleted. Long-term overexposure to cortisol causes your skin to become thin, your bones to become weaker, your muscles and connective tissue to break down, your body to develop abnormal insulin metabolism, your tissues to retain fluids, your arms and legs to bruise more easily, and your moods to tend toward depression.

෯

In these paragraphs, we see how stress undermines physical well-being, both present-day stress from fast-lane living and long-term stress that we carry in our biological systems from our unresolved early life experiences.

WOMEN'S UNIQUE RESPONSE TO STRESS

According to a cutting-edge UCLA study, women have a range of responses to stress that goes beyond *fight, flight, freeze,* to what researchers now call *tend and befriend.* In stressful situations most men and women produce the hormone oxytocin also known as the "touch chemical," the one that makes both people and animals "calmer, more social and less anxious," says the study's main researcher, Shelley E. Taylor. But that's where the similarity ends. The testosterone in men counteracts the calming effects of oxytocin while estrogen enhances it. Oxytocin can also promote maternal behaviors, making women want to grab the children, gather with other women and cluster for safety.

This research may turn on its head our notion of how stress affects men and women, and may also contribute to explaining why women live an average of seven and a half years longer than men. Oxytocin is a calming chemical that leads women to gather, talk and support each other through stress. Conversely, men, with their *stand-and-fight* stress hormones (such as adrenaline), tend to isolate in order to calm down from their unmitigated release. All of this was evolution's way of parceling out roles to maintain a tight "family of man" survival system. This is still more evidence of how women are wired to maintain and protect relationships.

SELF-FORGIVENESS

I think there are at least two types of forgiveness: One is a process of reconciliation with someone with whom one has an ongoing relationship, and both parties want that relationship to continue. The other type involves an injury by someone with whom one is no longer in relationship, and in this case the process is more of a one-sided "releasing."

I question whether the sense of "atonement" (or, at-one-ment) can be achieved in the second case. I even doubt that an absolutely complete or full release is possible—though a partial or significant degree of relief from the near-obsessive burden of resentment can be achieved in many cases.

~Adam Blatner, M.D.

Emotional and psychological pain is held in our bodies, recorded in our neural networks. This is why, when we're scared, anxious or angry, we have physical reactions like muscle tension, stomach churning, shortness of breath, head pounding, and so on. Working through emotional and psychological pain toward forgiveness allows our bodies, as well as our minds, to let go of pain. This is not to say that all physical pain is emotional, but certainly some of it is. Most of us know the feeling of self-recrimination, being mad at ourselves, and how it makes us feel in body, as well as mind.

It's one thing to consider forgiving someone else, but what about all the stuff we're holding against ourselves? Do we owe ourselves the same consideration we may be giving to someone else? There are two manifestations of self-forgiveness that I see clients struggle with. The first is *rational*. When our actions have directly hurt others, and we need to forgive ourselves in order to restore our inner equilibrium and move on in our lives. Addicts, for example, inevitably wound those close to them during their addiction. Until they forgive themselves, they may have trouble staying sober because the guilt and remorse they'll feel will trigger them to want to self-medicate. This is why the amends part of the Twelve Steps is so important: Addicts need to make amends to those they've hurt and take responsibility for their own behavior. The second is *irrational*. We hold ourselves responsible for pain that others have caused us, even though we could do nothing to change the situation and did not deserve to be mistreated. Sure, there is always something we might have done to make a bad situation worse, but the victims of child abuse, spousal abuse or rape did not deserve what their abusers inflicted upon them. The same goes, in my mind, for excessive criticism, manipulation or neglect. Especially for children who are totally dependent on their parents, these can constitute an abuse of authority. And they, too, leave us feeling bad about ourselves and in need of redemption of some sort. For many people, self-forgiveness is the hardest to come by. Often, we're harder on ourselves than we are on other people. The feeling that our actions have caused another person pain can be very uncomfortable. So rather than feel it, we do one of those pathological rewrites we talked about earlier, "What I did wasn't all that bad. They'll get over it." Or maybe, "They're being too sensitive," or "I don't really care if they're in my life, anyway." But even if we tell our minds a story, our bodies usually know the truth of our deeper emotions.

And when it comes to pain that we've internalized from childhood, though whatever happened may not be our *fault*, it is our *responsibility* to work with it and resolve it, and forgiving ourselves is often an important piece of that resolution. Many of the clients I work with get marooned at this juncture, where pain from the past is getting mixed up with pain from the present, causing a sort of psychological and emotional logjam. At some level, they may still believe themselves to be "bad" as the victims of abuse. Though they blame the abuser relentlessly, underneath that is usually the unbearable feeling of the unhealed inner child, that something they did or something they are drew this abuse toward them. In this case, they need to forgive themselves, even if it's only forgiving themselves for being to blame in their own minds:

⁓

Forgive me for holding myself responsible for something that was out of my control as a small child, forgive me for my own self-hatred, for this dark narcissism that holds me in its grip and keeps me glued to a tragic place within myself.

⁓

This is a piece of forgiveness that we sometimes miss. We may feel we did nothing wrong, a friend or therapist may tell us we did nothing wrong, but this does not necessarily fix the deep and negative attitude toward the self that we carry. Our neural systems respond to reparative relationships, not only to insight; healing takes time and new relationships in which we can experience ourselves in different ways and explore new patterns of behavior, as we'll explore later in this chapter.

Until we honestly confront and work through our deeper truths, our bodies will hold us responsible. We may respond to situations in the present day as if the earlier pain were happening all over again. This is often referred to as "getting triggered." We'll meet the situations in our current life, bracing ourselves with our fight/flight/freeze (or tend-and-befriend) apparatus in full gear, assuming, at some unconscious level, that a crisis is at hand. Our adrenal system goes on high alert, and our bodies pump out stress chemicals and experience feelings that accompanied previous hurt, even if none is intended in the current situation. The line between the present and the past blurs, and we feel as if we're being hurt all over again, even though it may be mostly yesterday's pain that's being triggered. But we don't know that; we see it as belonging exclusively to today's offense. We get caught in a negative feedback loop, in which the stress chemicals in our bodies stimulate painful memories, and our painful memories stimulate more stress chemicals. This becomes a place that it's tough to get out of, and our thinking can become distorted and fuzzy. Our bodies and our minds are interacting in a way that sinks us further into a stuck place. This is why we need to resolve deep emotional issues that we may be carrying from our past. Otherwise, we interpret situations today through yesterday's distorted lens—seeing current situations as the sole cause of our emotional and physical upset, placing ourselves repeatedly at that center of our old pain, both physically and emotionally. And if the meaning we make of the situations of our current lives is based upon the meaning we made as helpless children, in circumstances we could do nothing about, we may also live by those old interpretations, whether currently appropriate or not. Our bodies, minds and spirits are living off an old script. Forgiving ourselves, whether or not we're actually at fault, can be harder than forgiving someone else; it makes us feel vulnerable, needy, confused and hurt all over again, but it is critical for full healing to take place.

Think of September 11 and the constant TV replays of the planes crashing into the Twin Towers. Many children across America thought that this disaster was happening over and over and over again. They had no way of understanding, as youngsters with limited capacity for reasoning, that these were instant replays. Their line between reality and replay was blurred. So many of the especially young ones experienced September 11 as being as many days' long as the replays that appeared on our television sets if no adult explained otherwise.

Our child minds are really not much different. They stretch out our past through the landscape of adulthood, replaying over and over again those memories that we found traumatic as youngsters. The adults in our lives may have been too preoccupied with their own pain to help us make sense of a painful situation; or they may have thought that because we were silent or uncomplaining we were not being affected. How often I've heard adults say, "Kids are so resilient." Because children have the capacity to laugh and seemingly let go of pain, we assume they aren't being affected. But nothing could be further from the truth. Children are like sponges, soaking up their environment and holding it in all the tiny spaces they have inside.

The brain is uniquely wired to best remember memories that are powerful in emotional content, whether the memory is of a wonderful clown at a child's fifth-birthday party, the circus with grandparents who made it seem magical, or repeated abuse by an adored or feared relative. However, if the memory was traumatic, the mind also has the capability to block it out, to selectively "forget" what made life as a dependent child feel too threatening. Here is a case in point:

Karen's Story

*K*aren has been working with issues of childhood sexual abuse for as long as she's been in therapy, which is a considerable amount of time. She was in therapy several years before the memories of her abuse could even surface. Karen regularly struggles with depression and moodiness, and she finds herself wanting to isolate herself from others. "I feel stuck here and I can't find my way past it.... I don't even know if I've made this up. You could tell me that I'd made it all up, and I'd say, 'fine.' I fight feelings like, *What kind of person am I who would make this up? Do I want attention? Am I crazy or do I not want to grow up?* This, Karen says over and over again, in spite of corroboration from more than one relative that this abuse regularly occurred. Can forgiveness play a role here in the darkest corner of Karen's heart, the corner that thinks she is a crazy bad girl who only wants to make trouble? The truth is, she may never have more information than she has right now. Somehow, she will have to find a way to "accept the things she cannot change and courage to change the things she can."

Karen's dilemma is that she was getting hurt by the very same people she looked up to. She believed the terrible things they said to her in their out-of-control anger. So she had to make some kind of crazy contract with herself to go on living as a child needing and loving the people who were wounding her. She had to somehow create a sense of safety with the very same people who were putting her in danger. Part of the contract she made as a child was that there was something wrong with her, that she in some way deserved punishment. The other part of the contract was that she was in some way chosen and had a special relationship with the person hurting her, an intimate bond (which, of course, she did have: a limbic bond, which we'll discuss later in this chapter, and a traumatic bond, as a result of her extreme dependency on her abuser and her lack of access to or support from other sources). The convoluted, emotional interplay between feeling chosen, valuable and valueless has left Karen with a confusing legacy. It is her body that remembers the abuse, and reacts, in sexual encounters, by either going numb and being unresponsive, or wanting to scream and push her partner away when touched in certain areas that somehow hold memories of her abuse. In her youth, she acted out her pain by being promiscuous. Today, she experiences her body as shutting down and her emotions as frozen. She has had back problems and a bout with thyroid cancer, and she is rarely free of physical pain of some sort.

HOW EMOTION TRAVELS
THROUGH THE BODY

"The body is the unconscious mind," says Georgetown University research professor Candice Pert in *Molecules of Emotion*. "Repressed traumas caused by overwhelming emotion can be stored in a body part, thereby affecting our ability to feel that part or even move it. . . . [T]here are infinite pathways for the conscious mind to access—and modify—the unconscious mind and the body."

Until recently, emotions have been considered to be location-specific, associated with emotional centers in the brain such as the amygdala, hippocampus and hypothalamus. While these are, in fact, emotional centers, other types of centers are strewn throughout our bodies. Emotions travel through our bodies and bind to small receptors on the outside of cells, much like tiny satellite dishes. There are many locations throughout the body where high concentrations of almost every neuropeptide receptor exist. Nuclei serve as the source of most brain-to-body and body-to-brain hookups. Nuclei are peptide-containing groups of neuronal cell bodies in the brain.

Emotional information travels on neuropeptides and is able to bind to its receptor cells through the binding substance of ligands. The information is sorted through the differentiation of receptors. That is, certain information binds to certain receptors. So our emotions are constantly being processed by our bodies. This clearly paints a dynamic, rather than static, picture of emotional experience. The brain and body are exquisitely intertwined systems that constantly interact with the environment. All five senses are connected to this system and feed information that determines our unique response to anything from petting a soft rabbit to being slapped. The more senses involved in an experience, the more the brain remembers it. The *smell* and *taste* of Grandma's cooking—as well as her gentle *touch*, familiar *voice* and the *sight* of her standing at the stove—all engrave themselves onto our memory systems, along with the feelings associated with them because every sense is involved. The same is true in the case of trauma: Karen remembers the smells of the house in which her abuse occurred, various details of how it looked, along with the sound of her uncle's voice, his touch, the bitter taste of fear in her mouth and how she felt (or shut down feeling) at the time.

One way the commonality among all humans of this mind–body connection can be illustrated is in the study of the universality of facial expressions. Emotions seem to have an inborn genetic mechanism for expression. Whether you are observing Hungarians, Indians, Africans or Eskimos, their facial expressions for anger, disgust, sadness, anticipation and joy will be the same. Not only are we a vast mind–body network for the processing of the everyday emotions we feel, we also carry a genetic coding for experiencing basic emotions. So the emotional system is more or less like the endocrine system, and moves throughout our mind–body.

Darwin felt this system was highly conserved throughout evolution because emotions were so critical to our survival. The cavewoman who got scared when she sensed danger from a potentially threatening animal and removed her baby, whom she wanted to protect and nurture into adulthood, was the one who survived and kept our species alive. She is the DNA strain that led to us.

THE POSITIVE FUNCTION OF FEAR AND ANXIETY

Sometimes, though one part of our bodies is clearly relaxing, another part may still be holding onto stress. This is part of the split between the conscious and the unconscious mind. The following studies show how blocking our anxiety or fear can put us at risk. Fear can be productive in aiding some part of our minds, conscious or unconscious, to prepare for impending events like childbirth or surgery. Larry Dossey, M.D., in his book *Healing Words,* cites these studies that illustrate our need to be aware of feelings like fear so that we can use them to warn us of impending danger or discomfort. In a study done at the University of Cincinnati Medical School, it was discovered that pregnant women who had anxiety-ridden, threatening dream images toward the ends of their pregnancies had shorter, easier labors than those who had only happy thoughts and blocked their fears. "It's as if the threatening dreams are acknowledging the painful event that is to come, while the more pleasant dreams deny that reality, just as perhaps the woman who is dreaming them is denying the pain that will be sure to accompany the birth," surmise Jayne

Gackenbach and Jane Bosveld who conducted the experiment. The women who were unable to block or deny their fears, even if only in their remembered dreams, could better use and integrate them in order to prepare for the pain they were about to experience, and that preparation served them well.

Similarly, British psychologist Anne Manyande of University College in London, "examined blood levels of two stress hormones, adrenaline and cortisol, in patients just before surgery and two days following surgery." The patients were divided into two groups. The patients in the first group were taught relaxation techniques, and had lower blood pressure, lower heart rate and required less pain medication after surgery than the second group, which received no training. *However, their bodies told a story with a significantly differing subplot.* The group who *had* used relaxation techniques had significantly increased levels of the stress chemicals adrenaline and cortisol, while, in the group that received *no* training, the levels for these hormones *did not increase.* In other words, though the "relaxed group" had lower blood pressure, lower heart rates and needed less medication (which is a good thing), their levels of stress, as represented by elevated adrenaline and cortisol went up (which is not such a good thing). Again, the split between the unconscious and conscious mind manifests in the body. Even though we can seem to be in control of our stress response, another part of us clearly is not. The hypothesis of the researchers was that our bodies seem to need a little worry and fear before surgery so that we can accurately plan for potential pain and immobility. Wipe out the worry and fear, and we wipe out some of our conscious connection with the real experience. Our unconscious, however, seems to be aware of what's coming up and expresses *its* fear through elevated levels of stress in the body.

So blocking our ability to experience feelings of, let's say, "normal" fear and anxiety—even with something as seemingly helpful as relaxation techniques—means we can't feel, integrate and interpret their messages to us. Again, in Candice Pert's words, "The body is the unconscious mind." We need access to our authentic feelings so that we can use them to guide us toward what we need to do to resolve our life situations. We need to know how we really feel, or our bodies will let us know in some other way, usually in the manifestation of body aches or dis-ease.

THE POWER OF THOUGHT

What we think about all day becomes who we are. We are the product of our own thoughts, at least to some extent. In a study done to explore the connection between thoughts and their relationship to health, people from similar backgrounds and of similar age were divided into two groups. The first group was repeatedly shown movies of Nazi war acts while the second viewed films of Mother Teresa's work attending to the sick and needy. After viewing for the same length of time, each group was given blood tests. Group one exhibited a reduction in immunity while group two showed elevations in immune function. These results persisted over a period of twenty minutes then returned to normal. When this test was repeated, the testers asked the subjects to continue to "rerun the movies or imagery through your minds throughout the day." When the groups continued to image what they had seen on the screen and allowed it to play in their thoughts throughout the day, the group imaging Nazi war acts experienced a *depressed* immune function *throughout* the day, while the group imaging Mother Teresa showed *elevated* immune functions *throughout* their day.

We are what we think about all day. The thoughts we think stimulate emotions, which stimulate specific biochemical reactions within our bodies. We can't get away from ourselves. And our bodies won't let us get away with negative thinking. Our systems translate our thoughts into biology. Positive mental attitudes and a spiritual foundation, if they themselves aren't overly dogmatic or repressive (which can just give us new ways to feel bad or to split off emotional pain that is unacceptable to our belief system), can help us heal. They give us a way to reframe painful life events as challenges along a path to enlightenment or a closer relationship with God. If we see life as a gift, and are grateful for the opportunity to live, then we are saying yes to all of life—accepting the problematic side and working with it, *and* accepting the easy side and enjoying it.

As in marriage, we are committing ourselves for better or for worse, for richer for poorer, in sickness and in health. Our contract with life is 'til death do us part—and beyond, depending upon our spiritual beliefs. *The meaning we make of the events of our lives can affect our health even more than the events themselves.* Spiritual belief systems also tend to encourage lifting our hearts and minds toward higher thought. The ritual accompanying services, or even Twelve-Step meetings, is designed to elevate us toward a higher plane, to encourage faith and provide a sense of community so we feel that we belong somewhere. That community also allows us to repattern our limbic bonds, as we sit with other people who understand more or less what we're going through and are willing to support us through healing.

One of the powerful effects of trauma is a loss of trust and faith. We lose faith in the people nature intended to sustain us and meant for us to depend upon. This critical loss of connection and trust extends itself into other areas of our lives. Spiritual communities of all sorts help to restore this loss of trust and faith. They reinstate lost or deregulated limbic connections, the bonds that carry emotional relatedness. Our health suffers when we are in a constant state of fear or feeling disconnected from other people. Our health benefits when we can let go, relax and trust, even if we are let down once in a while. Relationships are critical to our sense of well-being. The feeling of connection to other people and belonging has more to do with health and longevity than we may think. In long-term longevity studies done in Alameda, California, it was found that the single most important factor determining how long people lived was their relationships with family, friends and community. This held true even more than cigarette smoking. Making a choice to have relationships in our lives is a choice for good physical health and well-being. The positive impact of secure relationships is undeniable.

But relationships are not easy. Most of us live with the childhood fantasy that if those close to us really loved us, they would put our needs before theirs and see our lives as the most important in the world. We want the parent we had or the one we never had. We want our partners to do for us what we can barely do for ourselves. This does not often happen, and expecting it leads many relationships down the proverbial river of regret.

A more realistic and appropriate understanding of interdynamics with family and/or partners is perhaps to see our relationships as catamarans of a sort. We may not notice as we fly along the top of choppy waters that we are constantly staying in balance with the help of a partner or close, sustaining relationships, but we are. The presence of the other often allows us to navigate the waters of life more comfortably than if they were absent. Solid attachments help us feel secure and provide us with a sense of belonging. The internal security that we carry around with us makes the world feel like a safer place. Knowing that we can come home often enables us to face the world with more courage and less fear of failure because, no matter what happens outside, we have somewhere we belong. This can free us up to succeed in the world, in a way, because we need it less. How the world does or does not receive us is less critical if we have a secure place of our own. This is what a good home provides. When this corner of the world called home gets violated, we will do almost anything, including contorting our reasoning, in order to stay connected to these fundamental relationships, these limbic bonds, that we need in order to feel secure. We will become the perfect daughter, or worse, the scapegoat; or we may sacrifice our own needs in order to fulfill the demands of others. We will even go down with the ship.

But a family that acts as a safe harbor that we can drop anchor in when we want or need to and sail out from to explore the world, that keeps a lighthouse burning so that we can navigate in darkness or find our way back to safety when we're lost at sea, is doing what family is meant to do. It is providing a haven of love and support that we can call home.

We are living in both a difficult and a wonderful time for families. Difficult because technology and other forces pull at the infrastructure of a family from every direction. Wonderful because we are really getting down to the nitty-gritty and cleaning house (if you'll pardon the pun). We're putting our behavior under a microscope and examining it in order to better understand what works and what doesn't work. Though this creates a new set of problems, ultimately, it should enable us to keep pace with a world that is changing at breakneck speed. The family that worked yesterday may not be the one that will work well in today's world. But with faith and commitment, we will find what family structure does work, if we're willing to put in the energy, love and the commitment that it takes. And the forgiveness.

THE ROLE OF THE LIMBIC SYSTEM

Altering deep emotional patterns is slow and painstaking work. Limbic bonds imprint themselves onto our emotional systems. The limbic system "sets the mind's emotional tone, filters external events through internal states (creates emotional coloring), tags events as internally important, stores highly charged emotional memories, modulates motivation, controls appetite and sleep cycles, promotes bonding and directly processes the sense of smell and modulates libido," according to Dr. Daniel Amen, author of *Change Your Brain, Change Your Life*. Our neural networks are not easily altered. "Early emotional experiences knit long-lasting patterns into the very fabric of the brain's neural networks," says Thomas Lewis, M.D., in A *General Theory of Love*. "Changing that matrix calls for a different kind of medicine all together." Our emotional life is physical, imprinting itself on our bodies. When we have problems in our deep limbic system they can manifest in "moodiness, irritability, clinical depression, increased negative thinking, negative perceptions of events, decreased motivation, floods of negative emotion, appetite and sleep problems, decreased or increased sexual responsiveness or social isolation," says Amen.

Our neural system carries the imprint of our emotional sense memories from childhood into adulthood. Familiar smells, sounds or places can send a cascade of memories flooding through us that either wrap us up in their warmth, or challenge us to maintain our composure. Along with the memories comes the cognitive sense we made of what happened at the time. That's why when we go to the circus with our children we, too, can "feel like a kid again"; or when we get hurt by someone we love, we can also "feel like a kid again"—but this time, that may mean vulnerable and helpless. Our early emotional memories are being relived in each case. When the memories are wonderful, this is a great boon in life; our child selves color our current experience with innocence and gaiety. When the memories are painful, they can color our current experience in darker hues.

We were naturally disempowered as youngsters to a greater or lesser extent because of the inevitable power imbalance between parent and child. This power imbalance can affect us in all sorts of ways. We can have the wish as adults to restore that secure and comforted feeling we had as children, which is why most of us enjoy creating a comfortable home. Or, if we felt overly disempowered, we may have a deep wish to "get our power back," which can manifest in healthy or unhealthy ways. All of us experienced some sort of power imbalance—it goes with the territory—but these imbalances can vary greatly along the continuum. We need to find real and sustaining ways to feel whole and solid. Relationships are part of what helps us feel we have a comfortable place in the world. Damage from youth needs to be repaired so that we don't pass it along in harmful ways and so that we can have reasonably healthy relationships in our current lives. But this repair can require committed and deliberate work.

Psychotherapy is one way of repatterning our limbic systems, along with other healing relationships of all kinds. Because "Describing good relatedness to someone, no matter how precisely or how often, does not *inscribe* it into the neural networks that inspire love or other feelings," says Lewis. "The limbic system is associated with our emotions and the neocortex is associated with critical thinking. Both are operative in processing emotions." While the neocortex can collect facts quickly, the limbic brain does not. Physical mechanisms are what produce our experience of the world, and we need new sets of physical impressions to change or alter those impressions. Lewis continues:

જ્જ

Emotional impressions shrug off insight but yield to a different persuasion: the force of another person's Attractors reaching through the doorway of a limbic connection. Psychotherapy changes people because one mammal can restructure the limbic brain of another. . . . The mind–body clash has disguised the truth that psychotherapy is physiology. When a person starts therapy, she isn't beginning a pale conversation; she is stepping into a somatic state of relatedness. Evolution has sculpted mammals into their present form: they become attuned to one another's evocative signals and alter the structure of one another's nervous systems. Psychotherapy's transformative power comes from engaging and directing these mechanisms. Therapy is a living embodiment of limbic processes as corporeal as digestion and respiration.

જ્જ

The body is part of the therapeutic process. One of therapy's ultimate goals is to restore our ability to care and be cared for in reasonably functional ways, to learn to love and be loved. The three neural "faces" or "expressions" of love are limbic *resonance, regulation* and *revision*. It is *relationship* that heals. We've probably all had the experience of loving a subject in school, not because of the subject but because of *who* was teaching it; we responded to *them* so we responded to it. Most research done on the efficacy of therapy arrives at the same point: Ultimately, it is the quality of the relationship between client and therapist, or between group members, that is core to the healing process. Insight is certainly critical to understanding and cognitive restructuring, but the relational patterns encoded into the limbic system do not necessarily respond to insight; they respond to the slow repatterning or recoding of the complex brain and body systems that hold the story of us, the sum total of our experiences, written on them. We take in information through all of our senses; the more senses that are involved in our learning, whether it's the alphabet or emotional learning, the more the brain absorbs and stores it. The more powerfully the memory is encoded in us, the more it takes to alter the patterning.

All self-help books should probably come with a warning that reads something like: *Caution! This book must be accompanied by a network of sustaining relationships. Do not attempt to get better in isolation.* Most women don't need to be told that relationships are core to our sense of well-being; we're wired to understand this. And most therapists have always understood intuitively that there is a repatterning of neural networks that accompanies a long and successful therapeutic relationship, no matter what name or discipline it has operated under.

IT'S NEVER TOO LATE TO
LIMBICALLY REVISE

My own discipline is psychodrama, sociometry and group psychotherapy, the brainchild of Viennese psychiatrist Jacob Levy Moreno and later his wife Zerka Moreno. It is essentially a role-playing method and a group-therapy method combined to allow clients not only to *talk* about their lives and passions, but *act* them out as well. In psychodrama, clients have the opportunity, for example, to speak to an empty

chair or a role-player representing a person to whom they have something to say. This allows more senses to get involved more directly in
the therapeutic process which, we believe, creates more opportunities
for healing. To quote Moreno again, "The body remembers what the
mind forgets." If it didn't, none of us would breathe, walk or ride a
bike. Scene-setting is also important in psychodrama. Memory is
"state dependent"; that is, we tend to recall something more fully
when similar conditions re-present themselves. Creating the environment in a psychodramatic enactment tends to encourage a more complete recall of a particular situation which, when used properly, can be
therapeutic. This of course assumes that clinicians will keep in mind
that recalling something with full intensity is not always desirable and
should be used carefully. But therapy that allows us to reconnect with
our deepest selves—our passions, hopes and dreams—can open a
door to living more fully and passionately in the present.

So, if it's the relationship that ultimately heals, let's take a deeper
look at what's going on with this process of neural repatterning.

LIMBIC RESONANCE

We are always giving off emotional signals or rather an emotional
essence for other people to pick up on. Our brains are designed to pick
up on these signals and translate them. We know much about people
without exchanging a word; we get a sense about them, what their
essence is, and how we relate to them. In psychodrama we call it *tele*,
the connection between people that is nonverbal but says everything,
what we "get" about another person and they about us, even with no
words spoken. Lewis likens it to listening to a piece of music:

                    so

*The first part of therapy is to be limbically known—having someone with
a keen ear catch your melodic essence. A child with emotionally hazy parents*

finds trying to know herself like wandering around a museum in the dark. . . . [S]he cannot be sure of what she senses. . . . Those who succeed in revealing themselves to another find the dimness receding from their own visions of self. Like people awakening from a dream, they slough off the accumulated, ill-fitting trappings of unsuitable lives.

The experience of being seen for who we really are, of feeling understood and "gotten" by another person or people can be fundamentally altering and healing.

ঽ৹

LIMBIC REGULATION

We, as humans or mammals, are physiologically patterned to resonate to each other at a deep neural level. Lewis says:

ঽ৹

Our neural architecture places relationships at the crux of our lives, where, blazing and warm, they have the power to stabilize. When people are hurting and out of balance, they turn to regulating affiliations: groups, clubs, pets, marriages, friendships, masseuses, chiropractors, the Internet. All carry at least the potential for emotional connection. Together those bonds do more good than all the psychotherapies on the planet. A parent who rejects a child's desire to depend raises a fragile person. Those children, grown into adulthood, are frequently those who come for help. . . . If patient and therapist are to proceed down a curative path, they must allow limbic regulation and its companion moon, dependence, to make their revolutionary magic.

ঽ৹

Working in the addictions field over the past three decades has taught me endless lessons about limbic regulation. People who have been traumatized by inadequate parenting, who are living with addiction or are addicts themselves, need to put in the time that it will take to heal in therapy and Twelve-Step programs. The ones who do poorly are invariably the ones who, for some reason or another, won't put in their hours. Maybe they go to Twelve-Step meetings and are bothered by what people do or don't say; maybe the idea of groups creeps them out, makes them feel vulnerable, but sooner or later they will need to come to terms with their aversion to connection that makes them want to pick up a book, read it and walk away better— just like they wanted the drink or drug to do the job. Books like this one can point us in the right direction, but words alone don't make for a full healing; people need to open the door to deeper, more mean- ingful connections with others, to light a path toward the right kind of healing *experience*. In Lewis's words:

> . . . *people do not learn emotional modulation as they do geometry or the names of state capitals. They absorb the skill from living in the presence of an adept external modulator, and they learn it implicitly. Knowledge leaps the gap from one mind to the other, but the learner does not experience the trans- ferred information as an explicit strategy. Instead, a spontaneous capacity germinates and becomes a natural part of the self, like knowing how to ride a bike or tie one's shoes. The effortful beginnings fade and disappear from memory.*

As a client depends, she internalizes this regulation, and it becomes a part of her. Gradually, she feels more whole, capable and confident, until eventually she is ready for independence and self-regulation.

LIMBIC REVISION

According to Lewis:

❧

When a limbic connection has established a neural pattern, it takes a limbic connection to revise it. . . . [C]oming close to the patient's limbic world evokes genuine emotional responses in the therapist—he finds himself stirring in response to the particular magnetism of the emotional mind across from him. His mission is neither to deny those responses in himself nor to let them run their course. He waits for the moment to move the relationship in a different direction. . . . And then he does it again, ten thousand times more. Progress in therapy is iterative. Each successive push moves the patient's virtuality a tiny bit further from the native Attractors, and closer to those of the therapist. The patient encodes new neural patterns over their myriad interactions . . . with enough repetition; the fledgling circuits consolidate into novel attractors. When that happens, identity has changed. The patient is no longer the person he was.

❧

This underscores the notion that a therapist's first responsibility is to do her own personal work so that she can pass along as resolved a self as possible. The same would apply to parents, partners, teachers and so on. Who we are speaks louder than what we say on a neural level. It is the total self that instructs and enlightens, not simply the right words. This is also why we can't will ourselves to forgive. As Lewis says, "A person cannot choose to desire a different kind of relationship, any more than he can will himself to ride a unicycle, play *The Goldberg Variations,* or speak Swahili. The requisite neural framework for performing these activities does not coalesce on command." It takes time to change our neural patterning and learn new relationship styles and skills. Lewis continues, "The physiology of emotional life cannot be dispelled with a few words." As we've already discussed, "*describing* good relatedness to someone, no matter how precisely or how often, does not *inscribe* it into the neural networks that inspire love." Or forgiveness.

Many people miss this critical aspect of therapy, and our current health-care system misses it as well. Deep limbic healing cannot occur in six office visits; rather, it happens slowly and over time. When I work with clients I do my best to help them to understand the importance of a safety net, a network of recovery relationships and activities that will support their personal growth. This network can include Twelve-Step programs or faith-based groups. I also find that exercise and good nutrition play a critical role in a client's healing. Oftentimes, clients want to get better fast, a let's-figure-it-out-and-get-out-of-here sort of thing. And that can work to some extent for some people. But this quick-fix mentality ignores the limbic repatterning that is so critical to full healing. New awarenesses about how your parents' divorce tore you up inside doesn't necessarily heal the tear. It may be the awareness that starts the wheels in motion for other emotional movement, but healing is a process and it takes the time it takes. Twelve-Step programs are one self-help option that have had a transformative effect on the lives of millions of people worldwide. People changing people.

I myself attend Al-Anon and have for many years. In the early stages of coming to terms with my father's addictions, it felt like enough just to sit in the rooms, share small pieces of my story and have the room still remain orderly and not be catapulted out of the state of New York. No one walked out, no one yelled, collapsed into tears or took another drink. No chaos. Just "thanks for sharing" and on to the next person. For me, that in itself was enough for a long time. It repatterned me from expecting that sharing my authentic feelings would somehow lead to chaotic emotional scenes, to learning, on a neural level to tolerate my own intense emotions and those of others, and to expect that others could tolerate mine, if all shared in a reasonably considerate manner. Therapy and recovery encompass a process of neural repatterning. So do our relationships in life. This is how we can plow through the emotional pain that's blocking our ability to experience pleasure in the present.

◦◦◦

The human brain is exquisitely sensitive to thought. The mind exerts continual "cognitive caresses" on the millions of neurons that make up the brain.

～Sir John Eccles
from *Healing Words: The Power of Prayer*
and The Practice of Medicine

The Body Holds the Secret

*J*anet is an analyst in private practice. An analyst with a very sore back. Now this is easy enough to explain away when you imagine the long hours of sitting and listening required for the job, or the commuting by train into the city every day from her home in Westchester, or the paperwork, or the lack of large muscle movement in general that has become the fate of homo sapiens trapped in a modern technological world. Bodies, built for one kind of work, are evolving into another evolutionary mandate. As Janet's back pain grew worse, her visits to the doctor became more frequent, until eventually her back pain became so serious that it interfered with her ability to function. The doctor said that the only option left was surgery, that her diagnosis was spinal stenosis, a condition in which oxygen is cut off from the nerves. Her condition was chronic and degenerating. This was her nightmare, the surgery she'd been trying to avoid for years. Janet opened up to a friend about her condition. Her friend looked her straight in the eye and said, "Why don't you read John Sarno's book on pain?" Dr. Sarno, from the Rush Institute in New York City, had taken the rather radical position that most back pain is psychosomatic—that the body's ability to provide a physical pain that is real, physically painful and distracts from the emotional pain that is being denied, and hence somatized, is quite remarkable.

Janet read the book.

That evening she woke up in the middle of the night. Her husband lay fast asleep while Janet went through the tortures of the damned, time-traveling through her childhood to the eleven-year-old child who had lost her father before she ever really had him. Janet was not a big crier, but the floodgates opened, and thirty-five years of tears poured out. She felt the biting loneliness that she could not feel then, the differentness she felt vis-à-vis her friends in the small Midwestern town where she'd grown up, the longing for a father she had never gotten to know or fully internalize, and the guilt of the daughter who sometimes wished her father would die rather than keep hurting her and her beloved mother with his coldness, meanness and lack of attentiveness. That guilt had kept the full measure of her pain at his loss from surfacing. How could she let herself grieve when she had many times wished him away? How could she be such a bad child, having these evil thoughts? Did her thoughts have the power to destroy, and had she succeeded in devastating their lives? How could she forgive herself, be forgiven and hurt as much as she did hurt after such a profound loss? And how could she ever let herself enjoy the freedom of childhood, of having her mother all to herself, of *not* missing the bite of her father's tongue when it lashed out at her and her mother. How could she be at peace? The tears continued to flow, from her *heart,* from her *soul* and from her *back,* where the pain had settled all these years in a physical throbbing that had lost its real voice and spoke out in a somatic one. Her body ached because her mind could not.

The next morning, Janet's back pain was reduced to soreness. During the following days, the soreness gradually wore off. Within a week, her pain was gone, and it hasn't returned. Miracles sometimes seem to happen, and this surely appears to be one of them, though, upon closer examination, it came along with a very solid program of therapy, meditation and appropriate physical exercise. Consequently, when this healing occurred, Janet had the support in place to accept it and sustain it. And she was willing to believe that healing had actually occurred and make the cognitive connection between her past hurt and her present pain. As the Italian saying goes, "The mind is hurt and the body cries out." The collected wisdom of an emotionally attuned culture has created a proverb to describe this common, human phenomenon.

Our bodies are like "smart cells" that store information on all levels. If the body's ability to operate unconsciously were not so incredible, we would have to think every time we took a breath, plan out each step or refer to a manual on digestion every time we ate a meal. But we don't have to do that because our bodies do it for us; they know what to do because all that information is carefully coded into them, so we can go about the business of living without being encumbered by all sorts of details associated with our survival. Our bodies function on the more basic levels, so that we can devote our attention to higher functioning. Our basic emotions of trust and mistrust, or connection and disconnection, are equally fundamental.

Trauma is allied with that basic type of functioning. Our fight, flight, freeze responses are physical; the body reacts in times of stress, and the body stores that information so that we can avoid danger at some later time. Fear is one of the easiest responses to condition in any animal. An electric shock paired with a loud sound, say of a slap, will train any dog to avoid either the sound or the feeling of a slap. Even the sound by itself will send the dog into hiding. Equally, emotional sounds can send people into hiding if they carry a fear message connected to them. The body, heart and mind are designed to work in elegant syncopation to accomplish the tasks of living, weaving all five senses together in exquisite symmetry, and adding emotion and intuition to their subtle, efficient mix.

THE LIMBIC BONDS BETWEEN PARENT AND CHILD

One of the most fundamental human bonds is the one between mother and child, with that between father and child a close second and in some cultures, grandmother and child. A serious disruption in these primary bonds can affect the child. According to Amen:

... hormonal changes shortly after childbirth ... can cause limbic or emotional problems in the mother. They are called the "baby blues" when they are mild and postpartum depression or psychosis when they are severe. When these problems arise, the deep limbic system of the mother's brain shows abnormal activity. (The phenomenon has long been detected in animals as well as humans.) In turn, significant bonding problems may occur. The mother may emotionally withdraw from the baby, preventing the baby from developing normally.

Other life events can also cause problems in the limbic system, such as divorce, death or loss of significant relationships or children in the home. Divorce can actually be "a source of one of the most severe kinds of stress," according to Dr. Amen. Partners and family members are inevitably limbically connected, and can feel a deep sense of *rupture* or serious *fragmentation* when they are separated, and likewise with the children involved. He feels that this may be a part of why it's so hard to leave even an abusive relationship, where partners have shared the same bed, table and life for years. The kind of deep fragmentation both partners and children experience over these sorts of separations or breakups can be with us throughout our lives. When we try to ignore the sense of fragmentation that can accompany significant loss, when we do not go through the grieving process, we condemn our unconscious to carry it in silence. The part of us that is fragmented may have no voice or expression. However, it does not disappear, as we'll see in our next case study; it waits for some circumstance in life to trigger it. It may then speak, but in the wrong words. We need to link it to the child's voice that was silenced to make sense of what is being refelt. When there is a longstanding problem in our bonds from childhood, the unresolved pain associated with it can seem to lie more or less dormant for a time, as we focus on getting our careers going, for example. But when we reenter intimate relationships or have children of our own, that early emotional conflict gets triggered, along with all the thoughts and feelings associated with it. It's important that we get some help if this is the case so that we don't sabotage our relationships in the present with unresolved pain from the past.

[In appendix I, we discuss parenting styles that teach forgiving attitudes toward self and others at each stage of development. It is the way we *treat* our children that creates the neural network patterning that they will take with them into adulthood.]

The Drama of the Stepchild

*S*ondra's history of relationships was not easy. Her parents divorced when she was seven, and her father remarried. Her father now had two stepchildren with whom he spent the bulk of his time. When Sondra visited her beloved father every other weekend she had to share him with two stepsiblings who had him full-time. Her previous, deep bond with him was disrupted, and she had the feeling that their relationship and the part of her that carried it were fragmenting, falling apart. She was quietly grieving the constant loss of her father; she just wasn't with him enough to sustain her sense of him as her dad, protector and friend. She experienced her parents' divorce and her life that followed as limbically shattering and fragmenting, and that feeling generalized itself into her daily life in lots of little ways. She felt confused and out of the loop. Wasn't he her father, really, and why did *they* get to live with him when she didn't? She felt jealous of these siblings she didn't even ask for and furious that they lived the life that was supposed to be hers. She felt like the outsider, the one who sang slightly out of tune, who hesitantly mouthed the words to the song that everyone else knew by heart. Her inner world felt fragmented, as if pieces of her were scattered in different places and she couldn't pull them all together.

And it was tough to resolve the natural competitiveness she felt toward her stepmother, which she might normally have felt toward her mother. Tough partly because she didn't love her stepmother as a mother, and her stepmother did not love her as her child; partly because her own mother seemed lost and depressed, and Sondra felt sorry for her and guilty about her wish to be with her father. She saw her father as choosing her stepmother and rejecting her mother, which made her feel all the more rejected and confused. Her mother didn't remarry, which Sondra was grateful for, but at the same time, she felt almost too important to her mother, responsible for being her missing partner, her friend . . . and she had no real sibling of her own or father to share the job with. She sort of vacillated between overwhelm and underwhelm, and longed for that family in between where she could relax and let down her guard.

Because she had nowhere to talk these feelings through, they never consciously arose. Because she didn't want to "cause problems" by bringing up "unpleasant" subjects that upset people, she somatized her difficult emotions, and they got plowed into her physiology. She had been deeply hurt over her parents' divorce, and felt powerful feelings when at her father's house and sadness when watching her mother working harder than her stepmother. Why was her stepmother living her mother's life and her stepsiblings living hers? And they all looked so pleased about it, and she felt like a fifth wheel. She had fantasies of one of them dying, of her stepmother becoming terminally ill, of somebody disappearing and a space finally opening up that was big enough for her to have a place in all of this, too. But it never happened, and two half-homes somehow didn't make a whole one.

Sondra dreamed of having a family of her own someday that no one could take away from her, where she wouldn't be divided from the people she loved and from herself. Where she wouldn't have to share her beloved person. But, as so often happens, she seemed to be attracted to the very people who re-created exactly what she came from. The men she fell in love with invariably felt she was "holding on too tight" and found other, less needy women. So again and again, Sondra found herself losing the one she loved, hanging on until it all blew up and ended. Then she would have to start all over again. Overtly, Sondra blamed the guys. She'd just made another bad choice, and it would be better next time because she'd find a better guy. But privately, she blamed herself and wondered what was wrong with her. And the worse she felt about herself, the more she blamed the guys; and the more she blamed the guys, the faster the relationships tanked. Each time, Sondra found it harder to keep the faith that something could work out for her. Her fragmenting self became her fragmenting life.

In this climate, when Sondra's heart got engaged, she was hypervigilant, waiting for the roof to cave in. At the first sign of a problem in a love relationship, she felt her throat go dry, her stomach churn and her head start to pound. Her palms would sweat, and if things accelerated into a fight, her heart raced. (All symptoms of PTSD from the trauma she experienced over her parents' divorce [see appendix II for a list of these symptoms].)Then she'd either blow up and blame, or shut down and withdraw. Or cry and get inarticulate. She got overwhelmed, not necessarily with what was going on outside but with what was going on inside. The more scary thoughts she had of feeling alone and rejected—with quicksilver, hardly discernible images of the hurt seven- and ten- and thirteen- and nineteen-year-old flashing through her mind—the more her body responded. And the more her body responded, the busier her mind became warding off the painful images of past loss and rupture that her body state was restimulating.

Once she got caught in this feedback loop, it really didn't matter who she was talking to; it all got sort of blurred together. She couldn't listen to herself or to him because she was flooded with her own reactions, though she was not conscious of their origins. So nothing got worked out. She just felt hurt and defensive, and the fight accelerated until she was caught in a place she couldn't find her way out of. Caught in a negative feedback loop.

Sondra's thoughts, hopes and dreams had combined with the day-to-day experience of her early relationships to form her relational world, and that is the world that she carried into each subsequent relationship. Her early experience had been cumulatively traumatizing, so connection and intimacy became triggers for pain. The more strongly she felt for someone, the more she got triggered. Her feelings of vulnerability, her deep wish for closeness, and her increasing feelings of need and dependency all triggered her earlier unresolved pain from other love relationships.

And forgiveness became distorted for her. She was supposed to forgive her parents. But she couldn't. Every time she forgave her father so she could be closer to him, she faced the stark reality that his heart belonged to others as much as (or maybe more than) it did to her. So she'd opened her own heart only to find out that it hurt a lot. Forgiving her dad was a bad idea; it was easier to stay mad so she didn't get blindsided. And she was supposed to forgive her mom, which she did really, but her mom seemed like the one who lost out in Sondra's eyes, so she didn't really want to identify with her. She wanted to do things differently from her mom so she wouldn't end up alone and lonely (childhood reasoning), but didn't really know how. So this, too, went with her into her own intimate relationships. Consequently, the tiny moments of conflict that are a part of any intimate relationship became laden with all sorts of stuff that made them seem like huge moments. Sondra didn't really see her parents in a close, satisfying relationship, and she resented the idea that her father's heart had been given to another woman and children. So the functional forgiveness and emotional processing that were part of that family just made her angry, hurt and envious. She couldn't make good use of it for herself because her own pain at feeling like an outsider blocked her from doing so. And underneath it all was the feeling that she carried from watching her mother's struggle, that she wasn't as important as everyone else, that she would never be able to hold a man's love (again, childhood reasoning). So she couldn't forgive herself for all the terrible thoughts and feelings that were now part of her psyche, and she gave herself a bad time in her own head.

This is where therapy is a real godsend. It takes time to tease out the myriad small details that make a life. And seeing them is not the only task; the feelings, thoughts and behaviors that have grown out of the ways in which we have interpreted the events of our lives need to be revisited and reworked as well. They have wrapped themselves around our development, our relationships and our lives. Forgiveness can be tremendously helpful at this point. It is like finally laying a burden down that we have been carrying in our hearts, bodies and minds. It is a way to disentangle our spirits and free them, so that our energies can go into a new direction. We may feel that we are too far along to change, but as a therapist, I have been amazed at how young people with this feeling sometimes are. Even clients in their twenties with their whole lives ahead of them can feel it's too late. Telling them that their life is just beginning doesn't necessarily help; they already feel old and tarnished. They have to methodically go back and pick up the discarded or lost pieces of themselves one by one, hold them in their hands, work with and understand them, construct new meaning to counterbalance the old, learn to take in caring and support from others, and then take a leap of faith into a new self.

In Sondra's case, these issues from her early life got restimulated when she married and began to have children of her own. She actually avoided marriage for a long time, unconsciously fearing another violation of the affiliative bond. While her focus was on career and single life, she felt relatively safe and secure. But when she did marry and have children, the intensity of the family experience triggered all her old pain from growing up. What occurred in adolescence resurfaced in early midlife. Luckily, she was in a therapeutic process and used the emotional information she gained from it as an opportunity to better understand herself, and to heal and move on. And she slowly underwent a limbic repatterning through long-term therapy and staying in and with her own growing family.

In the next chapter, we'll discuss the five stages of forgiveness.

THREE

The Five Stages of Forgiveness

The act of forgiveness involves a multistep process comparable to the one associated with grief. In the forgiveness process, the person first feels anger and hurt, then finds a way to forgive the specific offense. Ultimately, the person develops the ability to forgive more easily and to take less umbrage at the words and actions of others.

People who are unable to go through this process can experience not just emotional difficulties and interpersonal problems but also impaired cardiological, neurological and immune systems.

"When we get hurt, we get hurt not just in our minds but also in our bodies." The more readily we experience anger or hurt, the more our bodies secrete "stress chemicals" that, over time, take a toll.

If we have too many things that disturb us or that make us feel tense or uncomfortable, what it really does is rob us of our joy.

~FREDRICK LUSKIN, PH.D.
DIRECTOR OF THE STANFORD FORGIVENESS PROJECT
AUTHOR OF *GETTING DOWN TO THE HEART OF FORGIVENESS*

A s described in the introduction, *forgiveness is a process, not an event.* The very fact that it's a process is what makes it so worthwhile: It forces us to honestly confront feelings that are clogging up our emotional systems and work through them.

Maybe we're forgiving something small—ourselves for not getting something done on time or for inadvertently hurting someone else's feelings because we were in a bad mood. Or maybe we're forgiving something large—a deliberately inflicted hurt, the pain of which has been with us for many years. This is just the kind of deeper, more layered forgiveness that takes time. Often, we want it to happen overnight, to be over and done with. By now we've learned, however, that a significant amount of repatterning, resolving and relearning needs to happen before we'll really feel free. Breaking up the process into stages makes it easier and more efficient. And once we begin, the process gains its own momentum and motivation, and begins to feel right and good and full of hope.

The process can take many forms. We may be forgiving something that happened and hurt us, something that we wished would happen but never did, or ourselves for our own feelings of victimization or wrongdoing. Some people have been so seriously wronged that the prospect of forgiving their perpetrator seems inconceivable, and what they need to do is finally allow themselves to experience the anger, hate and hurt that they had to shut down at the time because they were too scared to even feel, let alone express those emotions. Still others struggle with forgiving themselves for what they may perceive to be their own weakness in the face of wrong, inability to make their case known or, as is so often the case with children, for feeling like they are fundamentally bad, that something about them is flawed or unlovable. There are many faces to forgiveness, and each one appears with its own unique needs and struggles.

But a couple of factors appear to be consistent. True forgiveness can be difficult, and require time and work if the offense is significant, *and* true forgiveness generally leads to a restoration of our ability to make new kinds of emotional connections and choices, an emotional free-dom that most people, once they attain it, value far more than the resentments they carried.

In this book, I primarily deal with forgiveness as it impacts inter-personal relationships. As we've discussed, deep ruptures in primary relationships are traumatic and leave us with the residue of trauma. Emotional, physical or sexual abuse, neglect, divorce, living with addiction or mental illness, are all either traumatic events in and of themselves, or cumulative traumas, and they can leave people with the symptoms of posttraumatic stress disorder (PTSD). [See "Symptoms of PTSD" in appendix II.] Even feeling inept in school, consistently on the spot not knowing what you're supposed to know, can become a cumulative trauma. The effects of these types of trauma, if they go untreated, get passed down through the generations right along with personal habits, food preferences and personality traits. According to Bessel Van der Kolk, author of *Psychological Trauma,* some of the symptoms of PTSD, aside from somatic disturbances (body aches), are a loss of trust and faith, depression accompanied by feelings of despair, hypervigilance (waiting for the other shoe to drop), extreme fear, free-floating anxiety, loss of ability to conceptualize a positive future, traumatic bonding, and the black-and-white thinking that grows out of the numbing versus high-intensity emotional responses that are part of our fight, flight or freeze response. That is, we alternate between states of shutdown/freeze and intense emotional reactions such as rage or extreme fear, two states we can get "triggered" into when we get scared. Trauma can affect our ability to take in love and support, so the things we need the most in order to heal or feel better paradoxically become the hardest ones for us to accept and integrate.

The more senses that are involved in a traumatizing experience, according to Mark Gold, M.D., of the University of Miami, the more it affects us. If you think of traumas that occur in homes, many senses are involved—sight, smell, touch, sound, maybe even taste. If we are being slapped, for example, we *feel* it, *hear* the yelling or words of rejection that are probably accompanying it, *see* the person and surrounding situation, *smell* whatever scents are part of the environment (like alcohol on the breath) and even sometimes *taste* our own fear as it arises in our mouths. On September 11, the first responders to the Twin Towers were the most at risk for developing PTSD. They smelled the burning, saw the devastation, heard the crashing and cries, were in physical contact with those they were rescuing, and tasted the metallic air. When four or five senses are involved in this manner, the effects of a traumatic situation can be persistent and pervasive. For women who have been physically or sexually abused by parents or men who are larger and stronger than they are, there is the added feeling of powerlessness that comes through being smaller physically, as well as the confusion as to whether or not they did something to invite or deserve this negative attention, which of course they did not—no one deserves to be abused (even if they're told they do). When people contemplate working through blocks to forgiveness, they are also going to encounter these sense memories along the way. The more overwhelming the memories are, the more they may resist remembering them. Forgiveness, however, is not reserved for only serious situations; it is part of our daily world, part of how we live our lives.

I have divided forgiveness up into five stages to provide an emotional map to follow that, hopefully, will make the prospect of forgiveness seem a little less daunting. There is nothing sacrosanct about these stages, they are linear simply because they appear in a book form, but in real life they are dynamic and can overlap. Some stages occur more or less simultaneously, while others feel out of reach. In addition, stages may be leap-frogged or moved through in a different order than appears here. What is very consistent, in my experience, is that these approximate the phases that most people seem to go through as they travel the intense and often rocky journey of forgiving and letting go of something that has hurt them, made them feel small inside, unlovable, forgotten or misunderstood.

WAKING UP

Here we begin to entertain the thought that the resentment and wish for retribution we harbor toward someone else may be costing *us* more than it's worth. This is when we wake up to the fact that we are caught in an emotional bind that is keeping us from feeling okay and inhibiting our growth.

Part of what's keeping us from working toward a more forgiving position is our own fear of being hurt again. We get scared when someone acts in a hurtful manner, so we freeze up, disconnect or try to fight back when we get hurt. This fear reemerges, along with our fear of getting hurt all over again, when we begin to walk the path of forgiveness. Not only do we feel wronged, but we're scared of being wronged again, of being reduced to the same feelings of helplessness and vulnerability that we experienced previously.

ANGER AND RESENTMENT

The next two stages we face are anger and sadness, which are very closely linked to each other. (Although the stages are anger and resentment, sadness and hurt, for clarity's sake, I will refer to them as "anger" and "sadness" in the text, except where it is necessary to refer to all of them.)

Anger can create all sorts of problems at home and in the workplace. It can also feel empowering and organizing, and it can mobilize us to take action. Sadness, on the other hand, can feel disorganizing; we feel like we're "falling apart." Some people will be more comfortable experiencing their anger at feeling violated, talking about it and expressing it, while others will need to feel sadness first. Chronically angry people may have to get in touch with feelings of vulnerability that they don't want to feel, and chronically sad people may have to let themselves feel their anger.

On the psychological level, anger, resentment and blame can also be used as defenses to ward off feelings of vulnerability and perceived weakness, or as justifications for remaining stuck at a particular place in life. Giving up our anger can feel like giving up a piece of ourselves or a piece of our perceived powerfulness. We can initially experience it as a loss of self, probably because so much of us and our development is wrapped around or invested in it that it's become a part of our identity. And if we felt deeply wounded, it can feel like our anger, resentment and blame are all we have that's ours to hold onto, to keep us from falling apart, to protect us from that disintegrating feeling that overwhelms us when we give in to our sadness. Repressed or denied anger can seep out sideways [as we will discuss in chapter 5, when we examine anger in detail] and cause problems in work and relationships. Working through our anger and resentment are vital steps on the path toward forgiveness.

HURT AND SADNESS

Grief and sadness are a part of life, and very important emotions to be understood and embraced. People who can't grieve their losses— whether the loss is a sense of comfort, safety and security in the home, a cohesive family unit, feeling personally rejected, abused or wounded—set themselves up for later emotional and physical problems. People who cannot let themselves feel their hurt, and consequently cannot grieve, often erect walls around their wounds that are designed to keep out further pain. Unfortunately, along with refusing to feel deep pain goes the ability to feel deep connection and pleasure. Their ability to bond in future relationships can be impaired, or unconsciously they may guard against forming sincere and deep attachments because they fear another rupture.

When our trust and faith in a primary relationship has been shattered, we need to feel the pain and anger that shattering causes in us so that we can heal, move on and trust again. Denied grief, anger and sadness ask future relationships to carry those powerful emotions that remain unfelt. Feelings from the past get displaced onto situations in the present. They get projected onto today's relationships—whether covertly or overly—though their intensity may belong to yesterday. This burdens present-day relationships and makes it harder than it might otherwise be to work through the problems that any relationship faces. If a slight in the present triggers old sadness and anger, those feelings can explode with all the vehemence of a buried mine, and there will inevitably be collateral damage. We discharge our emotions at today's target, not realizing that their intensity (their power) belongs to yesterday, or we may get triggered and become cold and withdrawn, imploding our emotional intensity and isolating ourselves by creating distance or erecting walls. The especially gnarly part of all of this is that it's an almost entirely unconscious process. And that's where we get stuck: Circling the current situation again and again, hunting for evidence that this situation indeed deserves our high degree of wrath, or withdrawing and becoming disconnected, not recognizing that the reparation we yearn for belongs to a time and place that will never come again. And the wounded person or child demanding it will never be truly satisfied with the amends that will be extracted from the wrong mouth at the wrong time. And even if we get the perfect response, our ability to take it in may be impaired. We may feel disappointed, like "too little too late," so instead of helping us feel better, it only deepens our confusion. This is one of the ways that the past re-creates itself in the present. We need to feel our pain and *link* it to where the wound began, teasing out the meaning we made of the original situation, which we may still be reliving (and living by) today. Grieving allows us to separate the past from the present so that our today is not darkened by the shadows of yesterday. There is a purity to real grief; it cleanses us and puts us back in touch with what's real, with our personal truth.

ACCEPTANCE, INTEGRATION AND LETTING GO

When we go through the process of getting past our carefully erected defenses and feeling the feelings tucked away beneath them, we may find pieces of ourselves that we thought were lost forever. When we actually experience the intensity of the emotions we've turned our back on, we're able to gain new insight as to how the circumstances of our lives have impacted us and why. We *accept* and *integrate* those split-off parts of ourselves into the fullness of our being. Suddenly, we hang together better, we're more coherent and cohesive, and we grow to understand ourselves and what makes us tick in a new way. Through this understanding often comes a new compassion and self-acceptance. It is the rare person who hasn't blamed herself for what may be going wrong in her life. When we explore the stages of forgiveness, we inevitably meet our own self-loathing along the way. As we dive down into the feelings surrounding a forgiveness issue, we generally encounter our inability to forgive ourselves, even if it's only for being in the wrong place at the wrong time; for being vulnerable or needy, and unable to protect or stand up for ourselves; or for being so limbically bonded that we would do anything, even sacrifice ourselves, to maintain the connection—because the strength and connection of that limbic bond made it feel like losing (or the threat of losing) the bond was tantamount to losing ourselves.

By exploring these feelings and teasing out the complicated issues surrounding them, we experience a growing understanding and compassion for our own and another person's human frailty. Self-acceptance opens the door to accepting others more easily. Forgiving ourselves leads us closer to forgiving someone else, and forgiving someone else leads us closer to forgiving ourselves. In the words of Chief Seattle in his "Letter to The President," "We are brothers after all." If our sins of the flesh are forgivable, it must follow that theirs are, too; and if their sins of their flesh are forgivable, then it must follow that ours are, too.

Acceptance is inevitably a two-way street. However, even though we *forgive* we may still *remember,* and it is well we should so that we can adjust our expectations of what we can realistically expect from someone who's hurt us and let us down (including ourselves). But the poison and the sting will have gone out of our remembering, and in its place will be a kind of wisdom and acceptance, not the satisfaction of apology or retribution perhaps, but recompense, restoration and resolution nonetheless. So forgiveness is really a by-product rather than an act of will—a letting go or releasing of something we no longer wish to carry, rather than a moral decision made at a particular time and place.

By now, we've come to understand that a person can only come as close to us as they can come to themselves. Wanting and waiting for them to be who they cannot be is a waste of our lives. We can only do something about ourselves. We can remove our own mental and emotional blocks that keep our joy at bay, and that wisdom, if we embrace it, will lead us to where we need to go next.

We've accepted and integrated; now we need to let go. *Letting go* is the stage where forgiveness is happening naturally. The term is more of a convention than what might actually take place. Letting go is a sort of releasing of the past, a by-product of acceptance. What happens is that whatever it was that we're forgiving moves from the foreground to the background. Simply put, we're just ready to move on. We take stock of our lives and suddenly realize that we're no longer carrying as many emotional burdens. We're freer to make choices that have less to do with the past and more to do with the present and the future. We're emotionally lighter and have renewed stores of energy to invest in our own lives. We think and feel more clearly because our mental and emotional vision has been reordered and reworked.

People arrive at this stage through many channels: therapy, spiritual beliefs and practices, or simply through the process of living, but once arrived at, the benefits are clear and sustaining.

REORGANIZATION AND REINVESTMENT

Having freed up energy that was weighing down our creativity and passion for living, we're able to reinvest that energy in satisfying life pursuits. Our desire to forgive may also have represented a yearning for connection, and this, too, can lead us to want to make a reinvestment in relationships. Often what happens is that we come to see things more realistically. Through the work of forgiveness, we may have adopted a more realistic picture of what we can and cannot expect from a particular person. Whether we are dealing with a parent, sibling, partner, grown child or friend, we may be able to reinvest in what is actually possible to expect without burdening the relationship with expectations of what it's not likely to offer. However, when we can free ourselves to receive the good that's there, we can set about getting other needs and desires met elsewhere, from surrogates with whom we can have a healthy give-and-take. There is nothing more discouraging than going to a dry well for water, and it's a great relief when we can stop expecting and wishing for what may never come our way.

Our own personal spontaneity and creativity are also freed up when we work through the pain and anger that have been blocking them. There is virtually no endeavor—whether it be cooking a meal, planning a day, raising children or working at a hobby or career—that does not benefit from enhanced creativity and spontaneity. Reinvesting this freed-up energy into the activities of our lives makes everything feel better and brighter.

As we have already established, these stages are not linear. Rather, they provide an overall picture of the territory we will likely cover and the issues we'll probably encounter on our path to forgiveness. They are normal and natural, and the best way to go through them is with an attitude of surrender and faith. It's important to develop a support system if the issues are deep and require time for healing. We need other people so that we don't feel isolated in our painful moments. Talking about our emotions and being with others creates new neural pathways and limbic connections, it rewires our brains and bodies. It can also elevate our immune systems, which helps us stay healthy.

Many people, when they ask for help with what they see as "their problems," feel they are admitting to being damaged or deficient, but it is these very people who are most likely to improve their lot in life. People who are strong and healthy enough to recognize that they need help with something are already halfway to healing. They have the humility to allow themselves to need and the strength to tolerate the feeling that something is wrong. These are the people with a positive prognosis. If you are reading this book, you are already beginning the process of forgiveness.

In the chapters that follow, we will examine, in detail, each of these five stages of forgiveness.

FOUR

Waking Up:
Moving Through Our Defenses

Forgiveness has nothing to do with forgetting. . . . A wounded person cannot—indeed, should not—think that a faded memory can provide an expiation of the past. To forgive, one must remember the past, put it into perspective, and move beyond it. Without remembrance, no wound can be transcended.

~BEVERLY FLANIGAN

FORGIVING THE UNFORGIVABLE: OVERCOMING THE LEGACY OF INTIMATE WOUNDS

I n waking up, we begin to move through those defenses we've erected around the powerful feelings of anger, resentment and hurt that we'd rather not experience. It's natural to avoid things that are unpleasant, whether it's the dentist, a midterm exam or a relationship wound. Nature encoded into us an aversion to danger, and digging into an emotional wound can feel just that: dangerous. Caution signs pop up all over the place: "Slippery road ahead"; "Watch out for rockslides"; "Heavily mined area"; but sooner or later, we can't escape the nagging feeling that something isn't working. Somehow, we're feeling stuck. But here's the tricky part: We're probably stuck because we're sitting on feelings that we don't want to feel. Whether the hurt is about something done *to* us or the guilt feelings of hurting someone else, our emotions are tugging at our insides. They make us feel vulnerable, needy, disappointed and angry all over again, or like we've been a bad person and we've done something terrible. Only a fool would go there willingly, right? Fear. Something that hurt is going to hurt again. And when we fear experiencing pain, we block it; we *defend* against feeling that pain again, perhaps with denial, minimization, rationalization, intellectualization, those pathological rewrites we talked about earlier. Or we might use behaviors like constant activity or self-medicating with food or alcohol to keep the pain from surfacing. Then we get locked in those defenses and they become a part of our makeup, part of the way we operate in the world. And when the fear comes up, it's generally not alone. It emerges alongside other feelings like sadness, anger or helplessness, which make us want to reblock all over again, every time the fear comes up. So we get caught in a loop of fear + a feeling = more fear + more feeling, which leads to more blocking. This is one way defenses get imbedded over time: like cement that is slowly hardening around our emotional feet, and when we try to climb out we feel like we're sinking at the same time that we're trying to claw our way to the surface, all the time fearing that we might make a wrong move and slip some more as it all turns to quicksand—or worse, hardens—around us.

Though it feels like the last thing we want to do, surrendering to these feelings can become our way through the fear. But this very act of surrender can feel terrifying because it brings up all our fears of hurting all over again. If we're stuck in anger at least we know where we are. Anger can feel organizing and empowering, but fear can make us feel small, insecure and powerless. Fear is not a place where most of us want to stay. Feeling frozen with fear is uncomfortable and immobilizing. Fear mixed with anger can create a potent cocktail of emotion that expresses itself in rage, a useless form of anger that obliterates the self and everyone around it, disabling clear thinking, and generally being paralyzing and nonproductive. The rage and intense fear become interwoven; deep anger and resentment get triggered when we feel scared, and they jettison to the surface as rage, a feeling we tremble in the midst of. Then bedlam: our painful feelings get expressed but not worked through, understood and integrated. We feel better for the moment, but make the long-term picture more complicated. And we provide ourselves with more evidence that it's dangerous to let our real feelings out.

The painful dynamics that keep repeating themselves in our lives and relationships send up a red flag marking a place of unresolved or hidden pain. It's what psychoanalysts call the "repetition compulsion," the compulsion to repeat the very same dynamics that hurt us the most, for example, those from our youth. Until now, we've probably been somewhat unconscious of what this emotional jam-up was costing us. Or perhaps we were feeling sufficiently gratified while nursing our revenge fantasies, that the arduous work of facing up to the fear, anger and sadness that forgiveness requires didn't seem like an attractive-enough alternative to contemplate giving them up. Long-term resentments can feel like familiar friends that we don't want to let go of, and more serious grudges can become part of our personalities. Giving them up can require reorganizing our sense of self and committing to moving forward in our lives, which can seem daunting. As long as we have "good" reasons for not "getting our act together," we can comfortably stay where we are.

The victim position can be very seductive and also very powerful. Self-righteousness may provide us with the feeling of being on a moral high ground, and that can be a lot to let go of. Sometimes, we may be innocent victims holding ourselves secretly responsible for what was done to us, and unable to tolerate the feelings of hurt and anger we're entitled to. At other times we may play the victim role for what it's worth and use it as a platform from which to operate. Maybe we had nothing to do with provoking a wrong done to us, or maybe we're involved in a mutual dynamic. But the tragedy is, when we can't resolve it in any way, we also become victims of our own negative emotions; we retraumatize ourselves. That's why we need to get a handle on what's really going on inside us. Lots of people in this bind feel that they are somehow unique, that they're the only person mired in conflicting, upsetting feelings; they feel crazy and fragmented. But, in fact, this is the internal experience that can happen when deep limbic bonds get ruptured. Either way, passing through some forgiveness process may be necessary in order to get free. We're taking a plunge into the uncharted territory of the human heart—often without a map, light or even a sense of direction. We just sense that we could do better if we knew how, and we're willing to give it a shot.

If we were hurt when we were young, it is probable that we have developed a complicated factory of defenses that allowed us to continue to live in a situation that was causing us pain. Some of those defenses may be denial, minimization, repression, rationalization, intellectualization, dissociation or self-medication. Moving past these defenses is part of the work of this stage of forgiveness. It's difficult to do because the defenses get encoded into us; we can't just will them away, we have to do the work it will take to undo them. Unfortunately, not being able to will them away can make us feel inadequate. "I *know* better so why can't I *do* better?" But knowing better doesn't mean you can *be* better. There's no shortcut; we need to become aware of the feelings that are being defended against, explore them, and reintegrate them with new understanding and meaning.

Before we're even ready to consider giving up these powerful strategies for "staying safe," we need to develop enough inner strength to tolerate feeling the feelings we've been keeping out of consciousness. This is part of why many childhood wounds don't even surface until we're well into adulthood and feeling like we can stand on our own. Other reasons they surface later are that they get restimulated when we reenter adult intimate relationships. When we open our hearts to love and feel vulnerable and dependent all over again, our defenses arise right along with our other feelings related to intimacy, not necessarily immediately, but "when the honeymoon is over," when the relationship gets real. At that point they can, and often do, get in the way of our ability to connect on a deep level. Another way issues surrounding forgiveness can get restimulated is when we become parents ourselves. Having our own children need and depend on us makes us remember what happened in our own lives around those issues. If we got hurt when we were young and felt dependent on our parents for our very survival, we needed to develop strategies for staying connected *while* feeling hurt. One of those strategies may have been to learn to hide our real and authentic feelings from those close to us and from ourselves as well.

As we begin to explore forgiveness we need to stop hiding our real feelings from ourselves, to admit how much something hurt. This is often done with a therapist in a healing process. When these feelings are raw, it helps to share them with someone who can help us understand them before we attempt to share them with people who may not find them easy to hear. We may nurse the fantasy that we can go back to the person who hurt us and tell him or her everything, or even to a sibling who lived with us or to our child if our ex-spouse hurt us. But all these people have had their own experience of this situation and developed their own complicated and deeply embedded strategies for staying out of harm's way. They will likely not forgive on our schedule, and they may see the situation completely differently from the way we see it. Sharing prematurely or, in some cases at all, may be asking more of those involved than they can give and may only leave us feeling more wounded. It's wise to give ourselves the time and support we need to heal *before* we attempt to take up a deep hurt from the past with others who were involved. Remember, ultimately we're forgiving for *our own* inner freedom. Once we've forgiven, we'll be approaching the same old situation from a different point of view. And our new attitudes and behavior changes will very possibly create shifts in others over time. Modeling new behavior is a powerful teacher.

BLOCKS TO FORGIVENESS

Clients get very blocked around the whole idea of forgiveness. Their emotions have become organized around their wounds, and tampering with that organization feels like asking them to reorganize their orientation to life. They're hurt; don't I get it? Don't I *see* them? Why am I betraying them by asking them to consider forgiveness as an option? I must be siding with their parents who hurt them. I must see them as they saw them, or worse, how they see themselves and spend so much time and money in therapy trying to undo. And I don't often ask. Because forgiveness isn't really anything we can make ourselves do as an act of will. Or because we are trying to live up to our ideas of what makes a good person. We can't force it. It comes as a by-product of doing deep emotional work. It's a statement about where we are in our healing.

If our pain is from childhood when our self was hardly developed or individuated, then our forgiveness may be confused with that of a child who will do anything to stay connected to the parent, who will bend into any shape not to lose what she loves. Forgiveness feels like a blow to this person, as if you're asking her to give up a part of herself, to give up her childlike wish that if she stays connected in any way possible, eventually that parent who wounded her will magically reform, will transform into the parent she has always wanted and needed, will turn around and see her, love her, nurture her and make up for all that didn't go well. Giving this wish up feels like giving up all hope. It's the final blow. Not only the adult sitting before me but also the child cries out: "Will I never, ever get what I want? What does that mean about life, about me, about my present and future relationships?"

The paradox is that it's in letting go of this wish that we *can* move on. And it's in letting go that we can open our hearts to receive what we long for through other channels. But the grief of the child within is real and has to be recognized, validated and worked through in order for the forgiveness to be real.

And then there is the Peter Pan in all of us, the wish to remain forever young . . . to find a place where dreams come true, where childhood never ends and we "never, never grow old." Giving up the wish for the ideal parents means we face going into adulthood imperfect, that we are taking responsibility for filling what's missing inside of us on our own without our parents' help. And forgoing revenge when we've been wounded is a lot to give up. All too often, clients feel as if forgiving their parent is tantamount to condoning their awful behavior. They fear that if they forgive they might be saying that what they did was somehow okay, that it wasn't as bad as it felt, that they're crazy for feeling hurt—those pathological rewrites again—and in forgiving, they lose their right to those feelings. So they hang on instead, continuing to breathe life into this dark place because forgiving feels like they are killing off some part of themselves, as if they're betraying themselves, snuffing out forever the voice of the child inside of them that weeps and waits for recognition and validation—again a paradox. It's only in working through all the complicated issues that are inevitably encountered on the road toward forgiveness that these wounds can be explored and dealt with. And it is only in exploring and dealing with them that they can be re-understood in the light of today and reintegrated into the self. So it is in losing a piece of the self that we gain self. But it's hell in the hallway.

THE FEAR FACTOR

Picture yourself walking through a forest. You hear the loud roar of a lion. Your palms begin to sweat, your stomach tightens and the hairs on the back of your neck stand on end. Now, imagine yourself strolling through a zoo and hearing the same loud roar from a lion. But this time, it only arouses your curiosity and interest. *Your powers of reason can control your ability to tell yourself that you have nothing to fear.*

In experiments done by Joseph LeDoux of New York University, it was found that while fear is associated with the amygdala, a tiny structure deep in the brain that is crucial for the formation of significant emotional experiences, input from the frontal region, or the cortex of the brain, can override the fear response. In *The Synaptic Self*, LeDoux says:

Studies of fear conditioning have shown beyond a doubt that the brain region that sits at the intersection of input and output systems of fear, and the key to understanding how danger is processed by the brain, is the amygdala. . . . We don't have to learn to freeze or raise blood pressure in the presence of dangerous stimuli, for the brain is programmed by evolution to do these things. We have to learn what to be afraid of but not how to act afraid.

In other words, it is the meaning that we make of an emotional event that governs our full emotional response to it. LeDoux's team found that when a loud noise was paired with a mild shock to the feet of rats, the rats soon showed fear whenever they heard the noise, even after the experimenters ceased pairing it with a shock. Eventually, however, the rats gradually lost their fear of the loud noise. Some part of the rats' brains outside the amygdala was helping to govern their fear response.

In subsequent experiments, researchers damaged a small region of the rats' forebrains, or the part of their brains that had modified their fear of the loud noise. Not only did the rats not lose their fear in the trials, they stayed afraid much longer. The input from the frontal region or the cortex of the brain helps modify the fear response.

Fear is a significant factor in blocking our ability or wish to forgive. We were hurt. We can be hurt again. "So if I forgive this person, naturally, I'm plopping myself smack into harm's way all over again. I'm not stupid, therefore I won't go there." This type of reasoning is not uncommon, in my experience, among those who genuinely want to forgive and move on, but feel blocked. And it's logical. And they're probably right: The person may well hurt them again. But it's okay to forgive *and* to remember; to forgive in order to free ourselves, and to remember in order to keep ourselves out of harm's way if the person we're forgiving is likely to continue their offensive behavior. Contrary to the popular expression, forgiving doesn't have to mean forgetting or letting our guard drop to the floor.

I have observed that a different sort of logic appears to work better in approaching the eternal question, "To forgive or not to forgive." Clients seem to do better with one of two approaches. The first is to create reasons to forgive that are, what I would call, intelligently self-centered. That logic goes something like this:

৵ৡ

I will forgive this person knowing full well that he will continue his offensive behavior. I'll do it because I'm sick of feeling glued to his insides and tired of letting him live inside my mind (rent-free; in fact, I pay him). I'll forgive because then I can think more clearly when I'm around him, and because it will release me from the constant expectation that he will some- how magically be different. I'll also forgive myself for being so preoccupied by him that I ignore my higher purpose, which is to make my own life better, to grow my own inner world and to live life fully and freely. In fact, forgiving him is freeing myself to put my attention where it belongs: on my own positive approach to life. Why should I wait around, stay stuck in this place waiting for another person to change when there are so many other things I could be doing?

This type of forgiveness is both self-protective and realistic. It takes us out of harm's way and frees us up for our own living. The second type is a more spiritual approach in which we accept a philosophy of forgiveness. We recognize that we are all human and make many mistakes. We realize that we, too, commit blunders and that there is a benevolent force that sees all and forgives all, and that forgiveness is available at all times, and it is given even to our enemies. In both approaches, the logical part of the brain is creating reasons to override or modify our fear response. They are, of course, not mutually exclusive. They can and often do work together.

Sometimes choices are made in the name of forgiveness while what is occurring isn't forgiveness at all. It is important not to confuse being forgiving with denying your own feelings, needs, and desires. Forgiving doesn't mean being passive and staying in a job or a relationship that clearly doesn't work for you or is abusive. It is important that you are clear about your boundaries. What is acceptable for you? If you are willing to allow unacceptable behavior again and again in the name of "forgiveness," you are more than likely using "forgiveness" as an excuse not to take responsibility for taking care of yourself or as a way to avoid making changes.

~Robin Casarjian
Forgiveness: A Bold Choice for a Peaceful Heart

FORGIVENESS AND MAINTAINING
HEALTHY BOUNDARIES

Forgiving doesn't mean that we should set ourselves up for being gluttons for punishment. Forgiveness is an inside job. We do it for ourselves. Nor does it have to mean that we choose to maintain a close or even a distant relationship with the person we're forgiving. It's something we do so that we can remove the psychological and emotional blocks that prevent us from having faith and hope in the fundamental goodness of life, people and the beauty of relationships.

In therapy, we encounter this situation frequently: Clients worry that if they forgive and reconnect they will only be setting themselves up for a continual dose of hurt, and that the wounds they are trying to heal never will. But as we've well established by now, we're forgiving not for the other person, but so that we can unhook ourselves from a particular type of connection—one that is filled with old pain and anguish, and that plays itself over and over again in our minds and hearts like a scary movie. Forgiveness should allow us some emotional and psychological freedom, some space to breathe and make choices. When we're consumed with a past unresolved hurt, we may only see two choices: total connection or total disconnection, black-and-white thinking. Once we confront the issues blocking forgiveness and process our grief and anger, we come to realize that we're more in charge of our experience than we might have thought, or at least we're more in charge of *our experience* of our experience. We learn to modulate rather than to either cut off or dive in head first. We get some balance, along with emotional and psychological distance, so that we can make some healthy choices about if and how we wish to connect. We also construct some healthy boundaries to replace our rigid defenses.

If we see forgiveness as meaning we have to stay closely connected to a person who continually hurts us, we'll naturally put off doing it out of self-protection. We may use chronic anger, resentment or avoidance as a way to stay safe—all eventually at great expense to our own peace of mind, our ability to have other more satisfying relationships and our willingness to take "calculated, intelligent risks" in life. (Note that I said calculated, intelligent risks to be differentiated from high-risk behaviors, which can be another defense against pain or symptom of PTSD.) In other words, we have a right to defend ourselves against being continually hurt by exercising boundaries that feel right to us, *while* letting go of hurt and resentment that are only eating up our own insides.

∾

Let's get one thing straight: Forgiving is not something you do for someone else. It is not even something you do because you SHOULD, according to the standards of religious belief or human decency. Forgiving is something that you do for yourself. It is one way of becoming the person you were created to be—and fulfilling God's dream of you is the only way to true wholeness and happiness. You NEED to forgive so that you can move forward with life. An unforgiven injury binds you to a time and place someone else has chosen; it holds you trapped in a past moment and in old feelings.

∾**Carol Luebering**
"Finding a Way to Forgive," *CareNotes*

In Christina's story, we see how this struggle manifests in her relationship with her family.

∾

There is no revenge so complete as forgiveness.

∾**Josh Billings**

Christina's Struggle: Carrying the Constantly Unraveling Mother in Her Inner World

*M*others are a strange, uncharted territory in our psyches. They live in us from cradle to grave, and try as we will, we cannot seem to move them from their core position in our inner world. The psychological theories of separation have been taken somewhat literally, I believe, with much emphasis on separation and not enough on individualization and self-defining. How can we separate from our own insides? For those whose relationships with their mothers have been tough, the idea of separation can come as a final blow, the death of the wish of ever getting what we want. But separation is a psychological and emotional process more than a physical one.

It's very hard to reject and hate our mothers without rejecting and hating a part of ourselves because, like it or not, our mothers are woven into the very fabric of our being as we are woven into theirs. Nature and physics are bigger than we are. And it's very hard to forgive our mothers without needing to entertain self-forgiveness. Even the guilt we feel over our angry, resentful or rejecting thoughts about our mothers can make us feel bad—let alone the actions we might have taken because we're feeling those feelings. Rejection is often laced into our own behavior as well. So do I forgive myself? My mother? Or both of us for our natural need to live our own lives?

And what does all this mean in terms of having dominion over our own selves? Do any of us have a prayer of being our own person? And if the relationship was problematic, what do we do? One sure way to keep a problematic mother gaining power inside us is to deny her internal presence. That's when we're really apt to become her in a variety of unconscious ways. The other way is to reject her wholesale or reject the part of us that wants to be free of her. If we can understand what we have from her that's positive and feel good about that, and then explore and accept what we may have that's not so good and be willing to take responsibility for it now being a part of us (otherwise, why would it be coming out?), then we can become ourselves; we can understand that all of us are like mosaics, many small pieces from many different places shaped into our own version of wholeness.

We can't write our parents out of our life scripts. They raised us, and they had a big hand in creating who we are. We may go through a period of blaming them in order to make sense of why we do what we do, or so that we can stop blaming or hating ourselves for particular qualities that are clearly an outgrowth of how we were raised. But the goal is not to move blame from the self to the other and leave it there. The goal is to move past the assiduous assigning of fault toward compassion, empathy and a realistic acceptance of ourselves, our parents and our lives. Getting stuck in blaming someone else is ultimately no more useful than getting stuck in blaming ourselves, and no more freeing. Freedom comes with insight and understanding.

In Christina's story, we see a woman in her late thirties who gets stuck feeling she is bad for wanting to live her own life, for wanting to be her own person. But here is her dilemma: Her mother, with whom she has by all counts a dysfunctional relationship, is not improving with age. When Christina, after diligent and hard work, gets better and feels healthier, her mother resents it and undermines it.

Last evening, Christina came to group hurting, feeling like a bad daughter. Mother's Day was fast approaching and all she wished to do was avoid her mother, who had been a tremendous source of pain to her all her life. Christina had been the oldest girl of a single mother. She, her mother and older brother lived with her uncle and grandmother until Christina was six. Her memories of that time are happy and peopled with those she loved. She grew up in a Hispanic family with strong cultural and family ties, and she felt cared about and secure living at her grandmother's house, even though her life there wasn't easy. Then a big change happened. Christina's mother landed a steady job and wanted to get away from her own mother now that she could "afford" it. She moved to an apartment with her children and worked full-time. Christina became responsible for the care and feeding of her brothers, both the older and the younger one born after they moved. It was she who looked after "the baby," she who stayed home from school when he got sick and became his mommy. She adored him, needed him and was burdened by him. This was her childhood.

Though Christina got precious little mothering herself as a child, her mother fully expects Christina's support as she grows older. There is not a dollar

Christina earns, a job she's got or a relationship she has that does not have a lien on it from her mother. Her mother assigned her the job of caretaker first of her little brother and next of herself, and said only that this is how things are done in their culture, no further explanation required. The fact that she is asking her to give from an empty well does not seem to register with her mother, an alcoholic who is getting worse with age. Christina is from the same culture and feels like a very bad daughter for not wishing to meet the needs of a mother who physically abused her, emotionally neglected her and left her alone to care for herself and her brothers. These conflicting feelings make her feel torn inside and crazy. Christina is also smart and able to obtain and hold jobs, which makes her a further candidate for taking care of the family. She is competent. So her best asset becomes a liability, and she doesn't feel free to use her earnings to move forward in her own life (which is why she doesn't go for the master's degree she so wants to get). The pattern of Christina being the family caregiver follows her throughout her life.

Fast-forward to adulthood, and we see Christina sinking into a deep depression she can barely find her way out of, let alone continue to help anyone else. Falling apart herself becomes one of the only ways to keep her mother off her back. But now she needs help desperately, and she is actually rather adept at recruiting it. One unfortunate way that she has learned to get taken care of is to be in a chronic state of crisis, much like her mother. Though she cannot allow herself to yell, abuse and accuse as her mother does to get care (that would be too much like home), she falls apart, gets the help from others, then sabotages its success at every turn, replacing her mother's perennial "straw boss" demands with her own version. Once Christina identifies a person from whom she feels she can get what she wants or needs, she becomes obsessed with that person, barraging him or her with calls, requests and demands. She can get people to extend themselves in all sorts of unusual ways to help her, but at the end of the day, she never feels fed. She finds some way to make it clear that nothing they do really helps, inducing in them the deep frustration and hopelessness that she carries so much of the time. This is her way of asking for help, or rather, because she cannot ask, she asserts a demand through her behavior. This is, perhaps, a convoluted way of expressing the hatred and rage she feels toward a mother who wants more than she can ever or would ever wish to give, or to externalize the unrelenting anger she feels toward herself for being a "bad daughter," or being caught in a tangled web of emotion that she can't seem to steer clear of. It is also an unconscious attempt to get others to feel what she is going through.

Christina's Drama

In her psychodrama, we let Christina express her powerful rage and feelings of hatred outwardly so that she could stop beating herself up on the inside, turning the rage and hate loose in her own inner world where it was tearing her apart and locking her into her depression. This work occurred over a period of years, but one new twist seemed to represent a turning point for her. Tonight after expressing her own negative feelings more fully and honestly then previously and taking more ownership and responsibility for them, she reversed roles and played her mother. She spent most of the psychodrama ordering herself (played by a group member) and everyone else in her family system around. She was queen of the mountain, La Doña, the big straw boss of the family system, and she asserted her maternal authority with the gusto and finesse of a bullfighter. She was hilarious, bossing everyone around, sending family members in to put on the pressure when Daughter didn't do what Daughter was "supposed" to do, moving anyone over who got into her line of vision or her line of control. She was brilliant; no actor could have portrayed the part of an alcoholic, demanding mother with a hunger for power better. When overt orders weren't followed, she accused her daughter of not being a good girl; when that didn't work, she dissolved into tears; and when tears produced no satisfactory result, she got sick. She ruled from below, from the victim role, and no one was beyond her reach. She constantly cited her whole cultural system as evidence that it was her children's job to care for her, wielding an emotional, psychological and cultural whip to nutty perfection. She was the unequivocal boss lady of the family system.

Christina got to be, for a moment in time, the tyrant whom she had spent a lifetime feeling tortured by—whom she loved deeply and hated deeply. In experiencing the love, hate, envy, hurt and power-tripping of her mother, Christina was able to better integrate those powerful feelings rather than splitting them off or denying them or acting them out by becoming them. And through the magical, healing alchemy of laughter, she found pieces of herself that had been living in various disowned corners of her family system and claimed them as her own.

The next day Christina received a call from her mother, who called because she "just wanted me to have her phone number for Mother's Day, just in case I might want to call." Christina reported having a "nice conversation with her," then getting off the phone.

Forgiveness and compassion can enter a person in many ways. One tried-and-true one is to stand in the shoes of the offending party for a while, even if only in a role-play. Though Christina did not play the heartbroken mother, she was able, after having what we might call a catharsis of laughter, to move the tyrant aside and touch the woman living underneath; the one who could not ask but only demand; who could not survive her own vulnerability; who, no matter how much nourishment she was able to extract from others, never felt fed. Paradoxically, in standing in her mother's shoes, she was able to understand that her mother's coldness toward her was not a result of Christina's being a bad daughter, but rather of her mother's own history of pain. This cast a wedge of light into Christina's psyche, and she was able to entertain the possibility of forgiveness, of herself as well as her mother.

In Christina's Own Words

The following is Christina's response to her work:

I am recognizing I have spent too much time in separation and not enough in integration and individualization. I cut off all ties completely at eighteen and denounced my family, my culture (not aware it was my family's interpretation of my culture) and their superstitions to be able to survive in adulthood. I had to break away from what was stifling me, hoping that the rejection would set me free. I later studied my culture in school and found something I could reclaim.

I cut myself off from that which is so deep a part of me that I cannot run from it. It exerts itself often. I cut myself off as my mother had when leaving her mother. Wow, I did what she did. But differently. I went to college. I took on a second culture as if it were possible to cut out this huge part of myself. No wonder I cried all through college. I could not divorce myself from the part of me that was my mother and my family.

I did, however, progress toward change. I changed my thought process to be less immobilizingly superstitious and cripplingly negative. I worked at detangling the expectations that had me in life-draining knots and loosed the binds, but I could not fully break free.

Whenever my mother or the baby, Lucas, five years old, called my dorm room from their chaos, I felt the efforts of detangling myself defeated, and the knots tightened around me once again. I was still expected to be the hero supporting her as her alcoholism progressed and her destructive behavior escalated. The stress of the cultural expectations, that I would/should/must come to her aid, did stifle my success, postponing my undergraduate graduation eight years, withdrawing from my fiancé, withdrawing from graduate school, etc.

I like the image of "constantly unraveling..."; I felt each time I started to create something good in my life, I did fall apart slowly and painfully.

How could I hate her without hating myself? She *is* woven into me, and I into her. I have always known that. I can't hate her without loving. I can't hurt her without hurting too big a part of me. I need her, and she needs me. I do agree with the value of expressing the rage, but I cannot murder her emotionally. To want to kill her off inside me feels too devastating. I tried it, "acted as if," but it didn't feel good or right. It only heightened my "bad daughter" feelings. I felt no better than she. But this is not the part of her that I want coming out of me. She had many strengths and talents that I am proud to have flow through me. I am who I am because she was who she was, both good and bad. How do I express my rage without annihilating her and myself? We are woven into one another.

Each one of us is desperate for the piece of ourselves that is missing because of my need to protect myself through total physical and emotional separation. She and my brother desperately want and need me, but I need me safe and whole. But I am not whole. I am devoid of too big a part of me, because I am so adamant about my safety. I stand firm in my decision to keep me safe, but I acknowledge the pain and grief it causes me, them and the family.

I have felt it a goal to stay connected to my family and get what they can offer, even if it is not what I need/want. I am trying with my extended family. But with my mother and older brother . . . their aggressive, manipulative and abusive nature is terrifying. I won't allow abusiveness in my life, if I can protect myself from it. But I am lonely and hungry for love and nurturing. I know I need to work through this stuff so I can let in caring from others who are happy to give it. It is here for me in others. It is available, and I don't avail myself of it when I need it the most. Because of guilt or some neurotic habit of deprivation? I "turtle." I flip over on my back, my legs in the air going nowhere, and I can't right myself. "How do we work with what we got?" They live in me. How do I take what I need and leave the rest? How do I stifle the "bad" mother, the "bully" brother, that live inside me without stifling myself? How do I kill that and not myself?

Before my younger brother was born, my mother, older brother and I usually had our own apartment near my grandmother's house, but my extended family was so much a part of my life that everything revolved around Grandma's house. I "lived" there, in that we were always there in my experience.

You know I "lived" with my grandmother's eight children (seven teenaged girls and my uncle was my age), right? It sounded like we lived calmly with my grandmother and her adult son. I know you know, it was much more chaotic than that. And in my grandmother's home, it was me and my older brother (the baby wasn't born yet). The baby never "lived" at Grandma's house. He never knew the joys and chaos of the extended family. He is also not as emotionally connected to anyone as we were.

I was thirteen when the baby was born. Yes, I was expected by all in the immediate and extended family to be the mother of this child. Everyone knew my mother was ill-equipped, and I had been born to care for babies. I was good at it. Tons better than she was. I think it relevant to note that I was not the oldest and that I still had to be the caretaker. The Hispanic readers would relate immensely, and other readers need to hear this to understand the cultural expectations.

I liked the way you delineated that my mother left her mother and family for "separation." She did and cut all ties. I was about eight and was responsible for the care and feeding of myself and my older brother Victor, up through age eight. But with the extended family it was hard to see the neglect and over-responsibility clearly because there was intermittent support. Now totally alone in this new apartment, it was bitterly clear to me and everyone. This was prior to removal for neglect and the child-welfare fiasco. Child welfare thought I shouldn't be that responsible? I doubt they understood. They stripped me of my role, my fragile family, the only control I had in this abusive and dysfunctional system and the only successful part of my life at that age. I was good at it, even though I was never good enough. I was just a kid, but I still got enough crumbs to feel esteem from it.

Protective services never followed through, and I was once again responsible just a year later but with none of the crumbs of esteem (self- or family esteem) I once had, nor the fragile family cohesion. After thirteen, I got that responsibility and esteem back with Lucas, the baby. As you mentioned, I became his "Mami Yana."

I was a good mother, and everyone acknowledged it. My mother gave up a lot of power and control over the baby. The expectations of the older girl do come with its rewards in the Hispanic culture. Ideally, this begins the maturation process of the girl and gives her a supportive environment to practice, much like an apprentice, the mother/wife role. The young daughter becomes like the wife to the mother. My mother felt its rewards as the oldest girl, but she learned how to abuse that power. Learning from her example, I did not and would not.

This is how Christina attempted to break the chain of a set of dysfunctional relationships that she had internalized slowly and over time. It required self-forgiveness, along with forgiving others.

Issues with parents often arise in the process of therapy. After all, they're the people who raised us; they have a lot to do with who we are and how we experience the world. In forgiving parents, we're forgiving not just the people we know today who may seem pretty okay, but the ones who live inside us, the ones from yesterday. The ones who raised us when we were young, when the heat was on. The ones we experienced as dependent and vulnerable children, who held our lives literally in their hands. The ones who were larger than life, not our moms and dads of today but our mommies and daddies of yesterday. The ones who hung the moon.

Self-forgiveness and forgiveness of our parents are inextricably intertwined. They occupy the same heart-space. We need to do both in order to heal and move on.

∾

> When you hold resentment toward another, you are bound to that person or condition by an emotional link that is stronger than steel. Forgiveness is the only way to dissolve that link and get free.
>
> ∾Catherine Ponder

INTERNAL DISCONNECTS: HOW WE LOSE TOUCH WITH OUR OWN INSIDES

All of us have zones of privacy, places within us that we go for comfort, respite or refueling. This is part of being a healthy person; we should not tamper with it. Disconnection is another animal. Disconnected zones are places of numbness or muteness, places inside us that we don't dare to go. They represent internal disconnects. What we want to bring to these forbidden zones is a kind of emotional literacy, or the ability to translate what we're feeling on the inside into words, even if what we say is nothing more than, "I'm feeling numb and out of touch with what I'm feeling or might be feeling."

Emotional literacy or the lack of it tends to get trained (or untrained) within us. Children are only too in touch with their feelings: They shout them out at dinnertime, blurt them out (often to their parents' embarrassment) at family gatherings and stop simple outings dead in their tracks with their spontaneous outbursts. Part of maturing and becoming a civilized member of society includes slowly helping children come to terms with their feelings and learning how to experience them without *becoming* them, how to feel them and find ways of expressing them that allow them to function in society while still being authentic within their own skin. In order to take charge of our feelings, it helps if we can learn to translate them into words. It is only at this point that we can use our powers of reasoning to explore, examine and make sense and meaning of our experiences. This can also be the point of a fundamental splinter. The deep emotions associated with our limbic system do not always bend to the will of the thinking cortex. And in forcing them to do so, some feel that we lose a piece of contact with our deeper emotional self. This is, in part, why therapies like psychodrama or art, drama, dance or music therapy can offer avenues for expression, integration and healing that allow more of these aspects of self to come forward. Perhaps one of the reasons artists or "creative people" are seen as "eccentric" or somewhat out of the norm is because more of this limbic self, for lack of a better term, comes forward into the world. Their "governors" aren't as strict.

When the emotions we're experiencing feel too big, they can scare or overwhelm us, for example, if we get very hurt. Then, rather than translate them into words, we may want to flee from them, to shut them down or explode. When we do this, we don't eliminate reason, necessarily, but we postpone it. The Creative Arts Therapies, such as those mentioned above, or journaling [as we explore in part II], offer additional channels through which feeling can flow and integrate with thought.

Feelings are biological as well as mental. They travel through our bodies on neuropeptides [as we discussed in chapter 2]. We experience them physically as body sensations, anything from a queasy stomach to a tight chest. They vibrate out into space and affect those around us. Any one of us can identify with what it's like to be standing next to someone who's tense or angry. Feelings inform, inspire, drive and often determine many of our actions. We need to be aware of them, so that we can make conscious decisions about how to handle them; otherwise, they handle us. When we can't back up, we're setting ourselves up for a less constructive way of coping. We might project our emotions onto someone else, blame another person for what we're feeling, repress what we're feeling so we temporarily get it out of consciousness, deny it by rewriting what's going on so it's more palatable to us, somatize it so it expresses itself on the body level ("my aching back!"), or self-medicate by using alcohol, drugs, food, work, spending or sex as tools for mood management. If we can catch our breath, backtrack and use our intense reaction as a signal to us that something powerful is going on, or that some old hurt got triggered, we can still do the translating necessary to gain some clarity. The critical issue here is that we realize that pain from other areas or times in our life may be manifesting through situations in the present.

We walk a fine line as citizens of a social world. Some ways of managing feelings effectively enough so that they don't keep us from meeting the day-to-day demands of our lives is necessary. A little bit of repression allows us to go to work after a fight with our spouse or to keep functioning when we're waiting to get the test results as to whether or not a tumor might be cancerous. Too much repression over a long period of time, however, can undermine our healthy immune functioning, or lead to chronic states of depression or anxiety. In these cases, we're probably sitting on rather than processing our feelings. If, every time we feel anxious or depressed, we hide our true feelings behind psychological defenses or form a habit of eating or smoking or drinking or spending, we're doing two things: (1) Training ourselves not to feel (in which case our "feeling muscles" get weak), and (2) developing a habit that is going to lead to still more problems. Most pathology results from running away from what's really going on inside of us. We lose compassion and empathy with ourselves and others, and we undermine our ability to handle life circumstances that may require relational sensitivity. This generally shows up most strongly in how we "live" in our intimate relationships, in the quality of our connections.

When clients arrive at my office in this state, they often don't know where to begin. And to make matters worse, these are often the clients who want to solve their dilemma in a few sessions. They've been shoving things down and giving themselves quick fixes instead of meaningful help for so long that they cannot bear the thought of sitting with their emotions as they arise, slowly feeling them and translating powerful emotional states into words. They want the therapist to figure it all out and tell them what to do to get their life to work. Sometimes, the therapist joins in their frustration and tries to give them those answers, but this really isn't what's needed. What's useful for the long run is a sort of emotional learning and teaching that educates clients in the art of becoming emotionally intelligent and literate. "Give a man a fish and you feed him for a day," as the Chinese saying goes, "teach him to fish and you feed him for a lifetime." Learning the skills of emotional literacy transforms your life.

~

As long as you don't forgive, who and whatever it is will occupy rent-free space in your mind.

~Isabelle Moiland
The Long Search

PEELING BACK THE LAYERS OF THE ONION

So many of the clients I work with echo the same frustration about how long healing can take. "Why am I not done with this? I already did this work, now I'm here all over again. . . . Will I ever be finished? I can't keep doing this over and over again."

It seems as if many of us assume that we're organized on the inside in a linear sort of way, our internal qualities neatly stacked up or filed in sequence. But in truth, we're an evolving, highly complicated system interdependent on our core. So when we forgive, we operate sort of like nature does. Deep plates shift inside of us. Rainfall can both cause a mudslide and make things grow; it can become a flood or a lake to swim in. Fallen vegetation becomes the fertilizer for new growth. As we get stronger and wiser we see new areas requiring emotional work. Just because we forgive one set of transgressions doesn't mean that other issues needing forgiveness won't be flushed to the surface and suddenly appear floating on the waters of consciousness. One thing leads to another; thoughts and feelings lead to more thoughts and feelings. But this is an intrinsic value of forgiveness. It's not just the act of forgiveness that is necessarily so freeing, but also the processing and working through of all of the complicated emotions that are blocking it, and transforming those emotions into new awareness and insight.

The goal isn't to "finish"; in fact, the finish line is really an illusion. The goal is to continue to grow, and growth is a deconstruction and reconstruction of the self, which is constantly evolving. If we see life as a spiritual journey, and we recognize that the events and relationships of our lives contain lessons that continually present themselves, then it's easier to accept that it's never really over. If you are goal-oriented and want to achieve forgiveness so that it will give you the life you want, you may well get disappointed if it doesn't match up to the preconceived notion of what you expect.

The "layers of the onion" approach helps us to relax into the process of inner transformation. I first encountered it while studying Eastern philosophy in the early Seventies. The idea was that, through meditation, self-reflection and practicing spiritual principles, we peel back or reveal the layers of self one at a time and, in a sense, work through the issues or blocks that are in the way of our own enlightenment and inner peace. Enlightenment seemed to me, at the time, to be a rather unattainable state that, once arrived at, lasted forever, or at least for as far down the road as I could see. Today, I see enlightenment as an evolving state. We integrate growth as our own; practice new ways of being in the world and in our relationships with this more enlightened self; solidify or consolidate our gains, then move on from there and do it all over again. We grow.

Another thing that bothers my clients a lot is the backsliding that often accompanies a growth spurt. When they're in an expansion mode they see something new about themselves, do deep emotional work, experience themselves differently, have all sorts of insights, make a myriad of tiny, meaningful connections, feel better . . . then (whoops!) feel worse. Soon, their excitement gives way to anxiety, and their insights move from appearing momentous to humdrum. Instead of feeling like they're moving forward, they often experience themselves skating on thin ice again, dangerously close to falling into the freezing waters they thought they'd left behind forever. It's typical. It generally happens to a greater or lesser extent. Part of consolidating learning seems to be to gain it, lose it, panic . . . then find it again.

Thirty years ago, I was a Montessori teacher. Over and over again, I watched children go through what Montessori called "explosions in learning." It may have been in math, reading or science. The children became excited and involved in a subject that they had achieved a readiness to learn. They were enthralled and made a thousand small connections as, for instance, they decoded language. Suddenly, the world was full of signs that they could actually read. Places and experiences had names and could be recalled, thought about and communicated to someone else. They were able to make order and sense out of things they never understood before. One new insight led to another, and pretty soon, whole new worlds were open to them. Doors flew open, over and over again. They were thrilled, ecstatic, leaping into the unknown and knowing it. Then came the regression. *It invariably did.* Suddenly, the world didn't seem so rosy. What they now knew only pointed up more of what they didn't know, and they weren't even all that secure in their new knowledge. Lots of what they just learned other people knew better and had known for longer. Discouragement. They no longer experienced themselves as moving forward, but as backsliding. No longer as empowered, but as scared. No longer as smart, but as a whole new kind of dumb.

They were sliding back to their baseline of learning: They needed to practice their new learning in order to solidify it and wire it in solidly enough to alter the baseline. Emotional and psychological growth are similar. Montessori believed that children go through what she called "sensitive periods," when they are particularly sensitive to learning a certain subject. The sensitive period for learning to read, for example, is around three. It comes after the sensitive period for learning language. I observe that we have sensitive periods for emotional and psychological learning throughout our lives as well. I believe young adults are in their sensitive period for learning a profession or acquiring a life passion and developing partner bonds. Women in young adulthood are most certainly in their sensitive period for mothering, with both the skills they've learned from modeling their mothers and grandmothers and the ones newly acquired along with their biological mandate. And women in midlife appear to be in a "sensitive period" for resolving painful issues from the past and for developing wisdom, understanding and spirituality—for beginning to become "keepers of meaning," the wise older generation that helps those younger learn and move forward.

FIVE

Anger and Resentment: Embracing Our Inner Demons

All the years you have waited for them to "make it up to you" and all the energy you expended trying to make them change (or make them pay) kept the old wounds from healing and gave pain from the past free rein to shape and even damage your life. And still they may not have changed. Nothing you have done has made them change. Indeed, they may never change. Inner peace is found by changing yourself, not the people who hurt you. And you change yourself for yourself, for the joy, serenity, peace of mind, understanding, compassion, laughter, and bright future that you get.

~SIDNEY AND SUZANNE SIMON
*FORGIVENESS: HOW TO MAKE PEACE WITH
YOUR PAST AND GET ON WITH YOUR LIFE*

The next two chapters, anger and sadness, are where much of the work that leads to forgiveness will get done. They represent the place we most often get stuck in and have the hardest time working our way out of. Anger and sadness can manifest in many ways, which we will look at in greater detail. The material is dense and challenging, just as this part of the forgiveness process is. But it is in understanding our anger and sadness and their far-reaching ramifications that the key to resolution lies.

THE MANY FACES OF ANGER

Sometimes, our anger feels like all we have to hold onto. The thought of letting it go can leave us feeling like we're giving up a piece of ourselves, or our last bit of connection to someone. As long as we hang onto anger, there may still be hope for reconciliation and restitution. So we hang on for dear life because letting go feels too risky—like if we give in, we'll only be hurt again, the other person will use it somehow to their advantage, and we'll be left high and dry with nowhere to go but down. Or we'll lose our connection to them forever. We may be entirely unaware that we're using our anger as a way to stay connected. And if our anger is covering up hurt, giving in can make us feel like we might fall apart on the spot. But if we can't get through our anger, at least partially, we'll never get to forgiveness. And, to complicate matters further, one of the people we may be angry at is ourselves, even if it's only for getting dragged into something we wish we'd been smart enough to stay out of or for not being perfect in our reactions in some way. But nobody's perfect, not us or anyone else.

Stonewalling, criticism, withdrawal, whining, sulking, irritability, control, grumpiness, or a preoccupation with negative subjects can all be manifestations of unacknowledged or unprocessed anger. Three common things people do with their anger are expressing, suppressing and calming. In _expressing_, we find some way to articulate our anger, we're assertive; we use it to propel us to make some shift, however minor or major. In _suppressing_, we do not express it. We may repress, deny, dissociate, minimize or in some way hide what we're really feeling from ourselves. Or we may simply choose not to express it openly. _Calming_ means we take active measures to calm down, like using breathing techniques, attitude adjustments, counting slowly to ten or taking a time out.

Anger can be functional or dysfunctional. Functional anger generally moves a situation forward in some way; we recognize we're angry about something, and that motivates us to reassess. Maybe we make a change in the way we're handling something, or shift our expectations so we're not setting ourselves up for disappointment, and subsequently, anger. Or we process our angry feelings with someone we trust and make some choices about what to do with them. Dysfunctional anger, on the other hand, can be a place we get swept into, where our anger seems to multiply and feed on itself until it has a life of its own.

Anger is an emotional state that can range from mild irritation to rage. The biological changes that accompany anger are increased heart rate and blood pressure, and increased levels of the "energy" hormones adrenaline and noradrenaline, which are associated with the fight-or-flight response. And according to Christiane Northrup, "when we're constantly pumping out 'stress' chemicals we also experience increased levels of cortisol which can do anything from weakening our bones to locking in fat storage."

Anger can also be a secondary reaction to early narcissistic wounds or relationship wounds. These wounds occur for everyone; they are a part of growing up and developing a separate sense of self that is no longer just an extension of our parents. If we're separate, we can get hurt. Maybe the birth of a younger sibling with whom we had to share our mother was an early wound, or a childhood illness, moving too often, persistent parental absence, or a combination of such occurrences is what we're feeling wounded or angry about.

When we're separate and young, we're especially vulnerable to those we love and need because they have such power over our lives. Many of these early wounds resolve themselves naturally as we become secure in our sense of self and feel increasingly capable of finding other ways of getting our needs for love, attention and security met. Some wounds don't.

Here is a catch-22: While sharing grief and anger and expressing our old feelings of humiliation and outrage can be healing, there may be such a thing as overdoing it. Unprocessed anger can also manifest passive–aggressively, or in getting back at others indirectly, not telling them why we're angry. Even lateness, stony silence, constant sloppiness or "having an attitude" can be forms of passive–aggressive anger. And depression can grow out of anger that we turn inward on the self, that never gets processed or expressed, but instead fuels a sort of negative self-concept and a dark inner dialogue. Chronic anger can wreak havoc on our bodies, pumping out stress chemicals and keeping us in a state of fight-or-flight readiness. People who are constantly putting other people down, criticizing, or being whiny, irritable, sulky, or cynical, or bursting out in regular fits of irrational anger haven't learned to constructively manage their anger.

HISTORICAL VERSUS CURRENT ANGER

When our anger goes beyond what might be an appropriate response to the situation we're actually in, we need to take a deeper look at what might be getting activated. Are we carrying anger from a fight with our spouse into the workplace? Are we *getting* angry with our child, when we're really angry with our boss, *displacing* the anger we're feeling toward one person onto someone else? Or are we really mad at *ourselves,* and it's leaking out sideways? Chronic anger can become a quality of personality, a resting place within the self. We go there, and we stay there. If our anger is chronic, we probably need to look more deeply to see if there's a piece of historical anger we're carrying that might be getting mixed up with current anger and creating a ticking time bomb. "If you are a highly sensitive or suggestible individual, receptive to mental imagery, and you have a lot of cortisol in your bloodstream (as when you're stressed), it is very possible for you to incorporate new 'traumatic' memories into your brain and body that have no basis in your past experience," says Dr. Christiane Northrup. She adds, "Instead they may be the by-product of your current environment combined with the suggestions and imagery you picked up." If someone or something in your environment seems to suggest that a certain thing happened at a moment when you are bio-logically susceptible, "the scenario may then be encoded as a new trauma memory," says Northrup, "one that you'll have to cope with on top of the original memories that have arisen on their own." This is where the theory that expressing and talking about all our fears and anxieties in order to heal them may have some loopholes. While it may be desir-able to uncover and explore repressed memories, it may not be desir-able to make uncovering and exploring a way of life or an ongoing behavior. The idea is to explore and *move through and beyond* a pre-occupation with past issues. Likewise, talking about a trauma imme-diately can have different results for each person, beneficial for some and not others. Certain people do better when they "go about their business," waiting for another time to talk about their experience(s).

As Christiane Northrup pointed out, if we're highly stressed we may do better to calm down before we share our feelings and fears. Otherwise, the past and present can get confused and mixed up with each other and make it hard to unravel, which in turn makes it hard to solve a conflict because there's no bottom; we never feel we've really gotten something "off our chests." An attitude of forgiveness toward ourselves and someone else can sometimes create a wedge of light that allows us to let things go, even though they may never feel *completely* resolved. We understand that complete resolution may never come because our memories are all a jumble, and we may have to consider being satisfied with what can feel like a partial resolution, say some-thing above 50 percent. For people who've felt pummeled in the past, or as though they were always coming up with the short end of the stick, letting things go at this point can make them feel as if they will never get to set the record straight—they will never get the revenge and restitution they feel they deserve.

Oftentimes, anger opens the door to grief. When clients can begin to engage in the grief process, of which anger is a part, they often feel a burden is being lifted as their feelings emerge and they experience and understand them in the here and now. The dysfunctional version of this process happens when clients continue, in a sense, to retrau-matize themselves with their own cycle of anger. They get angry, in a state of high stress, and the old anger gets triggered to such an inten-sity that it makes the current situation very complicated to work through. The current situation and the past form a sort of amalgam, and become a self-fulfilling prophecy; past hurts get recreated in the present with new names and faces, and rather than moving past anger toward resolution, the anger comes to have a life of its own. And other emotions associated with the grief process, like sadness, hurt and a feeling of "falling apart," never emerge. Their chronic anger is blocking them from feeling their hurt. People caught in this bind can find themselves stuck in chronic anger or depression. Forgiveness, especially self-forgiveness, can be a way out of this chronic dysfunc-tional cycle. I have found that a combination of therapeutic goals seems to work best for resolving past issues of trauma. I try to get clients to engage in more than a therapeutic process. I have found that daily exercise and sunlight are critical to maintaining a stable mood. Also, actively taking steps to create a positive lifestyle by devel-oping meaninful (or at least sustaining) work—finding something to feel motivated and passionate about—and incorporating healing or spiritual communities into our lifestyles all serve healing better than therapy alone, in my experience. Some balance between therapy and lifestyle changes seems to work the best. [More on this in "Prescriptions for Happy Living" in chapter 8.]

TRIGGERS AND TRANSFERENCE

On the emotional side of things, when emotional and psychological pain remain unresolved, they often lie in wait, unconscious of their power and content, until some stimulus in the here and now *triggers* them and they jettison to the surface for quick expulsion. Maybe we react to a perceived threat (this can be as subtle as a change in vocal tone or the look in an eye) with a response that is far greater than the situation merits; or, if we were repeatedly humiliated, feeling humiliated by someone in the present can trigger an intense reaction that appears to be about the present, but actually has its origins in pain from the past that's getting *transferred* onto the present-day situation. When triggered, we may go from zero to ten with no numbers in between, a symptom of PTSD. This grows out of the numbing response that is part of being traumatized. Traumatized people may alternate between states of extreme fear and psychic numbing or shutting down. These states can get hardwired into the brain and affect future behavior. As they occur over and over again, they become part of the personality structure and the way traumatized people interact with life and relationships, a phenomenon sometimes referred to as black-and-white thinking. Then their current lives may come to mirror their painful past as the past emotional and psychological dynamics develop a gravity of their own, pulling the present toward them. This is the "repetition compulsion" that we talked about earlier, the compulsion to re-create or repeat in the present those situations or dynamics that hurt us in the past. Perhaps it also indicates an unconscious and misguided attempt to pull together a self that feels fragmented from the loss or rupture of a primary limbic connection and "master" feelings of insecurity of engulfment.

For people who have experienced chronic emotional and psychological damage, the body can get damaged as well; it gets deregulated. When these people get scared and triggered, they may experience some of the following: trembling, voice changes, breathlessness, palpitations and flushing. These are not under conscious control and may be out of proportion to the current emotional stimuli. It is the arousal state of the autonomic nervous system. Learning to sit with this state and talk from it, put it into words, can help us to make sense of what's going on inside of us so that the past does not continue to pollute the present. To decode states like this we may need to seek professional help and support groups. This is, of course, on a continuum; some of it is within a normal range, but if it becomes a life complication, it may be well to take a deeper look at the origins.

THE SEDUCTION OF RAGE

The rage state can take us over, obliterating reason and blowing past ordinary boundaries like a tornado leaving devastation in its wake. Our trauma responses are essentially fear-based; that is, we get scared or sense danger and react to stay safe. Fight, flight or freeze responses cause us to shut down from fear or aggress in anger if we can't get away. When both the fear and anger get triggered together, they can catapult us into a state in which we tremble with rage. "During rage attacks . . . those parts of the brain that are central to feeling and expressing anger, such as the amygdala and the hypothalamus, commandeer the rest of the brain. In this wholesale takeover, the cerebral cortex is overwhelmed and restraint and reasoning are impossible. . . . Although rage—by which I mean anger that is extreme, immoderate or unrestrained—may be adaptive as a response to severe threat, in most situations it destroys much more than it accomplishes," says Dr. Norman Rosenthal in *The Emotional Revolution.*

Chronic rage might also be an indicator of depression. It's been estimated that 40 percent of those suffering from rage attacks also suffer from clinical depression. Rage attacks can also be a part of the PTSD syndrome. Rosenthal continues:

ꝰ

Dr. Martin Teicher and colleagues at Harvard have found that adults who were abused as children, whether verbally, physically or sexually, show brain wave changes over the temporal lobe of the cerebral cortex. These changes resemble those seen in people with documented seizures in the temporal lobe, which surrounds the limbic structures. . . . Teicher suggests that early traumatic experiences might kindle seizure-type activity in this area, resulting in a storm of electrical activity in the emotional part of the cerebral cortex. . . . [T]he end result could be a brain that is cocked and all too ready to fire off a limbic storm.

ꝰ

If you were belittled as a child and abused in some way, being belittled again can trigger a rage attack. A stimulus similar to that which was originally traumatizing can act as a trigger, releasing a potent blast of rage, a discharge of emotions loaded with fear, anger, humiliation and helplessness. Though rage can feel gratifying and even integrating to ragers because they are finally giving expression to split-off feelings that they may normally push out of consciousness, its irrational nature keeps it from leading to any kind of true or useful understanding. Rage also can be highly damaging to those around the raging person. People can feel temporarily empowered by raging; they may have seen themselves as too weak, humiliated or beaten down to "let it fly" in the past, so it feels gratifying to release pent-up emotions. They may experience themselves as going from tiny to big, helpless to empowered because the source of the pain getting triggered is from a past wound inflicted or experienced when they felt disempowered. But ultimately, we need to make sense of our feelings in order to use them to grow from; simply discharging them and walking away doesn't do the job.

Because the cortex is overridden in the rage state, sense is not likely to accompany rage, and this is why a time-out is good—it gives the body a chance to reregulate. Perhaps the rage state sets us up for the hope of solving an old pain-filled situation, a variation on what Freud called an attempt at mastery. As long as we can stay invested in our anger, which over time fuels rage, there's still hope for ultimate resolution. But, contrary to the myth that modern psychology unwittingly puts forth, not everything can get resolved. Sometimes, in fact many times, resolution of past hurts involves a combination of working through painful emotions, making helpful lifestyle changes and learning to see an old problem through a new lens. That is, we don't necessarily *change* the problem; we learn as Carl Jung said, "to go to the mountaintop and see it differently." We explore it, tease out the meaning we made of it and that we have been living by, and feel some of the feelings that we may have split off and out of our conscious awareness, the feelings that blew our available circuits. We understand the problem in the light of today, and reintegrate our memories with new understanding and insight. This is mostly an inside job. When this doesn't occur, our past tends to get layered onto our present and woven into it.

TO YELL OR NOT TO YELL

Some people seem to be more angry, chronically grumpy or irritable than others. Easily annoyed people don't always curse or throw things. Sometimes they withdraw, sulk or get physically ill, or they may have a low frustration tolerance. They may feel they should not have to be subjected to frustration, inconvenience or annoyance, and may get infuriated if they feel slighted or a situation seems unjust; very likely it triggers previous pain around feeling unfairly treated. For those who have the illusion that getting angry will somehow help the situation or that they can't keep themselves from blowing up, "letting it rip" can escalate anger and aggression and does not necessarily help us, or the person we're angry with. In fact, according to Rosenthal, "an old myth is that it is best to let your anger out when you feel it. New evidence, however suggests, that releasing it only makes it worse. To your nervous system, the release may be more a rehearsal, enhancing the neural pathways involved. It is far better for your health to find ways to let the issue go, or to channel the anger in a constructive way."

In my experience, clients do need to allow themselves to get angry, both so that they understand they have a right to their anger and so that they can restore a sense of lost power at repeatedly holding it in. But the expression seems to best serve the client when it is part of an active plan of making lifestyle changes and of examing *all* the various feelings, thinking and behavior associated with the issue requiring resolution—and anger is only one of the feelings, albeit a very big one. There seems to be quite a difference between owning and expressing anger, and getting stuck in it. Different factors contribute to problems with anger:

Genetics: There is evidence some children are born irritable, touchy, and easily angered, and signs of this are present from a very early age. There is also evidence that repeated abuse or trauma can deregulate the nervous system making us more susceptible to having intense reactions.

Sociocultural: In some societies, anger is seen as negative and as *not* okay to express; anxiety, depression or physical ailments are okay. Women often live under this prejudice.

Family background: People who are easily angered tend to come from families that are disruptive, chaotic and not skilled at emotional communication.

STRATEGIES FOR MANAGING ANGER

Rosenthal outlines ten strategies for managing anger. I list them here with brief descriptions. I like his list because it's realistic, genuinely helpful and stays away from quick-fixes.

1. **Recognize that your anger is a problem:** Nothing will change if we

don't honestly admit to having a problem with anger. Even if we're not flying into rages, being angry on the inside keeps us in a fight-or-flight state, and undermines our health and our relationships.

2. **Monitor your anger level:** We each can keep an informal chart that marks down times of the day when we're most likely to get angry—coming home from work, for example, or around the kids' bedtime.

3. **Look for a pattern:** We each can see if there is a pattern that's identifiable, and if there is, we can take steps to remain calm using some of the tips listed below, so that we can avoid getting angry at the same old things. We can use a little prevention to head off a typical pitfall before it becomes a problem.

4. **Take a time-out:** The body physically responds to anger, so a time-out can allow the body, as well as our emotions, to calm down. This keeps us from getting lost in a vicious cycle, where our upset bodies are feeding our upset emotions and thoughts, and our upset emotions and thoughts are feeding our upset bodies.

5. **Challenge perceptions and thoughts that fuel your anger:** We may be looking at the world in an "awfulizing" way, expecting the worst and helping to create it. If we have a constant negative read on things, we also have negative expectations, which can become a self-fulfilling prophecy.

6. **Dig deeper to understand the roots:** As we've already discussed in this chapter, some anger can have historical roots. Maybe we came from families that were so angry, we got trained in it in both body and mind. Or maybe we're expressing the anger we had to hold in as children, in our adult lives today. Our anger might also be acting as a defense against deeper feelings of pain and helplessness. We need to get to the roots so that we can change the pattern.

7. **Change the messages you give to yourself:** Sometimes, our "self messages" make situations much worse than they have to be. For

example, if our boss is critical we may say to ourselves, "She/he has no respect for me; she/he thinks I'm not very smart, who does she/he think she/he is? I'm not at all appreciated." If we can change these messages to more useful ones like, "I'll listen to the criticism and see if I can use any of it to improve my work," or "I'm bright enough to figure out how to get this to work and I'll use these ideas to help me," we will be empowering ourselves, rather than running ourselves down, and we'll get a little distance from messages that feel hurtful.

8. **Use exposure and relaxation:** "Joseph Wolphe, a pioneer in behavioral therapy research, was the first to reason that it is impossible to feel highly aroused and relaxed at the same time. If you get a person to relax while exposing him to an unpleasant stimulus at the same time . . . you can recondition him. . . . The nervous system can be taught to greet that stimulus with relaxation, not the old, unpleasant emotions," says Rosenthal. Each time we get triggered, we have an opportunity to recondition our response by actively changing the way we're thinking and using deep-breathing techniques to stay calm. This way, over time, we can recondition how we're responding.

9. **Use humor:** If there is a funny side to the situation, use it to create some new energy. Mel Brooks said about *To Be or Not to Be*, his black comedy set in Nazi Germany, "If you can get people to laugh, you've won." This is different from using humor in a sarcastic or belittling way, or as a hiding place; it's using it to see things in a way that allows us to gain some emotional and psychological freedom and to maintain a healthy perspective.

10. **Listen to your limbic news and act appropriately:** This is where we can use our anger as information. Why are we angry? Is it justified and do we need to take action on our own behalf to change something? What is our anger trying to tell us that we can hear and think over in a constructive way, and what actions might we take to improve our situation?

SOME TIPS FOR MANAGING ANGER

- **Find out what triggers you** and **develop strategies** to avoid getting triggered. Work with the list above to gain a deeper understanding of your anger and the source of it and add some tools such as breathing deeply; repeating to yourself, "relax, relax"; counting backwards; using imagery to visualize a relaxing experience [see part II]; or reconditioning your responses using *exposure* and *relaxation.*

- **Cognitive restructuring** or "changing the way you think" can be helpful. When angry thoughts get exaggerated, overly dramatic and awfulized, try replacing them with more rational ones.

- **Don't:** "It's awful, terrible, everything's ruined; it's always like this; it will never work out."

- **Do:** "It's frustrating; it's undesirable that I'm upset but not the end of the world; I'm not pleased with the situation but I can back up, regroup and make changes to improve things."

- **Avoid words like *never* and *always.*** They alienate and humiliate people, and keep them from working with us. And they work us up into an unnecessary lather.

- **Remind yourself that getting angry is not going to fix anything;** it won't really make you feel better, and it may make you feel worse. Remember what you're doing to your body when you get angry.

- **Logic can defeat anger** (as it does fear) because anger can quickly become irrational. Remind yourself the world is not out to get you—you're just experiencing some rough spots of daily life.

- **Use *meditation* and *relaxation*** as part of your regular routine. In this way you'll reset your neural wiring to a calmer level and you'll create a reservoir of calm from which you can draw comfort throughout your day.

- **Do regular *exercise*:** the body chemicals that are released during exercise are nature's tranquilizers. This is a valuable resource for a

healthy form of mood management if it is done in moderation
and as a way to consciously calm down and relax.

- **Get twenty to thirty minutes of sunlight a day.** Research points to
our natural need for sunlight for mood stabilization.
- **Eat well and get plenty of rest.** Remember, our bodies can drive
our emotions if we deprive them of what they need in order to
operate well.

Anger is one of the most primary emotions, and working with our
anger is important. We need to be able to allow ourselves to feel it so
that we don't run into the kind of emotional and psychological problems that come when we disallow feeling it. At the same time, it's
important not to get stuck in anger, not to let it have too much power
in our lives. Like so many other things in life, it's a delicate balance.

You can't forgive what you refuse to remember, any more than
you can seek treatment for a disease whose symptoms you have
yet to notice.

~Carol Luebering
"Finding a Way to Forgive," *CareNotes*

Sometimes, getting angry can be a way to avoid feeling hurt. Living
with trauma can teach us to inadvertently (1) repress or deny our anger;
(2) express anger inappropriately; (3) be left with learned helplessness
from chronic disappointment and seeing no way of improving the situation that marinates over time and becomes frustration, resentment or

self-loathing; (4) turn anger inward, leading to depression; (5) somatize anger and create physical problems; or (6) self-medicate our anger with drugs, alcohol, food, sex and gambling. If we learned dysfunctional ways of dealing with anger, it can impair our ability to forgive.

THE MANY FACES OF ANGER IN REAL LIFE: STORIES AND CASE STUDIES

Anger can take many forms. The person who is yelling, raging or physically abusing someone is obviously angry and acting it out. But the person who is controlling another person's behavior or cutting someone off or even currying favor and smilingly sickeningly as they manipulate others to bend to their will—all may also be in a rage inside and acting out their anger in more subtle ways. And in these cases, if you were to challenge them, they wouldn't even know what you were talking about. They would probably deny they were angry, accuse you of being mean-spirited, and by the end of the conversation, you would be so confused you might agree with them. In the following case studies, we explore a variety of ways in which anger travels through our relationships.

Forgiveness of relationship problems that have traumatized us in childhood can be confusing and disorienting. And if parents themselves were responsible for the problems, then the people we would normally have gone to for validation of our hurt feelings, or comfort and solace, are the ones who are hurting us. So the child is left to find her own way through. Her need for retribution is subsumed by her need to stay connected to the very person who is wounding her. If she gives up on her parent, she risks abandonment and that feels too dangerous to contemplate. So she must find a way to stay connected and disconnected all at once. Consequently, she hides the parts of herself that might threaten her connection with her parent. She hides them from her parent and eventually from herself. Her fear and hurt, her rage at being so vulnerable and intimidated with no way to even the score, her neediness—all must be hidden in the mind of the child, defended against feeling because feeling it would make her feel too anxious and vulnerable. She is left to make sense of this painful situation with the reasoning available to her immature mind: *Maybe I did something wrong, and if I think really hard I can correct it,* or *If I don't show my hurt or anger, everything will be fine.* But, for example, if the parent is an addict or has some mental disorder, what was wrong one day may have been fine the day before. So the child gets locked in confusion, lost in trying to make sense of conflicting responses. Logic doesn't work: *I'll try pleasing. If I'm very, very good . . . perfect . . . then Daddy will not get so mad, and rageful and drunk or violent. . . . I'll please. That will be my way of staying connected, of getting what I need.* These strategies for staying connected can stay with us throughout life, and we may come to live by them long after they have outlived their original use.

Anger is not always obvious. Parents who emotionally cut off their children, control or manipulate them, may be acting out unconscious anger, and their children feel angry as a result. In the following case studies, we see some of these less visible dynamics.

The Narcissistic Parent

*O*ur identities are so intertwined with our parents that forgiving them, if we've been hurt, can feel like giving up a piece of ourselves. It's impossible not to have been hurt by our parents in some way or another while growing up; it comes with the territory. It gets complicated, however, when we can't resolve it either by talking it through with our parents or working it through on our own and letting it go. Narcissistic parents can be problematic in that it's difficult to hang onto a sense of self around them. While we're young and clearly extensions of them, our connection is less threatened, but as we become more separate people this connection becomes harder to sustain. That's part of what makes this kind of parent difficult; we often have the memory of a strong connection and don't really understand what we did to lose it. So we keep going back to get what we feel we still need, wanting to fill up where we feel empty. Over time, this can make us feel upset and very angry. But the narcissist is too busy filling himself to fill us and we get disappointed all over again. Going to a narcissistic parent to be seen for ourselves can be a lifelong struggle because narcissists, at their core, don't see *themselves*. That's why they constantly need an audience, but being their audience is no fun if you're their child. You can feel like an extension of somebody else's personality, unseen for who you really are, which can interfere with consolidating your own sense of self.

We all need a bit of healthy narcissism, to feel ourselves to be special and endowed with particular gifts that we can share with the world. Jacob Levy Moreno coined the term "megalomania normalis," to cover this, and it can be an important part of a dynamic or creative personality, giving us the courage to see the world through our own unique vision. It propels us forward. Too much narcissism can still propel us into great accomplishment, but it can deeply wound those close to us. Though narcissists themselves are wounded children yearning for attention, they are so wounded that they cannot ask for it. Instead, they must remove it from others, hoard or manipulate it to keep the spotlight on themselves. The only real solution with this type of parent is to see the condition for what it is and to stop trying to be seen or approved of, because trying sets up the cycle of putting the power for approval in their hands. Remove that power from their hands by giving up the wish to be seen by them and recognizing that they may not have the ability to give in that way. Unconsciously, they feel too small inside themselves to see you, or they would already have seen you and shared their good feeling about themselves with you. Your wish to separate and "be big" yourself may only make them want to cut you down to size (their own internal size). But the story doesn't end there, because if you do separate and succeed on your own, they will be the first ones to claim you as theirs, because now you're contributing to their positive image of themselves. Forgiving them for what they can't give—and forgiving yourself for still wanting it—can be the key to healing and moving on. We can have a relationship with them, but it's probably not a good idea to wait around for that seal of approval that may not be forthcoming; better to get it from somewhere else.

Forgiving the Narcissistic Father

*T*he fantasy or wish of the young daughter to be close to her father, to be "Daddy's Little Girl," and vice versa is a phenomenon as old as the theater of Ancient Greece. It's what psychologists sometimes refer to as "the oedipal wish," to be closer to the father than the mother is; to, in fact, displace the mother in his affections. This wish is naturally outgrown as the daughter matures and realizes that though Daddy indeed adores her, he is married to Mommy and plans to stay that way, and it is Mommy he turns to meet his primary needs for intimacy, understanding, sex and partnership. This allows the daughter to integrate her wish and move freely into her own life, and to find her own life partner. The love her father feels for her and his adoration and devotion give her something to look for on an emotional level. Like a heat-seeking missile, she moves in on what feels like home. The love, or lack of it, lights the target that she will move toward in choosing her own partner.

So what happens when the father himself is a narcissist and his ability to love anyone (including himself, ultimately) is impaired? Though the narcissist seems to be engaged in a never-ending love affair with himself, he is, in fact, like a broken record crooning the same love song over and over again, because he can't really hear it. He needs the world to constantly prove its love for him. The dilemma for a daughter like Corinna, who we will meet in our next case study, is that she may never be able to love her father enough so that she can get loved back as a separate person; she may never be able to see him enough so that she can get seen back; and she may never be able to value him enough so that she can be valued as her own self, though she may well spend her life trying. She will be valued, but it will be more as an extension of her father's world, as a reflection of her father and an incorporation of his sense of self, rather than as her own separate self.

Last week, Corinna came to group glowing, cooing, having finally broken through her image of herself as a "cool customer," unemotional and distant. She had just picked up her little boy, whom she had been in the process of adopting for nearly two years. In her wildest dreams, she had not been able to imagine herself as a good mother. Her own mother had been alcoholic, and though she was sober today and Corrina had a close relationship with her, the ghost of her drunken mother haunted her every time she imagined herself as one. With tears in her eyes and in her voice she said, "I just am so surprised at what a good mother I am. I'm being a really good mother." Her joy was moving and palpable. She had walked a long road to get to the point of being able to embrace the experience of motherhood, and she was being richly rewarded.

So this part of her life was bursting with joy, victory and the rewards of years of work. This part was in good form. The sticky part for her today was letting go of the love she still felt for her first husband, so that she could "be" in a full relationship with her second and current one, whom she had adopted a child with. Loving a father who is a narcissist affected her ability to be in love with the man she was married to (at the same time she was married to him), to choose a man who loved her and allow herself to tolerate the experience of being chosen, seen and loved. She hadn't wanted a baby boy, but that is what the birth mother delivered. And the love for that adopted baby boy made her feel, as she said, "whole"—whole enough to be intimate with a man ... and a boy who will some day grow into one.

She wanted to explore what might stand in the way of her feeling at peace with her husband. With appropriate trepidation, she embarked on an inquiry into her own heart. Her psychodrama began with talking to her first husband, "I wish I could have had this baby with you. You wanted one, and I just wasn't ready; I couldn't want one. I wanted to accomplish something, to be someone in the world ... like you were." We chose someone to play herself at that age in her first marriage. She spoke to herself at that time from the perspective of the person she was today. "You just weren't ready, you were scared and empty and drinking yourself. ... You were so empty inside, just so empty. You couldn't let yourself be loved and wanted, and you didn't have that to give a baby. And you can stop hating yourself about it. You can forgive yourself. Forgive yourself so you can have your life now; you have so much that's good." Back to her first husband, "I'm sorry, I'm so sorry. I miss you; I wish we could be together like this. I still love you, and I'm afraid I can never love my current husband the way I love you. I wish I could have loved you then and let your love in." Next she reverses roles (now she stands in the shoes of her first husband and talks back to herself). In talking from the role of her husband and experiencing being him, she came to realize that twenty years later he is remarried and still has no children, that he still drinks and that, though he professed the deepest wish to have a baby, somehow, he still doesn't have one. She has idealized the love that never quite happened for so long that she missed the obvious inconsistencies in the real relationship.

Then we chose someone to play her father. "I adored you, and you were never really interested in me. You left me with a drunk mother and moved to another state. Everything in your life is about your work and your charity benefits and your image. You never really took an interest in me. You liked to show me off in public, to dance with me, but not to know me and care about the content of my life. When I showed you the picture of my little boy, you were more interested in our property in the Hamptons where the picture was taken than in him."

She idealized her relationship with her father, filling in the missing pieces with an ideal image designed to keep her loneliness away from her consciousness, and to keep at bay the nagging fear that somehow she wasn't worth loving, that she couldn't attract the real love she wished for to herself. This, of course, affected her choice of partners and her own ability to be intimate, to tolerate the powerful and vulnerable feelings that accompany real love and authentic intimacy. Working through this scenario left her freer to love her husband—or at least be willing to try to—and made her relationship with her son, who was the motivation for the work in the first place, less potentially complicated.

Putting the Pain Where It Doesn't Belong: Forgiveness and Transference

The phenomenon of transference is well-known to therapists and at the core of much therapy. Basically, it's when we unconsciously project a set of emotions from a relationship in the past onto a relationship in the present. Forgiveness can get confusing under these circumstances: If we want to forgive the person we're angry with today, it never quite holds if we don't undo the pain from the past that is mixed up with it.

Following is a "mock-up" letter written by Corinna to her father after an upsetting encounter. The letter will never be sent; it is simply a vehicle for Corinna to unravel her own thoughts and feelings. Letter-writing is a powerful healing tool that allows us to say what has gone unsaid and see what we've been carrying in our hearts and minds with greater clarity.

Oh, Dad,

What I wouldn't do to have you see me, respect me, know me. Why do I want your approval so much? Why do I need it from deep inside my bones? Your blessing. My father's blessing to give me the courage to face the world, to be who I think I can be. Why don't you approve of me, Dad, unless I'm attached to you in some way, or some vision of yours? Is it because I'm not enough or you're not enough? Which of us is lacking? So many years of waiting and wishing and wanting. Are you the only one who gets enough, a big piece of the pie? The only one who will ever sit at the head of the table? How selfish of you not to move over once in a while. What is it that welds you to that role, that makes you want to be in charge of everything and everyone? It's as if you don't think anyone does anything worthwhile but you. And it makes me want to knock you over so I can get through. But I don't want to knock you over, Dad. I love you and I need you. And I want you to love and need me, too. I want you to wish me well so I can wish me well. Why can't you give it? Why can you only approve of what reflects directly on you—what's some extension of you? Why isn't it okay with you if I succeed on my own—separately from you—as my own person?

That place inside me that you could reach into feels so deep—and even depressed. I need your help to pull me out and give me courage. I need your vote of confidence, your support.

Do you need me to be less so you can feel like more? If I move away from you, does it leave a hole in you? Can you even feel it?

It seems to me that I only matter to you in my role of daughter vis-à-vis your father role. Not as me. You father best with an audience, when I fill in some part of your idea of yourself. Daughter for a day. But I'm here, Dad, as me. And I'm me every day of the week. I'm more than just your daughter, and it hurts to fill in for the role you want me in and get so little back. It's sickening, in fact. Don't you feel for anyone but yourself? If your ducks are in a row then your world is hunky-dory. But what about me? I'm here, too, and not just as your daughter, your little girl. I'm not only a character in your play. This is my play too, Dad. Can't you share? Can't you see? Can't you stand in anyone's shoes but your own? If your day is organized, I'm just supposed to fit into it in the time slot allotted by you. And if it doesn't work for me, then the deal is just off. Your way or the highway. No equal concern or adjustment. I don't want to be an understudy for my own role anymore, Dad. I don't want to be handed my lines for a play I'm not even sure I'm interested in.

But I layer your face onto so many men who aren't you. It gets me in all sorts of trouble. I do this strange thing of taking care of men, anticipating their needs even before they have them so that they won't have to ask or feel needy or say thank you or any of that. Then I feel so frustrated, hurt and angry when they don't notice how much I'm doing. But most of the time, I don't notice how much I'm doing. Then all I am is angry at the men in my life. I suppose it's you I'm angry at, but it's them I feel it towards, and it keeps me from ever feeling okay being with them.

I'm trying to make all of this more conscious, Dad, so I can forgive me for still being in this place with you after all this time, and I can forgive you.

Love,

Corinna

In this letter, we see what we mean by undoing. It's complicated: Corinna's not just angry with her father, she also adores him. Feelings don't tend to be that well isolated inside us, and the sense we made out of situations from childhood has all sorts of childlike reasoning, sometimes called magical thinking, entwined in it. This is the man who raised her, who walked her to school, tucked her in at night and called her Little Pumpkin. Like it or not, they shared the same heart-space; their destinies were woven around each other, so forgiving him is forgiving herself, and forgiving herself is forgiving him. Codependent or interdependent, that's the way it is, and it doesn't separate itself until it does . . . until it all gets pulled up for untangling like seaweed from the bottom of the lake.

Corinna refers to "layering your face onto so many men who aren't you." This is transference. And, to make matters all the more confusing, the more traumatic a relationship was, the more emotional numbness and memory loss we may have, and the less mature our reasoning was at the time it occurred. Flash-frozen memory. Freeze-dried for thawing out at some later date. "Just add water." That's why journaling, psychodrama and therapy are so useful. As we engage in a process of writing or role-playing, stuff just emerges from our unconscious that we didn't know was there, along with the strange web of associations we attached to it at the time. And as it emerges, our cortex gets a second chance, as it were, to look at it through the eyes of today and make new sense of it. If I had a quarter for every time a client gets to this material and finally strings it into amazingly coherent sentences, then says, "I feel like I'm not making any sense," I'd have a lot of quarters. Quite the contrary to what the individual may feel, group members are usually sitting on the edge of their chairs in quivering identification or glued in place afraid of seeing their own lives pass before their eyes in living Technicolor.

When all this subtext gets projected onto our present-day relationships without our conscious awareness, it's no wonder we can't get to the bottom of a conflict. When we can't learn to *talk out* our pain, we do what psychologists call *acting it out* instead. We might, for example, hit our own child when we get triggered and angry because that's what we remember and associate with that feeling state or that age in our own lives. When our child reaches the same age we were, we may unconsciously re-create the same dynamics that occurred for us at that age. It's called an "age-correspondence reaction." Or we might act it out through the many faces of anger, letting our feelings seep out sideways in any form from cynicism to rage. Still another way we act out unresolved emotional and psychological pain is to self-medicate. Drugs and alcohol work their dysfunctional wonders on this because they really deaden the pain. Food works, too, as do chain-smoking, sex, working to excess and gambling, to name a few. Ask any recovering addict. Unfortunately, not only does self-medicating make our pain impossible to get to and think about, it creates a false positive. We really think we've got the answer and the rest of the world just looks stupid, like they can't come up with a program for managing their pain. Nothing gets resolved and more problems get created. (A lot more.)

Experiential therapies like role-playing jog our memories as the "then and there" becomes the "here and now," and we revisit a moment from our past that needs healing. In our next case study, Emily revisits such a moment. I have used the psychodramatic technique of "doubling" in recounting Emily's work. Doubling, in role-playing, is standing behind the client whose psychodrama is being role-played and speaking her inner life, what she is thinking but not saying, subject, of course, to her editing. I have "doubled for" Emily in italics: Everything in italics and parentheses is Emily's *inner voice* and the goings-on in her inner world. And, at times, Emily has doubled for herself, saying through the role of the double what she wouldn't feel comfortable saying out loud.

◌

Forgiveness is giving up the possibility of a better past.

◌ Mike D.

Forgiving the Narcissistic Mother

*E*mily hit that wall again. She came to group wanting to "work on something," but, as always, felt like her issues were really nothing compared to those in the group who had been sexually abused, hit, abandoned, addicted, or even yelled at all the time. These were not her issues. She must seem like a whiner. *("Poor me . . . What happened to me really? I'll just sit here and be a good listener . . . after all, no one abused me, really. I'm just exaggerating, being dramatic, a baby and a brat. . . . What else is new?")*

She was disappearing into the wall. In a few more minutes, she would be completely colored in with invisible ink, and no one would have to worry about her. But this time she caught herself. She opened her mouth and forced words out and into the container of the group. "I want to do some work. I'm not sure on what I'm going to need some help figuring it out *(gag)*. Is that okay to ask *(gulp)*? I just think I need to claim some space *(wanting to flee now, stomach churning)*. I want to try to talk to my mother, but I don't know what I want to say. *("I'm here.")* I don't really know where to start. *("Look at me please when I'm trying to talk to you.")* I'm at a loss for words *("Goddamn it, look at me.")* I'm losing it now.

I just went away again . . . *("h-e-l-p . . .")*. Does anyone else have anything they want to do? I'm sort of losing my warm-up. Maybe this isn't the right night." This was Emily's typical way of announcing she needed some attention: to ask, get horribly self-conscious and confused *("I feel like I'm shouting")*, then cool down, disappear and withdraw into herself.

Emily spent long hours listening to her mother talk about herself, or sometimes talk about Emily, or her fundraisers or relatives or clothes or random thoughts or *("just about anything")*. Emily got bored in places in her mind most people don't even go. She even got bored in her body. Her thighs, for example, could get very bored. Her shoulders often fell prey to a kind of ennui. Her neck turned permanently at an angle where she could seem alert but really be in her bedroom flipping through magazines or on the phone with a friend. *("Don't let her know I couldn't care less about anything she's saying. I'm bored stiff with her stories.")* Emily had devised more ingenious ways to listen than anyone on Earth. She had been the good little listener of a mother who lived within the walls of her own psyche, who never left to visit or truly enter Emily's world in a meaningful way. She often explained Emily's world to her. "Emily you're so . . . ," but always from within her own garrison, from behind her glass enclosure. And Emily felt alone on her own side of the room that contained her mother. Alone and very, very sad. *("Mommy, couldn't you come and find me over here? I can't find you. I can't reach across the fog that separates us, can't see you clearly through it. I feel like you don't even know I'm here. So I don't even know I'm here.")*

Growing up with a narcissistic mother becomes a complicated forgiveness project. Unless you are a saint living on vapors because you're so evolved, it generally takes time first because you don't feel you have a right to forgive anything at all. Emily feels she is the one in need of being forgiven, for being such a bad listener, for feeling such rage toward a mother who she should feel only good feelings toward, no bad feelings. She should "make nice," swallow her bad feelings, eat them for lunch, hide them, deny them, feel guilty about them and then, when the guilt becomes too much . . . start all over again at the beginning. She should turn them against herself, because if she really lets her mother know how much *("shhh . . .")* anger . . . *("shhh . . .")* she is feeling her mother will BREAK in two right in front of her eyes, and it will be all her fault.

All of this is going on in Emily's head. The guilt she feels and the fact that she came to the conclusion as a girl that she was bad for feeling all these horrible feelings and thinking all these horrible thoughts keep her from opening up and seeing that she was, in fact, traumatized by her mother's narcissism, by her inability to empathize with Emily in a million tiny ways that should have added up to a whole relationship, stretched out over time. It was cumulative. Her mother's narcissism shaped the way Emily saw herself, her mother and much of the world. Emily needed her mother to tune in to her so that she could learn how to tune in to herself. Emily tried her best to understand and attend to her mother, but because her mother was not able to truly tune in to anyone but herself, it didn't go back and forth. She could see Emily as an extension of herself but not as her own person. So Emily was left feeling like an appendage, unseen and feeling a lot of rage that she thinks is her fault and the result of, at best, an overactive imagination, or, at worst, a seriously *bad little girl who no one will ever love.*

So she smiles and supports other people, and another group session goes with her leaving feeling empty. It all gets re-created. *She wants to scream.* But then again, she doesn't want to scream because it would be unladylike, she wouldn't like herself in the morning, and everyone would think she was nuts, or worse—a self-centered, ungrateful girl. After all, who is she to have such rage? She wasn't hit, or sexually abused or humiliated with words (much).

But this ignores the deep wound that grows inside you when the person you most want to be seen by in life doesn't see you or take the time to get to know you, when the light is always shining in another direction and your turn never comes. When Mommy is the star and you're the wardrobe lady. When you feel all alone in the world because the person who is supposed to be protecting you is so busy protecting herself that her psychic schedule is just too full to fit you in. And then there's always "the big risk." If you do pipe up and ask for something, you might get ignored, in which case you'll feel worse than before, overtly rejected. Then you and your body will have to contain humiliation all over, or get yelled at for being selfish, in which case you'll eventually have to agree or risk being cut off for who knows how much pain-filled time.

So you learn the rules of the game, and you stay beneath the radar and you stay close to your mother by being there for her and putting yourself aside. Another complicated part of all of this is that the narcissist is not there for herself either. If she were, she wouldn't be a narcissist. She wouldn't have to spend all her time shoring herself up and convincing herself and the world that she is really there. She would just be there and would know, by deduction, that you were there, too. But the child senses the lonely world of the narcissist; she feels the unshed tears of the mute, little girl who lives inside her mother, and she weeps *for* her and sometimes *as* her.

The daughter is trying to shape an identity off of a hollow model, and she feels hollow, too. But it seems to Emily as if it's taken a lifetime for her to stand back and see her mother's hollowness, and by now she's so mad at her mother, at what happened or what never happened, that she doesn't know who needs forgiving: her mother, herself, or a world that asked all women to forgo laying claim to a self and handed them a role instead.

Though Emily didn't act out her anger per se with her own children, she became very controlling and possessive of them. As long as they remained close to her she felt okay, but as they went through the natural separation process of adulthood, she had a hard time supporting them in their autonomy. Because she hadn't really established her own identity, she couldn't comfortably allow them to have their own.

Again, it's the layers of the onion, peeling them back one at a time, deconstructing the self that was or wasn't built, reconstructing it, and when forgiveness does happen, it is slowly and over time, in a thousand little ways—in as many ways as the hurt happened to begin with.

Dear Mom,

This is just too long. I don't know where to begin. I haven't even started this letter, and already I feel as if I've said too much. Today we had an argument. Well, not really an argument, a wanna-be argument. That almost happened, that vibrated beneath the surface, that threatened to emerge and blow up if I said anything wrong. I feel so bad. I heard the depression in your voice. I've just lived through too many sad years with you, and I cannot stop wanting to make you better. So I can finally relax, I guess. So I can finally breathe. I hear it in your voice, in all that you say, in all that you avoid saying. I just want that sound to go away so I can stop feeling so responsible. I imagine that you're mad at me for not wanting to help. I don't, you know; I want to get a million miles away from you. But then I want to get so close to you, to snuggle up to you and make you stop feeling pain. But you get so angry, God, you are so angry, so angry and so in denial of it, it's infuriating. I want to scream. You get to be the good little girl while I scream for you. Then you back up and point and shake your head and say, "Oh my, my, you seem angry." I am angry, but I don't want to say it until you admit to a lifetime of your own anger, rage, subterfuge and manipulation. I want my self back, I want to wrest it away from you . . . . it's all tangled up in your insides, and I want it back. You can't have it. I'm so sorry, Mom, that I can't help you feel better. So deeply sorry. I've given my life trying, but I just can't do it. I feel like a failure, like I'm not big enough, good enough, loving enough. I see myself doing anything to stay close to you, providing you with a diversion so that you can get upset with me instead of you. Our relationship, let's make everything about our relationship. Great. Okay, I'll do it. Then I'll hate you. Then you can hate me. Then you won't have to feel your pain anymore, and I can be relieved for a moment because my mommy won't feel sad for a day. We can fight and recon-nect, and that's how we'll do it. That will be the story of us, and they'll be no story of me, because there's really no story of you. Endless women without lives of their own, borrowing each other's lives, identities, hearts because there just isn't enough to go around. It would feel easier if you clung to me and made me your reason for living, or hung on me like a stage mother who I could hate, but you turn me into a problem that you can fix so you can get angry and sad, and dis-avow your own depressed insides. Then you get to feel strong, and I get to feel weak. And you get all your feelings out at my expense. Now, they're about me and not you.

Angry again. Then guilty. Then sad and empty. Forgive me, Mom, I have to go and be my own person. Will you even know?

Love,

Emily

Emily felt relieved after putting pen to paper and allowing her inner world to spill freely onto the page. Though the letter was not to be sent, it allowed her to see her own process more clearly and relieve herself of some inner pressure. Contrary to what she expected, her relationship with her mother actually improved after doing this work. She doesn't expect her mother to be someone she isn't anymore, and she is better able to enjoy her for who she is. Emily feels less robbed of a self and more satisfied in her own life. Bottom line, she is glad to have her mother still in it.

Frozen Memories:
The Legacy of Significant Trauma

*T*hink of trauma in evolutionary terms. Early woman had a lot to worry about. So nature, in its infinite wisdom, built a protective apparatus into her. When she sensed that she was in danger, she went into the protective modes that nature encoded into her. Extreme states of fear cause the body to spurt chemicals like epinephrine and norepinephrine, both of which are associated with standing and fighting or fleeing for safety, commonly known as the fight-or-flight response. In women, however, more recent research reveals that oxitocin is also released. According to a recent UCLA study by Drs. Klein and Taylor, women even "respond to stress with a cascade of brain chemicals that cause us to make and maintain friendships with other women." In other words, our survival mode is tend and befriend, not only fight or flight. This "touch" chemical encourages women to bond with other women, and to take care of children and get them to safety. Jean Houston further confirms that as women perform these activities, they release more oxitocin, which strengthens them, as well as the *tend-and-befriend* response, and serves to buffer the stress, or the fight-or-flight response (in men, testosterone undercuts the oxitocin). These responses were encoded into the brain of early women and were meant to keep us all alive. So when threatened by a large bear, the cavewoman who bonded with other females and got the children to safety was selected by evolution to be our foremother. Nature favored her over the one who didn't (for obvious reasons).

Traumas in today's world are met with more or less the same equipment. But, as we've discussed, at the time that nature devised these defensive strategies the brain had not yet evolved enough to have a fully developed cortex. The frontal cortex is where we do our critical thinking and long-range planning. Fight, flight or freeze, along with *tend-and-befriend,* are a part of the old brain, whereas critical thinking is part of the more recently evolved brain, the cortex. This means that, even today, when we're scared stiff, struck dumb or in a rage, we're mostly in our old brain. We're reacting in order to stay safe. We're not using deductive reasoning or reflective thinking (cortex functions) to sort out a situation. We're frozen, fleeing, fighting or running around tending and befriending like crazy. These feelings that we experience while being traumatized don't get thought about and put into context. Instead we hide them, deny them, repress them or split them off, out of consciousness. Then, later in life when they get triggered and reemerge, they seem impervious to reason. They splatter themselves on the scenes of the present, and they splatter in their original form because, most likely, they were never processed with the skills of reasoning; they didn't get thought about and categorized in a reasonable manner.

The reason that triggered pain is so confusing to decode and deal with is that our emotional responses to trauma are recorded primarily by the parts of the brain that were developed early in our evolution, often referred to as the "reptilian" or "old" brain. The cortex, which is where we do much of our critical thinking and meaning making, where we *think* about what we're *feeling* and make sense of it, was an evolutionary afterthought. Consequently, when we were deeply hurt, say as children, we may have been too scared or frozen to process what was happening around us. The cortex did not get a chance to modulate the memory, reflect upon, think about, quantify and categorize particular painful events, so that they could be worked through and integrated along with a rational read on the situation. We may have been left to make sense of it on our own with only the powers of reason and the emotional maturity and capability for insight available to us at the time. The adults in the situation may have been too preoccupied with their own problems to take time out to help us understand what was happening around us. As a result, when these fragments of unprocessed memory get *triggered* in the present they have no context, they're all out of order and can get mindlessly blasted onto the surface of our current lives.

We feel like we felt when the original events happened: defenseless and vulnerable, with whoever hurt us having all the power. All this intense feeling that seems to relate only to the current situation but, in truth, has many of its origins in the past, gets interpreted as if it belongs exclusively to the present, and we may try to make sense of an adult situation through our child mind.

All of us have these little people inside. It helps if we're on speaking terms with that part of us, so that when the child self gets scared and wants to hide or hit or cry or yell, our adult self recognizes what's going on and extends a secure hand to their small fingers. This is how we grow, and this is also how we can keep the innocence, talent, spontaneity and creativity that is also part of this side of us, and still function as reasonably healthy adults. You notice I say *reasonably*. I think psychology has unwittingly put forward some unattainable idea of the "model" person that is about as far flung from the actual norm as a size four is for the average American woman. It just isn't what's out there, and if we hold ourselves to that standard we'll only feel bad. We're all only human, why should we kill ourselves trying to be perfect?

Little girls who witness parental rage or abuse over and over again like Adrianna, who we will meet in our next case study, experience trauma. Women who have been traumatized often don't have clear memories of the incidents because these memories remain outside their consciousness. Memories are blurred into each other if recollected at all. Instead, they tend to emerge as body sensations (head pounding, queasy stomach, heart racing, sweating). Or as feelings of helplessness, rage, memory flashes (flashbacks) or overreactions to circumstances in the present that act as triggers of past pain. Even subtle cues like a change in someone's voice or a particular look can drive a previously traumatized woman into a state of shutdown, anxiety or anger if it hits that nerve. In other words, we react to situations in our current lives with an intensity that belongs somewhere else in our past experience. We overreact when exposed to stimuli that are in some way reminiscent of the traumas we experienced.

Adrianna's teeth sometimes chatter when things get intense in group. She fears that a fight will break out. Her hands perspire, and her stomach goes into knots. Her body remembers what her mind has forgotten. But here's the catch-22: If her mind had really forgotten, her body wouldn't be remembering. So where did the memories go? Are they unconscious, semiconscious or jammed into a bunch of buried brain cells? Is out of sight really out of mind? I think it's safe to say that no one knows exactly. It's also obvious that wherever they are, they're not gone. They are as alive and well as within the Vietnam vet who covers his head when he hears a car backfiring because his "trauma" mind interprets the sound as gunfire.

Sexual Abuse: A Complicated Legacy

Sexual abuse is not just sexual abuse. It is an abuse of power, a robbing of innocence, a distortion of reality and a tearing at the very fabric of truth, until the victim cannot tell the innocent from the guilty because truth and lies are woven together with everything she loves, hates, needs, wishes for and rejects. Most little girls who are sexually abused are abused by people they love or trust, and are often living in a family system that is not as attentive and protective as it should be. How else could they be convinced to lie still while a person they look up to touches them in ways that feel strange, drawing from their young bodies sensations that both hurt and thrill, but do not feel as if they belong to them? How else could they be convinced to maintain and keep silence over something so big, when their habit has been to take even their tiniest hurts to their mommies or other grown-ups? How else could they believe that this strange and frightening experience was somehow fun or good, or in any way to their benefit? It is because those who hurt them are those they look up to and adore, those whom they wish most to please, for whom they wish to be good little girls. So the scars from sexual abuse are trained across their dreams and wants, their way of getting close or staying far, their mode of operating in the world at large or in the bedroom, their way of being.

A complicated maze of wounds that build on each other occurs in cases of childhood sexual abuse. On the limbic level, we can only extrapolate the effect of, for example, a limbic bond with the father that includes sexual play of some sort. Confusion, a fragmented sense of self, numbing versus intense emotion. Dissociation is a very common response to being sexually abused: The victim leaves her body mentally and emotionally because she cannot integrate the horror of her abuse into any framework that she knows as normal. Depending upon the level of abuse the dissociation can range anywhere from feeling like there is a sort of mind–body split (feeling like she's "somewhere else but she doesn't know where"), or splitting off into separate subpersonalities who "know the truth but don't tell it," as can be the case with multiple-personality disorder. Physical numbing can also be part of the abuse response. Having no other way to get away from the strange sexual feelings being stimulated in her body, the child learns to numb herself, to shut down her response system. Or she may do a combination of both: *freeze* and psychological and emotional *flight,* since *fight* is clearly not an option. These fundamental flights from the core self can produce a deep sense of fragmentation within the self of the survivor and can be carried with the survivor into adulthood. Because of the numbing versus intense responses associated with trauma, the sexual abuse survivor might find herself acting out in black-and-white ways, anything from promiscuity to frigidity. Zero to ten, shutdown to high intensity are what characterize the trauma response. No shades of gray. Adrianna's story illustrates the tangled path that sexual abuse can follow.

We have to call her by her childhood name, because that is where the story begins, that is where the seeds were planted. Adi was the youngest of six children and by the time she came along much muddy water had already passed under the bridge of her parents' relationship, but she didn't know that. As far as she was concerned, she had arrived feet first into the best family in the world. And it was a good family, a good family with a bad problem. There was nowhere in the world better to be than by her father's side as far as Adi was concerned, or perhaps in the middle of her family playing on the rug listening to the sounds of conversation and laughter as they washed over her and her pets. She was in her own world, contained by the world that she loved.

She had no way of knowing when her father had been drinking; she didn't know what drinking was, and as for what was or wasn't there in her parents' relationship, this was as far from her childhood mind as Latin. Everything simply *was.* She was surrounded by shapes and sizes and sounds and scents and feelings. Good ones. Warm ones . . .

The warm glow her father had when he was drinking just seemed like *his* warm glow, like she had done something especially pleasing to elicit his laughter and generous praise. And her mother seemed to join in the party, too. Not by drinking but by being part of the gang, going along, not making waves, keeping the home feeling like all was okay. Everybody doing what people do to keep things moving along, everyone doing their best.

Footsteps . . . Adi also remembers something about footsteps. There were the lighter footsteps that meant a good-night kiss, tucking in the blankets so they were very snug and saying a big enough good-bye to last all the way 'til morning. There were the heavy footsteps, the sound that she still hears, that woke her out of sleep and made her want to go back to sleep, to sleep through everything that was about to happen. These are the ones she identifies today as drunken footsteps, but at that time were just Daddy's heavy steps. These were the steps that made her freeze up and get ready to make herself numb all over, so the feelings that Daddy made go through her body wouldn't hurt or scare her so much. In her child-mind, love got fused with sex, which got fused with fear, repulsion, arousal, play, fantasy and the physical urge to freeze up. When we're traumatized, feelings get fused together in this way. This is why sexual abuse has so many strange tentacles that stretch into different areas of life, reaching everywhere.

Adi told her mother that Daddy was visiting her room. Her mother did nothing. "He's your father, he's just playing with you. Let him." So now Adi lived in a triangle with no way out, freezing up and coping on her own was going to be the only solution she could come up with. And along with a loss of healthy connection with her father, she lost access to her mother on some deep level. Adi learned to forget. She learned to go into deep states where she was far away in her own world. She learned to dissociate. She learned to forget by day what she experienced by night. She did the best she could with the choices available to her. If you had asked her if anything like this was going on in her life, she would have looked at you dumbfounded. If she had heard the story of this happening to another little girl, she would have felt terrible for that "other" child. None of this existed in her conscious mind.

It wasn't until she herself was married that the power of love, intimacy, vulnerability and the wish to connect drove not her but her body out of hiding. Certain ways in which her husband touched her made her want to scream bloody murder and push him off her.

But I'm jumping ahead. We must go back to the complications that followed along this line. When Adi was nineteen, she traveled with a friend. One night her friend wanted to go out on a date, and Adi, not wishing to be either alone or a third wheel, made plans to tour the city in the late afternoon and early evening. She felt safe doing this and comfortable with her guide. He was an older man, old enough to be her father, and she truly imagined that touring with him in the early evening was a good plan. See here how normal signals get paralyzed in the wake of sexual abuse? Even when this man's leering matched her father's, she instantly rewrote it as "the way older men look," which not only set off no alarm, but if it had, the wires to the alarm sound had long been clipped and were lying useless on the basement floor. If the alarm had rung, it had so long ago been muffled, turned off by her father and kept off by her mother, that she wouldn't have heard it. The man drove the car to a remote area, and when Adi grabbed for the keys and climbed out the car window, he went after her, struggled with her, became violent and raped her. So the early abuse got reenacted at this point in her life.

The only way that Adi really was able to validate that her early abuse took place was through her sister, who had been older when their father abused her and remembered it clearly. She also remembered getting a similar response from their mother when she went to her for help. The boat of their alcoholic family was going to remain unrocked at all costs.

Adi did what a lot of sexual-abuse survivors do: She wore baggy clothes and put on weight. Another abuse response can be the opposite, becoming overly sexualized. Adi was hypervigilant every time someone acted "attracted" to her. She liked feeling attractive and being attractive, but the feelings that went along with it set her spinning inside. She felt both gratified and guilty when men found her appealing, but never knew what to do with it. She had fused sex with rage, fear and a wish to distance, and her unconscious didn't know the difference between the bed and the workplace, so this caused complications. In the workplace when she felt these vibes coming toward her, she panicked inside (while feeling flattered) and created "issues" that allowed her to distance the men with whom she was dealing. She also felt guilty and sad that she could not gratify them, as, on some level, she felt that was her job. If they were depressed or lonely or unhappy (as was her father) she felt especially sorry for them because it was her job to keep her father happy. So the more she liked the man she was working with and the deeper her feeling of connection, the greater the probability that some cluster of these fears and distancing behaviors would emerge.

These are some of the strange permutations that sexual abuse can take. Early abuse sets us up for later abuse, and the power violation sets us up for later power struggles, fears or ambivalence around authority and problems integrating sexual feelings as safe and okay. They have been fused with feelings such as pain, rejection, rage, deep violation and hurt. This is a legacy of trauma. Feelings get fused together and become hardwired in the brain. Stimulate or trigger one and the others come along with it. They have been wound together, seared into one in the white heat of terror.

All of this is Adi's complicated and intertwined legacy from sexual abuse. Working with it requires flexibility, knowledge and compassion. And time, lots of time. Forgiveness becomes so complicated here, and to suggest that the survivor forgive her abuser can make her feel victimized all over again. Another painful point is that sexual-abuse survivors often blame themselves and feel in some way complicitous; they irrationally feel as if they did something to bring this attention on. If, for example, a four-year-old child like Adi was abused, she may feel that because she adored her father and wished to possess all his attention, as any child does, that this wish came true—that she was more special to Daddy than Mommy was. Her wish for specialness was granted through her father's perverted attentions, and it could feel as if she was more powerful and important than Mommy, which was very confusing for her. She was granted a special status that she both wanted and didn't want at all. Again, when she attempted to make meaning of it all with the intellectual equipment available to her, she might come up with a variety of scenarios in her child mind. This describes why self-forgiveness is so important, as the child can feel irrationally responsible, in some way, for what happened. The rage of the sexual-abuse survivor needs to be understood and felt; she's lost a lot and she has a right to be very, very angry. It can be empowering and healing for the survivor to own her anger and let herself off the hook, but there is further work to be done around feelings of guilt, sadness, helplessness and lost innocence. Forgiveness, in this case even more so than others, hinges on letting go. The survivor deserves the liberation and freeing up of energy that working through these issues can grant, and this is more important as a focus than forgiveness of the abuser. In time, the survivor may come to realize that these were the actions of a sick individual, or individuals who, rather than work through their own pain, acted it out at the child's expense. Though it can feel like the death of a dream of innocence, it can also help to free the survivor of feelings of being sick themselves. They were, in fact, unwitting victims and have to cry the strangulated tears of the innocent.

∽

Even a fruit is bitter before it is ripe.

∽**Italian Proverb**

INTEGRATING LOVE AND HATE

Good and bad are both a part of life, and so are love and hate. We need to accept both so that we can integrate them. It is possible to have feelings of both love and hate toward our parents, our spouses . . . those to whom we are closest. Great love gives rise to great hate. Think about it. When we love someone deeply we're vulnerable: "I have spread my dreams beneath your feet," said W. B. Yeats, "tread softly, because you tread on my dreams." Our hearts are open when we love; in fact, we can't really love through a closed heart, we only go through the motions of love or play out a fantasy of what we think it should look like. Cultivating forgiveness as part of our relationship skill set can allow us to keep our hearts open in our close relationships.

But in order to do this, we have to live with knowing how hurt and angry we are if we feel we have been wronged. We have to hold our own broken heart in our own hands. We have to feel the power of our conflicting feelings so that we can integrate them along with insight and new meaning. We have to accept and integrate these powerful, conflicting emotions with some of the power gone out of them, so that they don't create unconscious conflicts that get played out in our lives. Most of us don't like to acknowledge the depth and intensity of these contradictory feelings. That's why we have complicated defense systems like denial, minimization, repression, idealization and dissociation, to name a few. They keep us from knowing how hurt we really are and how crazy we feel when we can't make sense of a situation. These defenses also allow us to stay connected in our meaningful relationships. When we're deeply hurt, our instinct is to run, to freeze up or to retaliate. Rare is the person who stands in his or her own tears and converts his or her hurt feelings into words on the spot. And when the hurt is from childhood, we can't really run—where would we go? If our parents are perpetrating the hurt, as with abuse, we're stuck with them so our emotions have to do some fancy footwork to figure out a way to keep breathing. We may cajole, please, try to be perfect, forgive before we are ready, then stuff the resentment, or give up, or we may become the acting-out child whose reenacted pain becomes a personality style that we take into our world. In fact, all these methods of coping become personality styles that we take into our relationships, our schools, our work lives and every other place we go. Working through these emotions toward resolution allows us some healthy emotional distance from what hurt us, it gets worked through and put back into memory storage in a more resolved way, a way that creates less inner conflict. Because distance through anger is really no distance at all. It's a constant, pain-filled connection.

The grudges that have been nursed from childhood may have been all we had to hold onto that felt like our own. And even when we've peeled back the layers of the onion and worked through the pain, hate, grief and loss, there may still be that wish of the child that the parent we longed for would somehow emerge through the ether and grant us absolution by finally seeing us in the way we needed to be seen, by holding us in the way we yearned to be held. This wish, too, needs to be understood, then laid to rest.

We may come to understand that even if that perfect parent fought her or his way back through time, sailed somehow on angel wings toward us, it would still not be enough. Getting what we think we wanted may feel good for a moment, but it is a wish that belongs to another place and time. Getting now what we didn't get then could feel, over time, infantilizing and invasive. We have fought our way through life without what we felt this desperate need for, compensated for its absence in a thousand ways that are now a part of who we are, and getting it now would require that we somehow put all that aside. In this way, taking forgiveness into our own hands leaves us with our dignity. We're not postponing living and loving again until such time when our parents, siblings or lost loves finally take responsibility for the hurt they've caused us and turn around and see us. We're seeing ourselves. The best defense is a good offense. We're accepting responsibility for our own state of wholeness, which, at the end of the day, any sage will tell you is the quickest way to enlightenment.

This is the spiritual paradox wherein a kind of personal transformation takes place. We learn that, in giving up our attachment to something, we experience a kind of freedom, and our souls grow larger and stronger as we gain another piece of wisdom. We are human, all of us, after all. We don't have to be perfect in order to be loved. What freedom! We can have faults and succeed at some things and fail at others and still be numbered among the just.

SIX

Hurt and Sadness:
Finally Letting Our Tears Flow

Forgiving does not erase the bitter past. A healed memory is not a deleted memory. Instead, forgiving what we cannot forget creates a new way to remember. We change the memory of our past into a hope for our future.

~Lewis B. Smedes
*The Art of Forgiving: When You Need
to Forgive and Don't Know How*

Let mourning stop when grief is fully expressed.

~Chinese Proverb

WHY IS IT IMPORTANT TO FEEL SAD?

We experience many types of loss in life. Feeling sad when we are separated from someone or something we care about is natural and has an important, adaptive function. Feeling sad doesn't mean we're unhappy people, ungrateful or whiners; it just means we've lost something that's meaningful to us, and we're healthy and secure enough to feel it. It means we have the capacity to care and form significant attachments. Sometimes, we're afraid to admit to feeling sad out of fear of being labeled "depressed." But when we experience a loss we are meant to feel pain. Without feeling that pain, a mother wouldn't know when she had lost her child, and a kitten wouldn't *meow* to signal her mommy cat that she was out of reach. Nature intended us to experience pain at separation so that we could reunite. A baby alone doesn't survive. Both mother (or parent) and offspring need to have something coded into them so that they will not separate until such time as the young can survive on their own. The same phenomenon occurs in around 50 percent of all monogamous creatures, whether they have scales, feathers, fur or skin. Birds flocking, mammals running in packs and fish swimming in schools are all illustrations of attachment in the service of survival. There is no more plaintive a sight than a loon swimming alone on the moonlit bay he once shared with his lifelong mate. And hearing a flock of geese *honk* to signal stragglers of their whereabouts is one of nature's captivating wonders. The day that we can't form strong, meaningful attachments is the day our world will fall apart, because nothing will mean anything. There will be no motivation to work hard to put our children through college, stay the course in marriage or lay our parents to rest with love and prayers. Attachment, as much as love, "makes our world go 'round."

ATTACHMENT STYLES

British psychoanalyst Jonathon Bowlby, in his seminal work on the attachment bond, observed that baby monkeys, chicks and humans alike exhibit similar distress when separated from their mothers. When, for example, a chick is separated from her mother she'll *cheep* loudly. Bowlby called this the *protest* phase. If her mother doesn't come back she'll enter a phase he calls *despair*, becoming silent. If the mother still doesn't return, the chick will show signs of *reattaching* with a surrogate. All these strategies are designed to ensure survival.

Johns Hopkins psychologist Mary Ainsworth made a ground-breaking contribution to the research on attachment between mother and infant. She was able, with her research, to delineate three types of attachment: *secure, insecure avoidant* and *insecure/ambivalent/ preoccupied.* Basically, she set up a room with toys in which mother and child played and grew comfortable. A typical *securely attached* child will play happily with the toys while Mom is in the room. When Mom leaves the room, the securely attached child will show signs of missing her and cry when left alone. Then when they reunite, the child tugs on her leg to be picked up and snuggle into her body. The *insecure/ avoidant* child shows no distress at her leaving, continuing to play with the toys. When she returns, there is no warm reunion; the child may ignore, turn away from or stiffen at Mom's approach. The *ambivalent/ preoccupied* child behaves differently from both other groups. She does not engage in play with the toys, showing lack of interest, or being fretful and clingy with Mom. This child shows great distress when Mom leaves.

The mother's behavior varied in the development of each attachment style. Ainsworth found that in the first group of children, the mothers had been attuned and sensitive to the children's needs, responding promptly when they expressed need and having warm physical contact. In the avoidant group, though things seemed to run smoothly, the babies' bodies told a different story: Their heart rates went high during separations; they seemed angry at their mothers and were distressed at even minor separations. Mothers in this group often said they didn't like being touched and seemed to rebuke their children's attempts at connecting. In the third group, though the mothers reported feeling love for their children and invested in their welfare, they were unattuned caretakers who lacked good mothering skills. They appeared to give their children enough love to understand the feeling but not enough to feel secure.

As you already may have deduced, securely attached people feel hurt and sad when they lose someone with whom they have a secure bond. When people lose someone with whom their attachment is ambivalent (filled with strongly conflicting and opposing feeling), they may have more complicated reactions to loss. Anything ranging from a sort of emotional disinterest or numbness to intense bursts of emotion might be part of their more ambivalent or confused response, along with unusually intense and persistent feelings of guilt, resentment or remorse. (Loss from divorce, for example, can be more complicated than loss from death because of the ambivalent feelings that inevitably accompany a divorce.) When entering the sadness phase of forgiveness, these styles can either facilitate or complicate this grieving. Normal grief follows predictable stages like those outlined by Elisabeth Kübler-Ross. What psychologists refer to as complicated mourning, where there is more ambivalence around the loss, can take longer and be made more difficult; we may need to mourn not only what we lost, but also what we never got a chance to have.

THE IMPORTANCE OF HUMAN TOUCH

The experience of being loved in childhood echoes from cradle to grave. When pediatrician Harry Bakwin took over the pediatric ward of Bellevue in 1931, there were signs all over instructing nurses to wash their hands and not to touch babies and "spread infection." Baldwin recognized the horror of this, took away the signs instructing personnel not to touch and put up signs instructing nurses to pick up the babies. Paradoxically, the infection rates went down. Apparently, touch and caring are more useful to our immune systems than "healing" policies that isolate us from human closeness. In the thirteenth century, Fredrick II of Prussia conducted a strange experiment in which he had a group of children raised without being spoken to in any way, because he wanted to see what language they would "speak naturally." All the children died. We are meant to form secure attachments, and we're meant to feel pain when those attachments are ruptured. It is a matter of survival.

Tears shed in grief have a different makeup from other kinds of tears. Who among us doesn't know the feeling of relief in our bodies, minds and hearts after a good cry? Feeling sadness, hurt and grief is what allows a wound to heal. Just as we lance a boil to allow a physical infection to drain, we cry to relieve a swollen, hurting heart. An important thing to remember in grieving is that we're not only allowing our feelings of sadness, hurt, resentment, confusion and despair to surface and be felt; we're also allowing the meaning we've made of experiences in our lives to emerge. In a sense, the limbic system weeps in tears and physical sensations, and the cortex weeps in word and symbol. Both need to be experienced and made sense of.

Our early experiences lay down a neural template that impacts how we experience and what we do with our emotions throughout life. They influence our emotional fluency and the quality of emotion that we are capable of feeling and expressing.

EMOTIONS AND DECISION MAKING

"Does what we think lead to what we feel or does what we feel lead to what we think?" This has long been under debate. Emotions are essential to our ability to make reasoned decisions. The current consensus among researchers is that events with the potential for eliciting emotional responses must first pass the appraisal activity of the mind.

Pierce Howard, Ph.D., in *The Owner's Manual for The Brain*, explains that ". . . this appraisal activity is typically rapid. It may have several components and may be sequential or simultaneous, but researchers agree that it takes place between stimulus and response. When we receive 'news' from our environment, it is neither good nor bad until our appraisal process has 'passed judgment,'" and we have assigned it meaning and value as it relates to us—to our preferences, goals and personalities. Then we channel our appraisal into some form of coping mechanism that relates to our held values and goals. In fact, rational decision making cannot even occur without access to our emotions. Our ability to make reasonable decisions is knocked out if we have no access to our emotions. We need our feelings to help us to rate, decipher and assess information from the outside world, and relate it to our own needs, goals, desires and preferences.

According to Antonio Damasio, author of *Descartes' Error: Emotion, Reason and the Human Brain,* people who had brain damage that severed the frontal reasoning area from the amygdala's emotional resources performed perfectly normally on *traditional* intelligence tests, but were unable to *plan and make normal decisions.* Even making plans, which is normally seen as an operation of the cortex, doesn't happen without emotional input. Damasio found that people, over time, develop a set of representational markers such as opinions, values, traits and schemas that become associated with somatic markers that register pain or pleasure. His brain-damaged patients, who were unable to make these connections between the thinking and feeling sides of their brains, were unable to make decisions or choices. They had no gut-level pointers to favor one alternative over another. "They were unable to anticipate future pain or pleasure in connection with specific alternatives. With their decline in emotion came a concomitant decline in reasoning." Damasio points out, "The powers of reason and the experience of emotion decline together."

Our emotions are what enable us to evaluate incoming information and give it the emotional color, tone and value that tell us how to interpret everyday events. Joseph LeDoux uses the example of the first funeral he attended, which was also his first exposure to the scent of gardenias. The scent of gardenias still casts a melancholy mood over a situation for LeDoux because of his early association with a funeral. He still filters an event through this associative process or lens (the scent of gardenias equals melancholy), which illustrates the relationship between thought and emotion. And every real-estate agent knows that the smell of bread or cookies baking in the oven helps to sell a house because of the pleasant feeling of home associated with those aromas. Emotions color the events of our lives. Sadness casts its aura over the situations of our lives and can cause us to perceive or interpret events through that lens.

OUR BASELINE OF HAPPINESS

Research further reveals that people seem to have a "happiness set point." Those whose set point is high will tend to return to that point within a reasonable time frame, even when they experience a serious loss; while those whose is lower will tend to return to a lower point, interpreting even good turns of events from the point of view of a lowered set point. That is, people with a higher set point tend to put a more positive spin on the events of their lives, and people with a lower set point a more negative spin.

This begs the question of the possibility of an attitude adjustment, one that will set the wheels in motion for seeing the world differently or lifting a dark cast caused by sadness. Attitude adjustments, in my experience, work best in conjunction with therapy that allows us to freely and fully encounter, process and integrate our hurt feelings. When we attempt to adjust our attitude purely as an act of will, with no caring regard for the genuine pain we're in, the results are often brittle and don't hold. They are like a dike constantly being pushed on from behind. Eventually, a crack appears and all the held-back water pours out. On the other hand, if we make no deliberate and disciplined attempt to change self-defeating thinking for the better, we undermine every improvement we try to make. We need to fortify ourselves with daily doses of good thinking, which leads to good feeling, and vice versa.

DEPRESSION VERSUS SADNESS

Oftentimes we confuse depression with sadness. But, in my experience, people are more likely to be depressed when they are unable to feel their sadness or anger, when they are shut down. In working through depression with clients over the years, I've come to see depression as a variety of *different* states of feeling. It can be a sort of numbness, in which there is a strange detachment from our own inner world and the world that surrounds us. Or it may be an inability to grieve losses so that the pain remains turgid within the self, locked inside with no outward expression. Depression is commonly seen as anger turned inward upon the self. In all cases, it is deeply undermining and overwhelming for the person who experiences it. The person's life drones along, and he or she can feel hopeless or tragic, or alternates between feeling shutdown and flooded with too much feeling. Sadness is important to both identify *and* feel. Unfortunately, in our feel-good culture, we treat sadness as if it signifies a fundamental defect in a person. But if we can't feel real sadness, we're not likely to feel real joy. And if we feel like a failure every time we're sad, like we have to hide it, talk ourselves out of it or make it go away, we're training ourselves to be shallow.

One startling example of this phobia around grieving in America can be seen in the way we treat the loss of a spouse. The grieving process for losing a spouse is likely to take two years. During this period the griever can feel sad, angry, lost, empty, lonely, even desperate, and still be well within a normal range. But often, we get frustrated with this prolonged period of grief, and we worry when the person isn't "snapping out of it." However, if the person cannot go through this grieving process, she will not be able to successfully integrate the loss and move on with her life.

Then she might seek a *replacement* relationship, which can give rise to more problems. Having not grieved the initial loss, she may not be able to choose well in her next relationship because her emotions from the first loss are blocked and aren't informing her thinking for her next choice. Or the *new* relationship will be asked to hold the *old* pain.

Until we have mourned a loss, we're really not free to love again. We hold back unconsciously out of fear of pain from another loss, or leap in with an intensity or a neediness that doesn't allow the new relationship to develop naturally.

This grief process also needs to accompany loss through divorce, for both the estranged spouses and their children. Even if the person remains in our lives, we have lost the family as it was. So sadness is adaptive in these ways, too, allowing us to fully process a significant loss so we can form a new attachment that is less burdened by the pain of the previous one; otherwise, we carry our unresolved pain with us into our subsequent relationships. This can also apply to other types of loss. Loss of job, youth or moving may need to be grieved to greater or lesser extents, depending on their significance to us. Processing loss and the feelings associated with it are critical to living well in relationships. Not processing loss can lead to depression.

I observe that once clients who are suffering with depression are able to actually feel their anger and sadness, once they begin to make positive lifestyle changes (such as getting sunlight and exercise daily, and eating and resting well) their depression often begins to lift. Prior to that, their depression can color the way they experience the circumstances of their lives and saps them of the will and motivation to make changes for the better. And, if they've been traumatized, their faith that things can improve and their ability to imagine a positive future are undermined. These factors, along with trauma's negative effects on the limbic system, more or less coalesce to block things from getting better. Also, when people are depressed, they tend to withdraw from society and relationships, eat poorly and stop exercising on a regular basis. Research proves again and again that isolation contributes to everything from a shorter life span to increased depression, and exercise is one of nature's ways of restoring the self-soothing and emotionally regulating body chemicals such as dopamine and serotonin. Isolation means that we aren't near other people, so the benefits of the limbic resonance that can regulate our systems are unavailable to us. Also, we are, of course, not touching anyone, which means that our bonding chemical, oxitocin, is not being released. All of this inclines us toward further isolation. People who are depressed tend to be very hard on themselves; their inner dialogue can be very unforgiving. Helping them to be gentler and kinder to themselves, to forgive (not condemn) themselves for their shortcomings, can help them see themselves in a more compassionate light.

The deep limbic system is involved in setting emotional tone and coloring our moods. When the limbic system is quiet, a positive, hopeful state of mind generally emerges. When it appears to be overactive on a brain scan, according to Daniel G. Amen, M.D., it correlates with increased negativity and depression. It is important to remember, however, that our emotions are not confined to this system alone. Our meaning-making and decoding are also done in the cortex. The brain operates as a complex system that scientists are only beginning to understand. [Refer to chapter 2 for additional information on the limbic system.]

STRESS AND DEPRESSION

Cortisol has come to be seen as a major culprit in depression. "One of the most consistent biological findings about depression is that the adrenal cortex secretes more of the stress related hormone cortisol in depressed people. This simple fact, which can be determined from a cotton swab containing saliva, links depression to the biology of stress," says Antonio Damasio. When we're stressed the concentration of cortisol in our bloodstream goes up. "In the short run, stress responses are useful in mobilizing bodily resources to cope with danger. But if stress is severe and continuous, the consequences can be serious. Your cardiovascular system can be compromised, your muscles can weaken, and you can develop ulcers and become more susceptible to developing certain kinds of infections." Too much cortisol contributes to problems with short-term memory; it's elevated in elderly people, especially those with memory problems and depression.

[Part II offers practical techniques for reducing stress when it starts to take hold, *and* heading it off at the pass by developing stress-busting strategies for living.] The first questions to ask a depressed client may not only be psychological and emotional, but also biological, because biology *becomes* emotion, which, in turn, *becomes* psychology. A therapist might ask, How do you sleep at night? Are you working too much or too little? What are the relationships in your life, and how do you live in them? What are the stressors in your personal world? How is your support system? Describe your diet. What kind of exercise do you do? Having gone through this list and determined that the client is getting good rest, eating healthy foods, enjoying a strong support network, having adequate interests or work, and getting regular exercise, the therapist is ready to tackle other emotional issues. But so connected is the body to the mind that to ignore its impact and hope to get better without addressing these issues is like expecting to lose weight without adjusting our food intake or exercise program. If we want to get past depression, we'll need to address all of it.

According to Dr. Robert Goldman, president of The National Academy of Sports Medicine and author of *Brain Fitness:*

A study of forty women with a depressive disorder at the University of Rochester Sports Center found that an aerobic activity—running or walking—or working out on weight machines almost completely erased signs of depression. The women exercised about three times a week. Each workout consisted of a five- to ten-minute warm-up, a main session of either

progressing through a ten-station weight circuit, or walking or jogging around an indoor track, and ten minutes of cool down. A control group of women with similar signs of depression did no exercise. After eight weeks, the active women's scores on standard depression tests had improved dramatically, while their sedentary peers registered no improvement in their mental health. Moreover, the women were again tested for signs of depression a year later, and the exercising group maintained their rosier outlook.

Exercise kicks in the body's natural opioid system. Scientists at the University of Goteborg in Sweden feel that exercise is not only an effective treatment for depression but may also be one for alcoholism, drug addiction and anorexia nervosa. Exercise three times a week or more, along with thirty minutes of sunlight a day, is a very effective antidepressant and can be extremely beneficial. In addition, when we exercise and get outdoors, we tend to feel motivated and good about ourselves and our habits, while we're simultaneously getting our recommended thirty minutes of sunlight to further stave off depression.

If we can encourage prayer or a spiritual program to bring purpose and a higher meaning to our lives we'll do even better. In fact, prayer has as profound a beneficial effect on depression as drugs do. Over and over again, studies prove this, according to Larry Dossey, M.D., author of *Healing Words*.

I've also observed time and time again (and Amen's research bears this out) that people who have a spiritual belief system, meditate on positive imagery, and do daily imageries in order to learn to relax [see part II for details on these techniques] reeducate their brains, and seem to be able to locate the flip switch that leads to positive, rather than negative, states of mind. They become softer on themselves and others, forgiving themselves easily for mistakes and letting others off the hook for theirs. Forgiveness can help us cultivate uplifted states of mind because, though it forces us to confront negative emotions, its goal is to increase positive ones. When our brains and minds focus on positive goals, that is where we direct our attention, so we view the negative thoughts encountered along the way from a different perspective. We're not ignoring negativity, we're simply putting it into a framework and valuing it as something to get through and grow from rather than live in. Nor are we in any way denying the power of painful emotions. That would only drive the pain deeper inside us. The idea that there is a "better place" to get to can act as a light at the end of the tunnel, and can keep us going through the dark and narrow passageway of our own pain with a sense of purpose.

Americans experience a considerable amount of depression, and many of those suffering are women. The next case study explores one woman's pain-filled inner landscape.

The Dark Hole: Lydia's Story

Lydia describes herself as spending a lot of time "in a dark hole," from which she feels there is no escape. She reports feeling lonely, isolated from other people. Disconnected from her inner world and from the world around her. Hopeless. She says she's often tired and can have trouble focusing and organizing her thoughts, which often makes things in her life feel overwhelming or chaotic.

This way of seeing herself, life and the world strongly affects her thinking patterns, or her thinking patterns make her see the world this way—or both. Either way, she sees herself as flawed. The world, to her, appears cruel and aversive, and try as she might, she has trouble imagining the future at all, let alone a happy one. Feeling this way day after day obviously has a debilitating effect on Lydia, her life, her relationships and her career.

Lydia is depressed.

Another catch-22 is that her depression causes her to think in certain self-destructive ways, and her self-destructive thinking causes her depression. For example, the way she draws conclusions is very arbitrary and based on an absence of information. She'll selectively abstract—pulling, say, just one of many elements out of a situation and basing all her conclusions on that small bit of information without factoring in the rest of it. She'll generalize or come to some sweeping conclusions drawn on the basis of minimal data or a relatively trivial event. The way that she'll evaluate performance, hers or another's, can be quite unbalanced. She might magnify a situation or its impact or minimize it, not in accord with a balanced read, but based on her mood or state of mind at the time. Though it may almost appear that her thinking is confused or even shallow, it probably speaks to a loss of connection with her own inner depths and a fear of opening up a Pandora's box—in short, the fear of the power of her authentic feelings.

Today, Lydia comes into my office mad at her husband. He is a businessman who Lydia and the children rarely see. They live a life that looks good and feels bad. When we work with the situation psychodramatically, Lydia's entire focus is to want to apologize to her children for what she perceives as her own weakness and stupidity, and to blame her husband for everything that has ever gone wrong in all their lives. But what also becomes very evident as the psychodrama unfolds is the extent of her self-hatred, and her feelings of utter helplessness and inadequacy when it comes to effecting change in herself or her situation. She collapses in the face of it. She can ask for forgiveness from others, she can point a finger of blame away from herself, but part of her motivation and ability to do this is that, at an unconscious level, she feels such crippling self-recrimination and guilt. I ask Lydia to choose someone to play her anger. She reverses roles and becomes her anger talking back to herself. Again she collapses, alternating between shutdown and rage, black-and-white, all-or-nothing. Over and over again, she curls up, hiding her head in her arms and sort of crying, moaning, squinting and shaking her head. Her inner self wishes to take this concrete form; bringing it out of hiding, giving it a voice and a shape, is useful.

As Lydia has trouble expressing just anger—that is, her anger continually cycles into helplessness, shutdown, rage, self-recrimination, guilt, blame and frustration—she comes to remember her constant fear of her rageful mother. "She was angry *all the time*. I could never, ever be angry at all; there was no room," Lydia says. I ask her to find someone to play herself as a little girl. She reverses roles, becoming the little girl talking back to her adult self: "You can't get angry; if you do, you'll turn into her. You'll turn into Mom; you'll start raging, and you'll never stop. You'll be just like her." At this point, Lydia's work begins to shift as she is able to trace the helplessness to one of its sources. She was a child who was constantly overwhelmed by the anger and rage of her parents, and could do nothing to affect the situation, to make herself more comfortable or to change things for the better. So she gave up. She became helpless because there was nothing that she could see to do at the time to improve things. And this turned into a learned helplessness that followed her into marriage.

As a child, she received little positive reinforcement for who she was, so she built a sort of false self that was acceptable. And because she lacked the social skills to elicit positive reinforcement from someone else in her young world, her pattern of hiding her authentic self began to take root. She also learned that feeling her own anger was *verboten*. So she was in a bind: angry, wounded by the anger of others and silent about all of it. And to compound it, she decided that if she ever did express anger, she would turn into her mother.

All these threads began to unravel in the psychodrama, and Lydia was able to feel a compassion for herself as a child that she never felt before. As the connection between her way of being as an adult and how she learned to be as a child became clearer, some of her self-recrimination lifted and things began to make sense that hadn't made sense before. Maybe she wasn't so bad after all. Maybe there was hope for change. Maybe she could forgive that little child who was only doing her best, and have some compassion for the woman she had become. The clouds began to part, as she saw the possibility of forgiving herself. She also began to see the wisdom of it. If she couldn't forgive herself, she would lock herself into living out this self-destructive cycle. This was the true amends she wished to make to her children: not just words of desperation and compulsive apologies, but a shift in perception that could lead to a meaningful change in her own behavior. To let herself off the hook was to free those she loved as well. It had nothing to do with condoning what she saw as her own poor behavior; it had to do with understanding it. She had an opportunity to take a trip through time, to walk in her own moccasins—those of the girl she'd forgotten she was—and it freed her up. She understood, at last.

THE UPS AND DOWNS OF THE MIDLIFE JOURNEY

Midlife women can be at a higher risk for feelings of depression. Though some women experience very few problems in perimenopause and menopause, swings and dips in the female hormone estrogen appear to affect the neurotransmitters, brain substances that regulate mood. When the neurotransmitters are working well, our moods fit the situation. We're happy when it's appropriate to be happy, and sad when it's appropriate to be sad. But if the neurotransmitters aren't doing their job, we can have wild mood changes, depression or anxiety, all out of proportion to what's happening in the moment. Women can also have more trouble with concentration and forgetfulness in midlife because estrogen affects the number of connections made in the brain. Studies suggest that the wiring that connects message-carrying brain cells doesn't work as well when our estrogen levels are lowered. These lower levels can also cause difficulty sleeping because estrogen affects the brain's internal clock and natural rhythms.

But midlife has other psychological and emotional challenges that can contribute to depression as well. We're at the sandwich period of our lives. Our children still need us for financial and emotional support, but now, so do our parents. The people we might have gone to for a little help are needing to depend on us now in ever-increasing ways. And their getting older every day means we're getting older, too; their facing death means some day we'll have to face it, too. Suddenly, all of this becomes very real. Our youth-oriented generation is getting gray hair and wrinkled skin, and we don't look so great in T-shirts and jeans anymore. Our mortality is coming into view and the view may not feel all that great for people who thought we would never die. The Peter Pan in us is under serious pressure.

However, there is a flip side to all of this. Studies have also revealed that many, if not most, of us defy the myth that midlife is all crisis and no fun. Both women and men report experiencing a new sense of self-confidence at midlife, and a greater appreciation and awareness of the value of life and relationships. Many midlifers feel a newfound freedom: We're old enough to know what we want out of life and still young enough to enjoy it. We've accomplished our primary tasks of childrearing and career achievement, and we're still able, thanks to modern science, to look forward to years of reasonable health, if we're willing to follow doctor's orders and eat well, sleep well and get plenty of exercise. Many of us experience a newfound self-assurance and composure. We know who we are and who we aren't. We are more accepting, of ourselves as well as others. It's the perfect time to do some emotional housecleaning because we're young enough to want as bright a future as can be ours, and old enough to know it doesn't happen by accident—we have to play our part in creating our own luck. Forgiveness can be a bridge upon which we safely cross over into a deeper sense of self and connection with others.

∿

Forgiveness is the act of admitting we are like other people.

∿**Christina Baldwin**
Life's Companion

∿

As difficult as it seems, you can be sure of this: At the core of the heart, you have the power to move beyond the old issues that are still hindering your freedom. The hardest things—the ones that push you up against your limits—are the very things you need to address to make a quantum leap into a fresh inner and outer life.

∿**Doc Childre and Howard Martin**
The HeartMath Solution

MORE THAN JUST A BODY: QUANTUM PHYSICS AND FORGIVENESS

Quantum physics puts forth the idea that we all share relational space. Through the waves and particles that surround us, and are us, we overlap into each other's worlds. Newtonian science follows the model that sees people and objects as the often-referred-to "billiard balls" suspended in space, acting upon each other through Newton's laws of physics, while quantum physics sees our world as active and alive in every aspect. There is no dead space.

I am putting forth the idea of "quantum" forgiveness because of what I have experienced over the years as a therapist and psychodramatist. The energy field around the people with whom I work seems most apparent to me; I feel it and I sense it. When people come upon a moment in a psychodrama in which they are remembering a struggle that has been stuck within them for decades, they release a certain type of energy that *feels* a particular way. It can even have a scent. Where did that come from, and why does one kind of energy get released when letting go of old, stuck pain and other kinds at other times? Then there's the energy that the group is generating as a whole. A stuck group feels constricted, while a "happening" group has a flowing, bubbly feel to it. Waves and particles are interweaving with each other, collapsing wave functions, creating new configurations of energy with new possibilities for connection. A sort of "quantum" openness. Group therapy is as much a function of what happens in the quantum physical environment, in the container of the group, as what happens with any one individual. In fact, separateness, according to quantum thought, is somewhat of an illusion. Our world is made up of waves and particles, according to quantum physics, not separate billiard balls suspended in the same lifeless environment. If we are made up of waves and particles, then so is everyone and everything else. If we aren't solid, then we are always in and out of each other's space. And what we need is to be responsible for what we put into that space and how it affects the space of others. Waves and particles interweave constantly with each other. When we are "in relationship" with others, we are interweaving our waves and particles with theirs. We become woven into the fabric of each other quite literally, when we are intimate, sharing space or connecting with each other. As Danah Zohar, physicist and author of *Quantum Self,* puts it:

๑

Intimate relationships, that type of relationship that gets inside the self, that influences and even defines our being from within, are the sine qua non of quantum self. Viewed quantum mechanically, I am my relationships—my relationship to this is the results within my own self of my relationship to others, my living relationships to my own past, the new quantum memory and to my future possibilities. Without relationship I am nothing.

๑

We often give voice to certain platitudes: "That was then, and this is now"; "It's all in the past, put it behind you." But the past is alive within the present at all times. We have no choice but to accept it, embrace it, feel it, experience it and give it a new meaning that, in turn, allows us to reconfigure our present with new insight and understanding. We rework our past memories by allowing them to emerge, to be felt and seen. Then we reintegrate the memory as seen anew through the eyes of today with greater maturity and insight. We reweave. We need to feel what we're forgiving in order for forgiveness to go beyond being a mental exercise. This process often leads to more compassion both for ourselves and the person we're forgiving. But this is not done once and for all. It's a mistaken notion of therapy that we "do our mother work," "get through our father issues," grieve the loss and get over it. In truth, we are constantly making new meaning and new connections, adding a new awareness to an old one, shuffling and reshuffling the past and present and pieces of the future that are ever with us. To see ourselves otherwise is to imagine that we are Newton's billiard balls, contained in a tight space, finite and solid. We are not. We are alive. And the price of our aliveness is to be constantly in flux. As Heraclitus said, "You can't step twice into the same river," and "All is flux, nothing stays still." The ancient Greeks understood that we are on an ever-changing journey throughout life. Our passions, our needs, our human drives and inter-actions with nature are all essentially one, issuing from the same stuff of life.

When we work in therapy, we work with all of this—all of who a person is, was or will be; all that the person inherited from the system in which he or she grew up, its passions, morals, hopes, dreams and its requited or unrequited love. All of this is woven into the quantum self. And all of this emerges in therapy, in the here and now, which includes the then and there. Zohar continues:

Reciprocities of quantum memory occur where the wave patterns created by past experience emerge in the brain's quantum system with wave patterns created by present experience, my past is always with me. . . . It exists not as a "memory," a finished and closed fact that I can recall, but as a living pres-ence that particularly defines what I am now. The wave patterns of the past are taken up and woven into the present and relived, afresh at each moment as something that has been but also as something that is now being.

Through quantum memory, the past is alive, open and in dialogue with the present. As in any true dialogue, this means that not only does the past influence the present, but also that the present impinges on the past, constantly giving it new life and new meaning. (It's never too late to have a happy childhood.) Zohar, who as a child was often separated from her mother for long periods of time, uses her own experience of motherhood to reflect on how healing takes place from the quantum physical point of view:

৵ৎ

During the first night in the hospital after my daughter was born, I missed my mother with a greater and more painful urgency than I had ever experienced before. I wanted her to be there with me and my new baby. As had happened often before, she was not. But then something began to happen. Even during that first night I felt myself becoming that mother—not simply the mother of the new baby I held in my arms, but also the mother of the baby within myself. As I held my own baby close, I also embraced the baby within me. I loved her and reassured her that I will always be there. . . . [M]y unhappy infancy was taken up into the present, interwoven with all the ministrations lavished on my own daughter, and she became secure. Reincarnated in quantum memory, the baby within received a new start in life; she was "born again."

৵ৎ

Zohar describes beautifully, in this passage, how the process of healing takes place.

Sometimes, life itself is the agent of healing, and sometimes, we create a healing environment in therapy. In the ever-alive environment of the group, our child selves emerge in the quantum moment. The desires of the inner child who wished to be seen and loved by her parents emerge as a wish to be valued by the therapist or other group members. Along with this may come all of the complexes, competencies and competitiveness that were a part of the family she grew up in, with siblings, parents, extend family and so on. Psychoanalysts also refer to this unconscious dynamic as transference. It has its origins in the past, but is alive and energized by the present situation. If misunderstood, if this past pattern that is being attached to the present is not linked to its proper origins in the past, it may be seen as solely a part of what is happening now. If the transference is not resolved, understood and reintegrated into the ever-alive present/past it may become a conflict in the here and now if the transference is a problematic one. This is another way in which the past becomes the present.

Quantum physics shows us why, when thoughts, feelings and behaviors that are ostensibly from the past get triggered into the present, we experience them as if they are happening in the here and now. The past *is* the present. Burying it is an illusion. That's why when we repress it, our health suffers; we are denying something that is as real as the sky around us. It is made up of the same waves and particles that make up our present, our world and our relationships. We have no choice but to experience the contents of our past experiences and integrate them with new insight and meaning. Though this work can be difficult and even frightening, the only other choice is to deny its very existence, which we now can see does not get rid of it. It merely makes us strangers in our own insides. Personal ownership means just that—owning who we already are.

As quantum selves, we make ourselves up as we go along, weave the fabric of our being in through our ongoing dialogue with our own past, with our experiences, with the environment, and with others. An important part of that dialogue is the reasons that we assign to the various choices that we might make and how those reasons fit into the whole context of our lives and what we value. Thus, while reasons themselves don't determine the choices we make, they play a crucial role in making some choices more likely than others. The particular reasons that we link to an array of possible choices influence the probability of making any particular choice.

Zohar's preceding description helps us understand more clearly why it is so important to confront those aspects of our past that undermine our present, to understand them in the light of today, and to create new and hopefully more enlightened meaning. The meaning that we unconsciously attach to our past experiences of life actually becomes our tomorrow and lives in our today.

When we imagine that we can "forgive and forget" without going through the natural process that is a part of creating, uncreating and re-creating—the process that is the natural imperative of being in a state of aliveness—we deny our own humanness and the intrinsic qualities of the world we live in. Forgiveness isn't forever, either. We may need to re-forgive the same hurt many times if it is living inside many parts of us, many internalized time zones, or if resentment and hurt have been woven into the fabric of our relationships. So it is never one thing. Not really. It's the layers of the onion. Trying to reduce it to one thing only denies the complicated truth: that we are a tapestry of many colors constantly unraveling and being rewoven. We will never figure it all out. This is why it may be more important to get good at the process of growth and forgiveness rather than to "get it right." Forgiveness is not an event, but a process, and the process is always changing. What we need to weather it well is not a fixed self, but a coherent, well-balanced, flexible self that can constantly adjust, yet still hold at the center (which is not solid). In other words, it's better to become a good "forgiver" than to focus on forgiving once and for all, because we will be constantly called upon to forgive and re-forgive and forgive again. Each time it will be from a slightly different place in the river that we can't step into twice, a slightly new configuration of waves and particles.

This means that we need to take a holistic view of life, we need to stay in shape for living the way athletes stay in shape for an athletic event. This includes getting enough sleep, enough relaxation and downtime, enough work, enough good nutrition, proper exercise, spiritual food and fun, and avoiding activities that sap us of our inner balance. It also includes working through those particular past issues that are blocking our healthy functioning in the present.

FEEDING PAIN INSTEAD OF FEELING IT:
THE CONNECTION BETWEEN
EMOTIONAL AND PHYSICAL WEIGHT

Why, when we have a multibillion-dollar diet industry and more leisure time than any other time or place in history, are we heavier, as a nation, than ever? Scientific studies clearly link stress with fat build-up. Stress releases cortisol into the body, which may contribute to locking in fat storage and is often a trigger for overeating. Emotional stress, whether the result of unpaid bills, unresolved pain from childhood or shame at not being perfect, has more to do with undermining our health than we probably want to know. One way to assist in maintaining a healthy weight is to live our lives in a balanced way that does not create excess stress. Stressful lifestyles, poor eating habits, lack of exercise and fragmented relationship networks may be contributing to this phenomenon. Maybe when we're stressed or lonely we're turning to food to feel better. We call it "comfort food." In addition to the obvious addictive substances such as drugs and alcohol, many people in our society use food to manage moods or painful feelings. Food is used as a sedative to quiet and comfort or as a drug to relieve emotional pain. We also use food as "company." But food isn't proper company; it doesn't give back or interact. Or maybe we feel secretly guilty for wanting to eat anything at all, so we eat unconsciously because we feel shame around food; or rather, we *don't* want to feel it, and that's why we're eating unconsciously.

When we eat instead of feel, we undermine ourselves on every level. We become somewhat disconnected from our inner world and ignore its true contents. We build up walls between ourselves and others because our growing preoccupation with food competes with other relationships. We lose touch with our bodies, which can alienate us from a significant part of who we are. In addition, we may tire more easily, have less energy and a harder time exercising. And our self-image often suffers. Unfortunately, our standard of female beauty is too thin. Twenty-seven years ago, models weighed seven pounds less than the average American woman; today, they weigh twenty-three pounds less. We need a new standard that's neither skinny nor overweight, but a livable in-between.

All of this can complicate forgiveness issues for a couple of reasons. Carrying too much weight, in my experience, can mean we're carrying extra emotional burdens, and extra weight is a metaphor for this. Maybe we're feeling angry and resentful. Or sad and filling a hurting heart with food. To start the ball rolling in a better direction, we may need to forgive ourselves for eating in a way that undermines our well-being. We may need to forgive others for the relational problems that are contributing to our use of food as a self-medicator, or examine our pasts to understand how these patterns of relating got set up to begin with. And we'll need to understand how food was used in our own families.

In a society that is obsessed with being skinny, it's no wonder that the shadow side (being overweight) has finally emerged. Any extreme that shuts out or clamps down on moderation gives rise to what Jung referred to as a "shadow," or the denied part. We have created so much psychological shame around not being model-thin that we've become its opposite: overweight. While we're looking at stressful or sedentary lifestyles, fast food and exaggerated portion size as contributors to our ever-increasing waistlines, why not also factor in the stress and emotional pain caused by holding ourselves to impossible standards that doom 90 percent of us to failure, or using food to self-medicate?

One has only to look at the cultures of the Mediterranean or Eastern Europe to understand that eating together or enjoying Grandma's comfort foods are sources of deep bonding and consolation. Being Greek myself, I have wonderful memories of long hours 'round my grandmother's dinner table and endless weekend breakfasts with my family. My sisters and I baked together and doled out chocolate-chip cookies or brownies with great ceremony and excitement. Food used in these ways has tremendous power for bonding and creating important and memorable moments of celebration. Food is so important: It can and should be a vital part of all of our lives. When we're sick, we need chicken soup; when we're bereaved, casseroles from caring friends nourish us in body and spirit; and when we graduate high school or college, we have a memorable dinner to celebrate. Holiday meals carry deep meaning in all our psyches. Eating dinner with the family is where we learn how to socialize, develop easy, natural good manners and internalize the feeling that we belong. When we use food functionally, we have it in its proper place. Weight control is not where we begin to make meaningful and lasting changes. We need to examine our entire relationship with food and perhaps restructure it. Forgiveness makes it so much easier to make the many tiny changes along with the big ones. It greases the path for lack of a better term. See in this next story how food can be used in problematic ways.

∽

Eating is never so simple as hunger.

∽Erica Jong
"The Catch"
Becoming Light

A Generational Legacy of Food

ℛena's mother was anorexic. Her obsession with food manifested in unusual disinterest, though the family always sat down to nice dinners. When Rena had her own children she longed to provide them with a normal sense of food. (Unfortunately, she didn't have one and didn't really know at that time that her mother had a serious eating disorder. She just thought she was thin and lucky that she didn't like food.)

Rena made cookies every day to welcome the children home from school. She married Jack, a nice guy who was basically quite preoccupied with his own life and not very available for his wife—a good guy, a loving father, less good on the husband front. At one point, Jack had an affair that almost ended their marriage. Emotionally for Rena, this repeated affairs that her father had. She witnessed the pain they caused her mother, but her father never acknowledged any of it, took no responsibility for the damage these affairs inflicted on his family. So Rena's old, unresolved pain got mixed up with her new pain, and she was immobilized. Jack and Rena got help, just enough to get *by,* but not *through.* Their marriage carried on, but resentments that were never fully worked through built up slowly over time. Their three children gave them enough to focus on so that the distance between them didn't feel all that pressing. Rena developed a close relationship with her eldest daughter. The talks she didn't have with Jack she had with her daughter J. C., instead. The sweet and sharing bond that she and J. C. had filled the intimacy hole that had developed between herself and Jack.

During Jack's affair, Rena had put on fifteen pounds. She ate the feelings of rejection that hurt too much to feel, and the more shame she felt about her preoccupation with food, the more unconscious and sometimes secretive her eating became.

J. C. (who didn't know about the affair) munched along with her mother, as they shared the events of the day, watched TV movies and went shopping together. She sensed her mother's pain and joined her in it by eating with her. Food was just part of the relationship. When J. C. grew to her full height, which wasn't very tall, the extra food she ate piled on all over her young body. Each of them was carrying an extra fifteen pounds or so. Once they had that much extra weight, the next five or seven they gained were hardly noticeable.

Rena shared her anger at Jack in a thousand subtle ways with J. C. over the years. It made J. C. feel anxious; after all, this was her daddy, these were her parents, her source of security and love. She couldn't share her anxiety with her mother because it just seemed too risky, and she didn't want to upset her. She hardly shared it with herself. She was quite young to sort out such things, and besides, she had her own issues with her dad. So she ate a little more than she might have had she not been a little girl trying to hold so much—her mother's hurt, her own worry about being her mother's chosen confidante, this special alliance that left out other family members (what would her sister and brother think, and her dad?). Gradually, over time, she developed the habit of putting food in her mouth when she was having a strong feeling. The extra weight became a part of her persona and her growing identity. The longer it stayed, the less she could imagine herself without it. It was just sort of who she was, who her mother was and a special connection that they shared, part of feeling close. She would feel almost disloyal to her mom to lose it now.

Meanwhile, Rena's weight and lowered self-esteem stood in the way of having the courage to confront and feel sadness; the unfelt sadness and lowered self-esteem and unexpressed resentment made eating in healthier ways too hard, too threatening, and the fear of the loss of intimacy made all of it feel overwhelming.

When J. C. finally had her own children, she desperately wanted to break this cycle of what looked like a weight problem. By now she had married someone with many of the same issues (of course), which both helped and made it harder. But the couple got help and did it together. They learned that their weight wouldn't stay off without doing the emotional work, and that they had to methodically change their eating habits (stop feeding their pain and start feeling it) in order to get in touch with their inner worlds. As the weight came off, the feelings came up. As they got thinner, the fear of the loss of intimacy (eating together can feel bonding) emerged, and their identity as a certain kind of person started shifting all over the map. The emotions that had been stuffed down surfaced. Understanding this helped them get through the tough and challenging work of recovery without blaming each other (too much) for the emotional and psychological upheaval and sense of disorientation they were experiencing. Slowly and with the help of professionals and support groups, they teased out the complicated issues that they had wrapped themselves in, around and through the weight and they forgave themselves, and the generations in back of them as far as they could see, for being human, for doing the best they could at the time with what they had to work with.

GIVING UP THE DREAM

Particularly when it comes to parents, many of us carry our child-like fantasy into adulthood that eventually we will get what we so deeply desire, the love, attention or approval, the "I love you, you're the best child this world has ever known," the support for our lives and the recognition of who we really are. Sometimes, this works itself out naturally. Children separate enough to be themselves, they don't particularly feel at war with the part of themselves that is their parent; in fact, it comforts them and gives them strength. Their connection with their parent evolves over time, and they evolve along with it, becoming more of who they are and less of who their parents are; they create their own identities and their own lives.

But for people who have been hurt, deeply and consistently, by their parents, giving up the dream of either a final reckoning or a magical transformation of their relationship is very difficult. These people have kept a part of their childhood hearts alive, waiting for their emotional ship to come in. And when they face letting go of the dream, they feel the pain underneath it. Ultimately, of course, it's a good and freeing pain that will allow them to move on and set about organizing their lives to fill in what's missing, though they don't necessarily see it this way.

The other side of the emotional coin is having our identities fused with our parents, as we saw with Rena and J. C. This can also make it harder to have our own secure sense of self because we lose track of where we leave off and they begin. Fusion and cut-off are two sides of the same emotional coin. In each case, *our* needs were overwhelmed by those of another person. This is another place where forgiveness can help us to work through whatever is in our way, whether it was being shut out and hurt by rejection, or absorbed and having our personal space impinged upon. But as we'll see in the next chapter, so often it is in *accepting* things as they are, *integrating* the complex thoughts and feelings that are attached to an emotional and psychological wound, and *letting go* that we can have the peace and sense of wholeness that we're yearning for. No parent is perfect, we got what we got or didn't get, and now it's ours to work with and take the next right step. We take this step not necessarily to get our relationships with our parents right but to get our relationships with ourselves *right* and in order, and to free the next generation—our children—from the burden of carrying unresolved, intergenerational pain. It's a lovely bonus if we can have it all, and certainly our relationships with our family of origin improve, but our real goal is to break the chain—starting with ourselves—and to free the subsequent generations. And it's often in this working through and releasing old pain that we somehow open and receive pleasure, hope and faith. Another paradox of the human heart. Something that we had thought we'd lost returns to us in a new and different form. In the immortal words of Shakespeare, "Nothing is lost that cannot be found."

If only there were evil people somewhere insidiously committing evil deeds, and it were necessary only to separate them from the rest of us and destroy them. But, the line dividing good and evil cuts through the heart of every human being. And who is willing to destroy a piece of his own heart?

—Alexander Solzhenitsyn

SEVEN

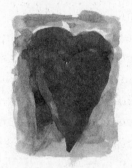

Acceptance, Integration and Letting Go: Coming to Terms and Releasing the Past

With a little time, and a little more insight, we begin to see both ourselves and our enemies in humbler profiles. We are not really as innocent as we felt when we were first hurt. And we do not usually have a gigantic monster to forgive; we have a weak, needy, and somewhat stupid human being. When you see your enemy and yourself in the weakness and silliness of the humanity you share, won't it make the miracle of forgiving a little easier?

~Lewis B. Smedes
Forgive and Forget: Healing the Hurts We Don't Deserve

Sincere forgiveness isn't colored with expectations that the other person apologize or change. Don't worry whether or not they finally understand you. Love them and release them. Life feeds back truth to people in its own way and time—just like it does for you and me.

~Sara Paddison
Hidden Power of the Heart

U nconsciously, we're all writing the story of our own lives. It's important that we unearth the details of our unresolved pain, tease out the meaning that we've made of the events of our lives and share our stories with others. We need to hear the sound of our own voices, to create, uncreate and re-create our own meaning, and write the next chapter with our eyes open.

Lying to ourselves about how we've experienced the events of our lives doesn't work; our unconscious will hold us to our own truth, whether we like it or not. The truth will reveal itself to us, consciously or unconsciously, that much is for sure. The choice we have is not whether or not the sins of our past will visit themselves upon our present—they will. The choice we have is whether or not that visitation will be conscious or unconscious. When it is unconscious, we live out our own cycle of hurt, blindly passing the pain on to others in one form or another, or keeping our own lives from flourishing. When it's conscious, we're choosing to use the circumstances of our lives to grow. We till the soil of our lives, turning over the contents of our inner worlds, digging deep, weeding, planting and nourishing new growth. We tend the garden of our own soul.

Integration, by now, has been happening naturally as we honestly *accept,* confront, explore and experience parts of our personal history that have combined to make us who we are. That exploration has taken us from meaningful moments in time to relationships that have shaped us and formative family styles that have acted as our classrooms on how to live.

By now we have learned what it means to process repressed emotions by feeling and understanding them, making connections between the past and present behavior, and identifying repetition patterns (dynamics from the past that repeat themselves in the present). When we allow ourselves to revisit these pieces of personal history and explore the impact the events of our lives have had on the person we are today, we reintegrate them with newfound awareness and insight. This allows us to use the events of our lives as opportunities for growth, to extract meaning from them, and to separate the past from the present. We learn to see how the past might be playing itself out today, getting in the way of our ability to have nourishing relationships and move freely and productively through our lives. We also learn to work through what was difficult and learn from it, while claiming what was good and using it as a solid foundation upon which to build a life. This is how we grow; it's an undoing and a redoing, a deconstruction and a reconstruction, a working through and a letting go. What preoccupied us moves from the foreground to the background of our minds, and though it may, at times, reemerge, it does so with greater understanding and less pain attached to it.

BREAKING THE CHAIN: HOW FORGIVENESS PAYS FOWARD

We do our partners, children and grandchildren a tremendous service when we own our own truths and fight our own tigers in the night, so they don't have to. "The sins of the father are visited upon the children," in more ways than one. If we are not willing to cry our own tears, someone else will have to cry them for us, but not by choice. We have learned enough by now about the dynamics of interrelationship and the impact of emotions on ourselves and, in turn, those we're close to, not to doubt what the impact on those around us might be if we *act out,* rather than *feel* and *talk out,* the powerful emotions that have wound themselves around our thinking, feeling and behavior. Unhealed pain from one generation gets passed along to the next in ways we hardly imagine, attaching itself like vines onto the foundations we build, seeding itself into the soil of our relationships, and disseminating itself into the irrigation system of the newly growing family.

The feelings that we walk around with are known at a deep level by our children, and affect both our parenting and partnering. What we can't move past within ourselves will inevitably be passed on to our families. They will have to live in our wound.

Parent and partner are two of the most splendid, meaningful and taxing roles that we can play. They stretch us to the max, and in the places that we're unhealed, that stretching can cause us to behave in ways we thought we'd never behave, to do what we swore we'd never do. This is the family legacy; the past gets re-created in the present in subtle, hardly perceptible ways, but their impact is more than felt.

People who have deep, unresolved pain from their own childhoods carry that pain into their parenting and partnering. Along with it may be a need to hide their fears of feeling vulnerable or needy, or of being "found out," so they put on a false face, drive their fears downward and play them out in dysfunctional ways with their own children and spouses. The emotions we deny have even more power because they make those close to us feel crazy. They sense one thing, and we tell them something else. What comes out of our mouths doesn't match up with what they pick up on at a more intuitive level. Sometimes, our loved ones try to make sense of this split by discounting their own reality and joining in adopting a façade.

Or maybe parents need to be needed a little too much. Since they haven't really self-defined themselves vis-à-vis their parents (that is, they live physically apart, but emotionally they haven't left home), they may have trouble fostering healthy autonomy in their own kids or allowing their partners to have a separate identity. The hot-and-cold emotional patterns from their childhoods can get lived out in their relationships with their own family members. They may connect, but not easily; or maintain rigid control to keep the chaos that they carry in their childhood hearts from erupting into their own homes. When the intimacy of partnership and parenthood makes their childhood feelings of sadness and loss vibrate beneath the thin membrane that separates their child from their adult selves, they may not know how to balance their emotions. They may withdraw, smother, explode, or all of the above. When parents don't make it a priority to resolve wounds from their own pasts so that they don't impact their ability to partner and parent well, they will inevitably seed their wound into the next generation, in one form or another. Closeness requires a secure sense of self. If significant pieces of our emotional world lie buried in silence, those zones of numbness will keep us from connecting fully with our partners and our children. Intimacy also offers us one of the most available passages toward personal and spiritual growth if, when we get triggered, we're willing to back up and use our emotions as indicators of where our work might lie.

So forgiveness can be explored as a way of staying connected in a manner that is ultimately self-preserving. Though we may feel like we're giving up a piece of ourselves—say our resentment, our wish for retribution or our anger—we may actually be preserving some more useful and valuable parts of self. Peace of mind, for one, or feeling good about ourselves as human beings. We give up the moral high ground that we feel we gain when we hold onto the anger we may feel toward someone we're constantly cutting down to size in our minds and, to our utter amazement, we're on a whole different kind of high ground. We gain solidity within our center. We no longer constantly feel torn up inside. Instead, we have a center that holds. We have, paradoxically, found a way to gain emotional space—through letting go. Our commitment and love for our partners and children motivate us to see things from another point of view, from their perspective. Children, especially, get us to do this because we identify with them so strongly. We understand them intuitively, so they train us in the emotional skill of empathy. Even before they can speak, we try to divine their needs and thoughts, and because we love them, we forgive them for everything from ruining the new carpet to changing the youthful shape of our midsections. They teach us to take the feelings of someone else into account, which actually is very freeing.

∾

It takes one person to forgive, it takes two people to be reunited.

—Lewis B. Smedes

The Art of Forgiving: When You Need to Forgive and Don't Know How

SIGNING ON THE DOTTED LINE

But forgiveness cannot be court-mandated. The courts are jammed with people who have found an arena for validating hurt, pain and anger through legal channels. Courts are being asked to handle and hold some of our most primitive and powerful emotions. But the courts do a poor job of healing a broken heart. What they may do is provide the time necessary to work through the complicated feelings involved in forgiveness by dragging out the proceedings for so long that all the pain and anger surface, in spite of our best efforts to keep them in check. We forgive out of exhaustion, disillusionment and a growing awareness that revenge is just costing us too much on every level. We're going broke—feeling bankrupt emotionally, spiritually and financially. It's a great metaphor, actually, for why we ultimately need to forgive, which is, of course, for our own preservation. As already discussed, what we don't work through in terms of painful issues with our own parents gets played out in our marriages and in our parenting. It's like clockwork; it resurfaces on schedule. With uncanny accuracy and punctuality, we respond to emotional triggers, whether it be a date, a season, a song, a smell, a word or a look. When we enter deep, committed relationships and begin building our own families, it all comes flooding back. Somewhere in our minds, we remember. We re-create the sweet and sustaining family rituals we knew: trips to the hardware store with Dad, sitting around the kitchen table, snuggling up with Mom. And the other rituals get re-created, too, the darker side of human interaction. This is why marriage and family offer one of our greatest opportunities for personal growth.

They tell us where our still unresolved wounds lie, giving us a second chance to work through them toward healing and letting go.

UNRAVELING THE LEGACY

If the stages outlined so far are worked through, forgiveness often happens naturally, as an outgrowth of the deep emotional work accomplished during these passages. Rather than an act of will, it is a dawning of awareness. We feel more separated from the intensity of the feelings of anger and hurt that were holding us down; our wish for revenge has diminished, and in its place is a growing compassion for our own and the other person's human frailty. We have more self-acceptance. We didn't die of awful feelings and the other person didn't either. We've gone to the center of pain and felt it, and we're humbled and relieved. Because we've accepted ourselves and come to terms with our vulnerable side that can feel weak, hurt or angry, we have an easier time accepting the same qualities in someone else. Because we've forgiven ourselves for our frailties—not through an act of will but through a willingness to see ourselves, warts and all—forgiving someone else feels more natural and possible. By the time we ask ourselves if we've forgiven someone, we already have. We see ourselves in humbler, more human terms, so we see other people in the same way. Suddenly, they aren't so big in our minds, they become right-sized. We have a growing sense of empathy for ourselves and the other person, and realize that their experience isn't the same as ours and that is natural—we're different people, and we can't expect to see things in exactly the same way all the time. They have a right to their point of view and we have a right to ours. Unbeknownst to us, we've let something go that we were hanging onto; we've moved on, and when we look back, we realize we're standing in a whole new place and seeing things from a different perspective. The issues we've been grappling with don't disappear exactly; that is, they aren't deleted from memory. Rather, they move from the foreground to the background of our consciousness. When and if they get triggered back into awareness, they are less potent and don't have quite the power to throw us, if we've done the emotional and psychological work to reduce their intensity. If they do return, it is with new awareness, understanding and meaning attached to them. We've accepted and integrated them.

When clients enter therapy, they do so because they want to learn something about life or themselves; they want to solve some puzzle and grow, or to fill in the ever-widening gap between themselves and the self they wish to be. When insight and self-awareness begin, the journey feels relieving, exciting and empowering. (First it gets better.) As they begin to peel back layers of the onion and get in touch with what it will take to do deeply transformative work, the task looks enormous, and the feelings that emerge, that have been let out of Pandora's box, can feel overwhelming. The hurt may feel as if it's happening all over again, almost as if it were happening right now. And problems today that are loaded with past issues can make the present feel unmanageable. Also, self-destructive thoughts about the self that were fossilized into habits—thoughts or ways of being—now start to become porous, rising up at every gain to undermine it. Clients feel awful as these thought patterns bombard the newly acquired sense of self with hardened self-talk designed for combating strong emotion more than embracing it. All this can hurt and make us wonder if there is any point in revisiting painful feelings. (Then it gets worse.)

But as the clients survive their own strong emotions and learn that such emotions don't kill them, a new dawning of awareness occurs. The thinking might go:

I am strong enough after all. I am mistress of my own inner world. If not I, who will be, who can be? I can experience my fears, anxieties, night terrors, wishes and disappointed dreams and live to tell the story. The story of me. I'm beginning to make sense to me, the world is not so bad after all, and relationships are possible because I am possible.

Then it gets different.

And finally, I am a somewhat new version of me integrated with the original me—an improved version. I hold in my heart all of who I am. I accept myself not as I wish I were, but as I am. I am willing to be real because being real is how I stay alive while I am living. I have a newly consolidated sense of self that incorporates and integrates the various parts of me, warts and all.

Then it gets real.

True love is always mixed with a bit of true hate. Forgiveness is the magic elixir that allows the two of them to swirl around and through relationships, so they can breathe and grow. Forgiveness enables feelings to emerge to the surface and be felt and understood for what they are, rather than to be buried and emerge in countless toxic forms. It provides a way out of the many little sins that we all commit daily, within the privacy of our own hearts, so that we can work with rather than deny them. The problematic truth, however, is that all too often the more something hurts, the greater our investment in hiding the truth from ourselves. To feel the pain is just too overwhelming a prospect, so it becomes disguised in varied and ingenious ways. But if we're willing to look, we will invariably find; if we're willing to ask, we will invariably receive.

There can also be a need to forgive the part of ourselves that remains young, vulnerable, needy and self-absorbed. The idealizations of our youth and our wish to be enveloped forever in the care of our parents, who will make us feel special and all-important, is a dream that has to transform in order for us to tolerate and survive the inevitable slings and arrows our flesh will surely be heir to as we establish our place within the world. Life is not easy, and the world can be a frightening and foreboding place. We will, if we choose to succeed, be rejected at least as often as we will be embraced.

But if we can stay with the process, we will grow; we may not get exactly what we thought we wanted but often we'll get what we never knew we were looking for. As Alice Miller says, "In search of my Mother's garden I found my own." Somewhere along the line, we stop searching for what we've lost and start exploring what we've found. That's when we "no longer regret the past nor wish to close the door on it." We actually are grateful for whatever led us into this radiant path of self-discovery and personal growth.

～

I don't think the psychological community looks enough at the best of what people can offer.

～Fredrick Luskin
Director of Stanford Forgiveness Project

TRANSCENDENCE, MEANING AND FORGIVENESS

Forgiveness often arises out of a transcendent experience that has allowed us to "see" things from a broader perspective, to take in the big picture and make decisions and choices based on a view from "outside the box." The physicist, Michio Kaku, in his book *Hyperspace*, describes a goldfish who spends her life swimming around in a bowl of water with other goldfish. From her perspective there is no bowl; this water, these fish, are her entire world, and she takes them for granted. But one day, this little fish takes a leap into the unknown, a leap out of the bowl. She looks back and realizes that she has been living in a bowl, in something called water. Having taken this leap, she is in a position to understand that there is something beyond the bowl that she previously thought was the whole world. She has *recontextualized* her experience and transformed her view of reality. *She sees her world from a new perspective.*

It is my feeling that forgiveness can, and often does, include this sort of recontextualization. As the French philosopher Jean-Jacques Rousseau said, "Death makes philosophers of us all." Often, the death of another person is what makes us aware of the finite nature of our own lives; it recontextualizes our experience of living, and we understand that life will not go on forever. One day, we will die, like they did. We face our own mortality. Life becomes valuable because we know we can lose it. That's why the Navaho tradition is to begin the morning with the statement, "Today is a good day to die." Not in order to invite death, but to invite life.

When we come to the awareness that hanging onto hate, pain and resentment is another kind of death, an inner death, we are seeing from outside the goldfish bowl. On balance the cost to ourselves of hanging onto anger and pain is too much. We see that it isn't worth it, that holding on is letting the other guy win because it hurts us not once, but over and over and over. We recontextualize, we transcend. Yes, we may have been traumatized once or many times by the other person, but we continue to retraumatize ourselves by the thoughts we think and the feelings we feel, or the situations we re-create in our own lives that either mirror our past or our attempts to get even with the past. We push away the good that could be ours because, on some deep level, we just can't let it in. We're living by an old script that says things won't work out in the end so why start, why invest, why care?

One of my favorite mottos is Oscar Wilde's quote, "Living well is the best revenge." If I let others who have hurt me win by stealing away my joy in life, my love for other people and my willingness to take risks, then they win and I lose. I'm not a victim, but a volunteer. And the thing to work on isn't just figuring out other people in all their marvelous complexity, but also myself, and why I'm still letting them define the parameters of my soul.

The road to spiritual wellness isn't easy because part of the road to freedom and transformation may include letting go of the anger and hurt that are a part of us now, that we feel we have every right to, that feel familiar and even warm. But if we will embark on the path of forgiveness, we can transform those feelings into the growth and understanding that will expand our souls. That's the magic. We don't have to let those feelings remain stuck and unconscious. Instead, we tease out their hidden messages, understand their intricacies and crazy wisdom, and let not only the pain, but also the joy of mastery and understanding, guide us through the struggle of recognition and the reward of understanding. Because what I get if I can jump out of the goldfish bowl long enough to see things differently is my joy and the ability to live in this magical world with my heart open to receive. And that's worth more than holding a grudge any day. I'm worth more. This is more often how *letting go* comes about, more as a by-product of *acceptance* and *integration* than as a singular event.

UNITIVE THINKING:
HOW OUR MINDS MAKE MEANING OF
THE EVENTS OF OUR LIVES

Because forgiveness very often does require a kind of transcendence, let's take a moment to have a deeper look at what that's all about. Danah Zohar, in her book, *SQ: Connecting with Our Spiritual Intelligence,* writes that, "machines mimicking neural networks can replicate some of our associative thinking abilities, and these machines will certainly get better as the technology develops. But there are a great many aspects of human mental life that no computer so far built, or even envisioned, can replace."

She calls these capacities "spiritual intelligence," our meaning-giving, contextualizing and transformative intelligence. *Computers can play a finite game, but we humans can play with infinity.* We can transcend into a state of awareness that allows us to see ourselves operating in our own lives, we can play with context and meaning, turning the prism in our minds over and over long enough to see things in a light that allows us maximum freedom. We can put things in perspective. We can play with light and shadow. Says Zohar:

We're able do all this because we have a kind of thinking that is creative, insightful and intuitive, we learn language with our serial and associative thinking systems, but we invent language with some third thinking system. We understand common or given situations and behavior patterns and rules with our first two kinds of thinking, but we create new ones with this third kind.

We have the ability to "bind" our disparate experiences, and to give them meaning and a connection to each other. Understanding is essentially an ability to grasp the overall context that links component parts. It is this kind of contextual understanding that is lacking in schizophrenics, who cannot unify their experience and so cannot respond appropriately. This "unitive ability" is an essential feature of consciousness and is the key to understanding the neurobiological basis of spiritual intelligence, this ability to transcend ordinary consciousness and rest in the infinite.

Returning to the neurological basis of spiritual or transcendent intelligence, here's roughly how it works. Most of the millions of neurons in our brains are connected in serial chains and circuits, and still more are connected to thousands of others in neural networks. But here comes the "binding" problem. There is no one system that connects all neurons, or even the separate modules and chains to each other. The brain forms what are known as "expert systems," some of which process color, others sound, tactile sensation, fear, and so on. Explains Zohar:

❧

When I look at a room in which I am working, all these expert systems are bombarded by millions of pieces of perceptual data—visual, auditory, tactile, thermal and so forth. Yet my consciousness sees the room as a whole: I have a unified perceptual field. The mystery of how this can be is known in neurology as the "binding problem." How does my brain bind its disparate perceptual experiences together?

❧

This binding problem has plagued neuroscientists and begs the question from Zohar, "What part of me is watching, making sense and complete meaning?" One possible answer to this question that has been asked throughout the ages may lie in the study of neural oscillations. Wolf Singer and Charles Gray from Frankfurt, Germany, found in their study (cited by Zohar) that

❧

. . . when we perceive, say, a coffee mug, the neurons in every localized part of the brain involved in that perception oscillate in unison. These synchronous oscillations unite our many different localized perceptual responses to the cup—its roundness, its color, its height, and so on—and give us the experience of a single, solid object. So there seems to be a connection between the level of neural oscillations and the ability to perceive in a holistic manner. When meditators, for example, enter what they describe as a state of unity and oneness, their neural oscillations bear that out by evidencing a unity in

neural oscillations. There is now good evidence that synchronous neural oscillations in the range of 40 Hz lead to particular states of consciousness, such as in meditation.

✺

"Such coherent states of oscillations, Singer and Wolf were able to show, give unity to our perceptions. At this neural level, this unity can be described as a transcendent dimension to the activity of individual neurons. Without it, our world would consist of meaningless fragments," says Zohar. This is that part of us that sees and binds our perceptions together into a coherent whole. Zohar continues: "If neural oscillations in the brain were a coherent version of a fundamental property pervading the whole universe, then our human SQ (spiritual quotient) roots us not just in life, but at the very heart of the universe. We become children not just of life, but, more strongly, of the universe."

Forgiveness seems, to me, to be connected to this state; that is, when we're in this transcendent place, little petty grievances seem unimportant and large hurts are put into a new perspective. We *recontextualize* the events of our lives, and they take on a new meaning. We transcend a situation and see it from a different perspective.

SPIRITUAL BEINGS ON A HUMAN JOURNEY

Forgiveness is an organizing principle that has the ability to transform the painful events of our lives into our own spiritual growth. The key words here are "our own." We have no control over people. We may wish we did, but it's a fantasy, really. People will do what they will do; they will live on their own schedule, not ours. But we do have control over our own choice to grow. It all is money in the bank that we can draw on whenever we need it, and the more we deposit, the more we have to withdraw. And like any sound investment, it grows on its own; it, too, is subject to the natural laws of growth. In ways we hardly realize, the time we put toward growth affects our inner life, which becomes our outer life. We become more mindful, gain more mastery over our inner world, get in touch with our bodies, learn self-discipline and more about what makes us tick. We slow down enough to know when we're hungry, when we need to rest, take action or sit back and watch the world pass by. We take time to appreciate the experience of being alive.

As we become more valuable to ourselves, forgiveness becomes easier. For starters, we hold less against ourselves because we come to understand the self-harm that holding resentment causes on all levels—physical, mental and spiritual. Then we hold less against others. Having given peace to ourselves, it becomes natural to extend that same goodwill toward others. Next, by being on more intimate terms with ourselves, we come to understand that part of maintaining that internal closeness requires an attitude of forgiveness and releasing. And we see that the same principle applies to intimacy with others. We lose a feeling of closeness when we harbor unaddressed resentments or pockets of unexplored hatred.

So going within is the time-honored path toward greater intimacy with self and others, mastery over self and a path to a more dynamic, focused and appreciative way of living. One of the ways to beat the system, if you've been hurt, is to consider forgiveness as an option; not just to let the other guy off the hook, but to do right by our own selves. To free *us* from the endless repetition of the painful dynamics that inevitably entwine themselves around so many aspects of our lives when we can't process, metabolize and move on.

If we really want, as Eliza Doolittle said in *My Fair Lady,* to "get a bit of our own back," the way to do that is not to live at the other end of someone else's mistake until it becomes our mistake, too—not to take up residence in another person's problem. The way to restore ourselves is to get out whole, with our sense of joy and our faith in love, humanity and a higher purpose intact. The wish for revenge that all of us harbor in our hearts when we've been hurt is a natural and primitive urge, and we need to reckon with it honestly. But the truth is that if we can't in some way forgive and move on, the revenge we seek is enacted on our own lives. We doom ourselves to repeat the painful circumstances we've experienced in ways that only debilitate *our* happiness. The daughter with the cold, critical father who falls in love again and again with men who can't love her back, or the girl who was distanced by the mother she wished to be close to and today either distances or smothers (two sides of the same coin) her own daughter, are people who could not find their way out of a painful past dynamic and move on. They are still reenacting the things that hurt them most in some form or another.

Forgiveness offers us a way off the wheel of karma, out of a cycle of pain. Christ, on the cross, made this his last order of business: "Forgive them, Lord, for they know not what they do." Eastern philosophy tells us that it is our ignorance that keeps us in an unenlightened state. Psychology talks about making the unconscious conscious so we can free ourselves from reenacting the painful circumstances of our lives. In a way, aren't they all saying the same thing? That becoming conscious of our own ignorance or lack of awareness is what provides us with the insight and understanding to heal the wounds of the past and take possession of our present happiness. Forgiveness is the alchemy by which what was shattered can become whole again, what was torn can be mended, and what was pain can open our hearts to joy. This is the magic of forgiveness.

EIGHT

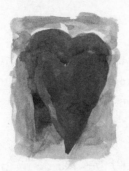

Reorganization and Reinvestment: Renewed Energy and Passion for Life

Forgiveness entails the authentic acceptance of our own worthiness as human beings, the understanding that mistakes are opportunities for growth, awareness and the cultivation of compassion, and the realization that the extension of love to ourselves and others is the glue that holds the universe together. Forgiveness . . . is not a set of behaviors, but an attitude.

~Joan Borysenko
Forgiveness: A Bold Choice for a Peaceful Heart

Having done the work of forgiveness, we may find we have a need to reinvest our newly freed-up energy into our current lives and relationships. Once issues from our past get resolved, they no longer consume the large quantities of energy that they formerly did; they move from the foreground to the background of our minds, they recede in importance. Though they may return from time to time, they come back with less power, and we deal with them with greater understanding. This means that we have room for other, more nourishing experiences in our foreground.

This is a time to make conscious choices about how to live our lives and be in our relationships. If the issue we were working through represented a yearning, that yearning can now be met consciously and by choice. Having come to terms with what we may never get from our father, for example, we're freer to have the relationship as it is, letting in whatever good may exist within it. In other words, the relationship is no longer blocked by resentment of what, realistically, we may never be able to get. And by extension, neither are we. We can also make conscious choices about how to live in our relationship with our father so that we can keep the good that's there and guard against continual hurt. That's the advantage of making issues conscious: We gain the opportunity to make reasoned decisions of our own rather than continuing to live mindlessly and reactively. No one can get everything they need or want from one source, and it can overburden our relationships and doom them to failure when we try.

The world is a big place with many opportunities for vast and varied experiences. Through reinvestment, we can set about filling in what we need or what feels missing from another source. As parents, we can reinvest new energy and love in our children and grandchildren; as adults we reinvest in partnership and friendship, and find professions, activities and projects in which to put our time and talents. We can make conscious choices. We can look for surrogate relationships to help round out our relationship network. This is actually a phenomenon that has been happening for some years now. With the advent of technology and the distance it has imposed upon our family systems (along with the ever-shrinking size of the nuclear family), people have been forming what I call "friendship families" to augment their relationship systems. We still have a need for a certain number of relationships in our personal world, and we naturally set about getting them there.

But all too often, I've seen that we tend to pathologize the distance that technology has put into the family system. Because it's painful to be separated, we more or less "make a case" as to why we're better off being far away. It makes it easier to separate—like when teenagers pick apart their parents so they can tolerate the idea of moving into their own lives. But why not turn this on its head, embrace the distance and work with it as best we can? Distance can also give us the opportunity to connect more consciously and to develop sides of ourselves that we might not develop if we didn't have a need to fill in what's missing. If we don't let our relationships be undermined by distance, we can find ways to strengthen them. Then we can have our families, our friendship families and whatever other special interest groups or passions we may enjoy in our lives.

PRESCRIPTIONS FOR HAPPY LIVING

At this stage of reinvestment, we're creating a sort of emotional marker, we're drawing a line in the sand between one way of living our lives and another, we're heading down a new path. It's useful to map out this new journey so that we don't slip unwittingly back into old habits of thinking, feeling and behavior. In the rest of the chapter, we will map out that path, based on the research of the last two decades. These are the ways of living well and aging well that research has repeatedly found to work, and which I elaborate on in this chapter. They are:

Have a Spiritual Belief System
Maintain Intimacy and Strong Relationship Networks
Pursue Good Goals and Find a Life's Passion
Stay Emotionally Current
Cultivate and Live by Good Values
Exercise and Get Thirty Minutes of Sunlight Daily
Develop an Attitude of Gratitude and Appreciation
Keep Expectations Realistic
Get Enough Sleep, Rest and Quiet Time
Eat Healthy Foods
Play and Enjoy Leisure Activities
Become a *Keeper of Meaning*

HAVE A SPIRITUAL BELIEF SYSTEM

Research has found over and over again that a spiritual belief system is beneficial to our health and well-being. Whether your faith is in God, Higher Power or nature, some sort of spiritually organizing principles help to give moral structure, spiritual purpose and meaning to our lives. They also provide us with like-minded communities to belong to. If we're willing to live with the mystery and release our need to know exactly how it works, we can share our burdens in life and ask for help and guidance from unseen hands. I don't see radio waves, but I hear all my favorite songs on the radio. Nor do I watch voices traveling through the air into my cell phone, but there they are, plain as day. It seems to me that in our quest to have official evidence of God, we may be missing the obvious evidence of the miracle of life, nature and our world that we live with daily. One has only to witness a beautiful sunset, see a horse and her new foal against the verdant green of a pasture or touch the heart of another human being to sense a higher wisdom, beauty and purpose to this experience called life. I've always thought that people who fight about who is the right God haven't themselves had their own personal experience of spirituality. "Be still and know that I am God," says the Bible. When we sink into our own reverie and meditation regularly, we do experience a deeper pulse of living. We do connect with the God or Guru or Higher Power that lives within us and through which we connect to the universe. And we do find and cultivate a kind of inner peace and create a reservoir of serenity from which we can draw peace throughout our day. Does absolute proof really matter?

While Larry Dossey spent a decade researching prayer, he found that cardiology patients who were in a prayed-for group were five times less likely to require antibiotics and three times less likely to develop pulmonary edema (fluid in the lungs). The results are so startling that, if it were a drug, companies would invest millions in it. Literally countless studies provide the efficacy of prayer in healing the body. Time devoted to contemplation and prayer is also a way of healing the self and relationships, it would seem. In addition, it is deeply calming and allows us to have a sense of control, because prayer is something we *can do;* it is an action of sorts that we *can take,* while at the same time helping us let go of a problem that we can't solve immediately by turning it over to a power greater than ourselves.

MAINTAIN INTIMACY AND STRONG RELATIONSHIP NETWORKS

Research bears out again and again that relationships are key to living a long and balanced life. People with secure relationship networks (as those in the Alameda, California, study) lived longer, in spite of undermining habits like lack of exercise or smoking. This should come as no surprise with all the talking we've done about the biology of connection. Essentially, this is the reason for writing, or reading, this book: to learn to preserve our relationships through rigorous self-honesty and a willingness to work through the kinds of issues that are blocking our ability to live comfortably in them. We all need to feel that we belong somewhere. These deep, limbic bonds allow us to stabilize our emotional world. Or our deep need for relationship can be seen by its opposite: how devastating it is when relationships rupture. This is why it's in our own best interest not only to learn to self-define and create healthy relationship boundaries, but also to learn to live and let live, to have a forgiving attitude, *in addition* to our healthy boundaries. Isolation tends to accompany depression, whereas a good network of relationships can help keep us from feeling disconnected from the world.

But intimacy isn't easy. Inherent in relationships, particularly in intimate relationships such as marriage, is a need to include another person in our thinking and planning. This inevitably requires a certain selflessness that we may experience as a confusing loss of self. We may wonder who we are now that we're in a committed relationship. We feel a loss of who we were, fear being overwhelmed by the other person, squeezed out of our own skin and into a shape we're not sure feels like us. But the truth of the matter is, this is a normal part of marriage or even a committed professional liaison. We grieve for the self we feel we're losing and don't yet know who we're becoming. We get confused and may ask ourselves, *Is this the right person? Am I giving too much of me?* Probably a more helpful and realistic question to ask ourselves is, *Am I getting enough in this relationship so that it's worth my letting go of what I'm not getting?* If the answer is "yes," then we step up to the plate and do our part to get things to work. This will entail asking *and* giving, listening *and* talking, loving *and* letting ourselves be loved. And it means enduring and having faith that building something worthwhile takes time and effort. It's also a recognition that if we continually tear down what we're building, we undermine our own happiness and the happiness of those around us. This is not to say that relationships don't need to be reconfigured or reconstructed from time to time, only that we learn to respect and value the stability and sense of belonging that they provide and become willing to do the necessary work to maintain them—and the forgiving.

STAY EMOTIONALLY CURRENT

Unresolved emotional baggage can really undermine personal happiness and zest for life. When pain is unconscious, we aren't able to make choices about how to deal with it. And it is just this unconsciousness that all too often gets us into trouble, reenacting painful relationship dynamics that result in our doing the same old thing (that may not have worked in the past) but expecting different results. Unconsciousness can also mean that we make partially blind decisions. The more information we have about ourselves, for example, the better able we are to make life choices that are right for us. Tailoring our lives to suit our particular personalities, needs, drives, desires and ambitions inevitably leads to a happier life. We are responding not to who we think others want us to be, but who we feel ourselves to be on the inside. We are making life choices that suit us and—lo and behold!—find ourselves living more congruently, and our relationships often improving, as a result. When we take responsibility for our own happiness, we tend to blame others less and support them more.

The other aspect of remaining emotionally current is that we feel lighter inside because we are not preoccupied with "unremembered" pain from another part of our lives. When we have an overload of unprocessed pain, we are probably defending against feeling it. This drains energy. And running away from pain often gets us into more trouble than facing it. It can also lead us into a style of defensive thinking that distorts our relationship dynamics and our attitudes toward life. Denial, for example, may be a way of defending against emotional pain that we don't want to feel, but this rewriting of reality keeps us from being able to be open and realistic in dealing with our lives. In other words, we are living in our version of reality rather than what is closer to the truth of the situation. While it's natural for each of us to see things in our own way, denial is really an attempt *not* to see something. This not seeing impacts our ability to see things clearly in our relationships and our lives. This is only one style of defensive thinking, they are many more. Unprocessed pain can also cause us to engage in high-risk behaviors or self-medicating. Staying emotionally current is our best insurance policy against unconscious living and for living well in the present.

A recent study conducted by Kennon M. Sheldon, Ph.D., of the University of Missouri-Columbia that appeared in the *Journal of Personality* and *Social Psychology APA* examined what made people happy. At the top of the list of what appears to bring happiness are *autonomy* (the feeling that your activities are self-chosen and self-endorsed), *competence* (feeling that you are effective in what you do), *relatedness* (having a sense of connection with others) and self-esteem. Staying emotionally current allows us the emotional and psychological freedom to live more consciously.

Pursue Good Goals and Find a Life's Passion

Goals organize and mobilize; they help us consolidate our skills and talents, and realize them in some concrete form. Self-esteem is enhanced by a feeling of competency and a sense of engagement in valuable activity. And once we've accomplished one set of goals, we can set new goals to work toward. For some, work and passion are connected. For others, work may be more of a "day job" and connecting with a passion might come through another channel. As women, many of us experience passion in our mothering and grandmothering, two of the most valuable, challenging and meaningful roles going. These roles aren't only natural, they also require us to learn and develop complicated new skill sets. Business studies reveal that women make excellent middle managers. Certainly, managing a home and family is some of the best management training you can get, and that skill set appears to carry over into the workplace.

Having a passion is one of the most important ways to give our lives meaning and purpose. It connects us with ourselves and other people, and we're lucky enough to live in a country that provides more opportunities for cultivating and pursuing a passion than most other places in the world.

Certain passions can produce in us what is called a *flow state.* Painting, writing, sports, cooking, teaching or whatever activity we're truly engaged in—can also allow us to enter what Mihalyi Csikszentmihalyi of the University of Chicago calls the "flow state." In his extensive research in this area, he has found that people are most likely to enter this state when their *skill level and the difficulty of the task itself are properly matched. Too little skill leads to frustration, and too little challenge leads to boredom.* In the flow state, time tends to disappear, as we engage in a deep, effortless involvement where ordinary cares are out of consciousness. Paradoxically, while receiving immediate feedback we're also goal-oriented. While in this flow state, our concern for self disappears; however, when we emerge, our self feels stronger. In my experience, many aspects of mothering, grandmothering or being with young children can also produce a flow state in which our preoccupation with ourselves can disappear temporarily, but ultimately, we emerge with a stronger sense of self.

CULTIVATE AND LIVE BY GOOD VALUES

Values are the road map for our journey through life. Without them, we would have to decide anew how to behave in our personal worlds each time something different occurred. Values ground us. They provide a solid foundation upon which we can build a self, a family and a life. They also keep us steered in the right direction when we're having weak moments or can't think clearly. When we have good values and live by them, we have a certain congruency; our actions match who we are on the inside, at least, much of the time.

All values don't necessarily make for the same level of happiness, though. Research has revealed that those who rate financial success, for example, more highly than self-acceptance, community feeling and relationships are less happy than those who don't. Once again, our human need to be a part of a relational network of some sort comes out on top as a value that leads to happiness. "It's good to have a forgiving attitude toward life and people so that I can stay open to what life has to offer," is a relational value. Even if our forgiveness doesn't lead to staying connected to the same person or situation we're having a forgiving attitude toward, it opens the door to other relationships. Having worked through our painful feelings and come to terms with them, we're better able to risk opening up to further relationship connections. We no longer need to isolate or cut off to attain a feeling of safety because we have developed some confidence in our ability to survive being hurt.

The kinds of values that tie us to a code of ethics, of basic human decency and care for others and ourselves, give us strength and a good feeling about ourselves and our world. And as what we believe and live by tends to manifest in our lives, we're creating our own, better world to live in, attracting those experiences toward us that fit our sense of a good life.

Exercise and Get Thirty Minutes of Sunlight Daily

Human beings were built to move and to need a certain amount of sunlight each day. We cannot deny our biology. Sedentary lifestyles mean our bodies can't operate as they were designed to operate. The soothing body chemicals that nature meant us to use as natural calming agents, don't get a chance to work their daily magic if we don't stimulate them through exercise of some sort. This affects our moods, our motivation and our pleasure in living. We need a healthy amount of daily exercise in order to feel comfortable in our bodies. We need dopamine and serotonin to be released into our bodies in order to even out our moods. This prescription, according to research, is as effective as any drug is for healing depression. In a recent study at Duke University, researchers Michael Babyak, Ph.D., and James Blumenthal, Ph.D., found that depressed patients who exercised had declines in depression equal to those who received anti-depressants. In addition, those who continued to exercise after treatment were 50 percent less likely to become depressed again.

A ten-minute walk gives you more energy in the long run than a candy bar. Researchers find that exercising in whatever way is most convenient works best. If it's a brief walk during a lunch break, walking the dog or biking to work, exercise seems to work well when it's combined with purposeful activity or works naturally into our lives. Research also reveals that exercising with other people helps us to make it a more regular part of our lives. (That relationship thing again.)

And thirty minutes of sunlight each day wards off depression, provides vitamins and gives us a much-needed boost to our immune systems. When we try to get our lives to work on strictly a psychological level, we ignore the fact that we live in a body, and that that body has significant power over our moods. This is one of the easiest places to start to turn our lives around or to get out of an emotional slump. A daily, brisk thirty-minute walk outdoors is free, and one of the best habits we can cultivate for our bodies, minds and spirits. It can elevate our moods, keep us fit, control weight, relieve depression and give us time with friends—to say nothing about connecting us with the great outdoors. There's just no downside to this one. And it's free.

Develop an Attitude of Gratitude and Appreciation

What we appreciate tends to persist and grow in our lives. It's like watering a plant. The universe is alive and growing, and so are we. Appreciation is like Miracle-Gro: It nourishes and feeds, it helps something to take root and get strong. Try it for yourself: If you want something in your life to expand, appreciate that something in thought, word and deed for the next three weeks, and silently send it your good thoughts, prayers and energy. Develop an *attitude of gratitude*. Like anger, gratitude is an energizing and organizing emotion that motivates us toward a particular way of thinking or acting. Because of this, it's a good antidote for sadness. While sadness can make us feel as though we're falling apart, gratitude can help pull us together. We still need to feel our sadness, but the trick is not to get stuck in it. Making a gratitude list or cultivating an attitude of gratitude in no way implies that we aren't accepting and processing our pain, nor should it. It simply allows us to stand on firmer ground when we do feel our pain. Gratitude helps us organize and mobilize our thoughts and emotions in a positive direction. And it helps us appreciate the life we already have.

KEEP EXPECTATIONS REALISTIC

Eastern philosophy tells us that expectation is the mother of disappointment, and research seems to agree. One rather surprising prescription for happy living may be to reexamine our expectations. Though at first glance this may sound defeatist, it actually can produce a greater sense of well-being in some cases. In studies done on animals, the relationship between expectation and the body's release of dopamine (also known as the pleasure or feel-good hormone), was explored. Dopamine levels went up when the animal received a pleasant surprise. The more unexpected the pleasant stimulus, the higher the rise in dopamine. However, when a stimulus was expected but did not come, the animals' disappointment could be measured by a drop in dopamine levels. Stable expectations produced stable levels, pleasant surprises elevated ones, and disappointed expectations a drop in levels.

One advantage of forgiveness in light of this research is that we're, in a sense, choosing to modulate this cycle of expectation and disappointment. Once we forgive, it should follow that we are more accepting of human frailty, ours and others, and consequently, are more likely to adjust our level of expectation to what is realistic. We've accepted that perfection is probably not likely (at least our version of it, anyway). We discover that if we expect a little less, we may be able to take more pleasure in what we actually do get. We may also come to realize that people aren't meant to live their lives meeting our particular expectations, and that to wish them to do so is not only a guarantee of disappointment, but also can be controlling if it gets out of hand. We have a right to our reasonable expectations; they're part of a stable relationship and important for our ease and trust, but the line between reasonable and demanding can get fuzzy and is worth reexamining from time to time.

GET ENOUGH SLEEP, REST AND QUIET TIME

When Shakespeare referred to sleep as " knitting the raveled sleeve of care," he may have been right on the money. According to Rosenthal:

Researcher Thomas Wehr at the National Institute of Mental Health conducted studies during which he had people lie down in a quiet, darkened room for fourteen hours each night, conditions similar to those under which we evolved during the millions of years before the discovery of artificial light. Under these conditions, the subjects reported a state of pleasant relaxation coupled with a crystal clear consciousness.

Also, while they were in these states of relaxation and clarity, their pituitary glands were releasing prolactin into their bloodstreams. Meditators also release prolactin, which is associated with a state of calmness and serenity. As the name implies, this is also a chemical that stimulates the breast tissue to release milk in nursing mothers.

But it's a delicate balance; even a slight, low level of anticipation during sleep was enough to keep prolactin from working its magic. In separate experiments, researchers told subjects that at some point a nurse would enter the room to take blood. This semiconscious awareness during their sleep, that they could be interrupted at any time, was enough to stop the release of prolactin. (Men also release the hormone prolactin when they meditate or are in a state of deep relaxation.)

One easy way to give yourself a little shot of prolactin, according to Rosenthal, is to take a warm bath because heat stimulates prolactin to be released into the bloodstream. You can also rest in a darkened room or meditate. I go into how to do deep relaxations and meditations in detail in the first section of part II. Following the instructions for deep relaxation and meditation is very revitalizing, and clearly has restorative effects on the mind and body. It's what nature built into us as a daily way to restore ourselves. Yogis use these techniques to "give their minds rest," and according to this research, these techniques also release prolactin. Because prolactin is secreted by the pituitary gland, which begins to be more regularly stimulated in midlife, we may find ourselves desiring more quiet time for reflection and reverie as we enter this period of our lives.

(Over and above all this, we are a sleep-deprived culture. If you feel anxious or depressed, one of the first questions to ask yourself may be, *Am I getting enough sleep?*)

EAT HEALTHY FOODS

This is a subject so well covered in the popular literature and media today that it's amazing we haven't all gotten the message. Our bodies are biological; they run best when we give them what they were built to use as fuel. Emotional eating or *feeding* our emotions, instead or *feeling* them, can make it hard to do right by ourselves when it comes to healthy eating. This is yet another good reason for working through the kinds of painful emotions that might cause us to use food in ways that are self-destructive. Food should feel like comfort, but part of the comfort needs to come from the enjoyment of thinking up something yummy to eat, imagining eating it, taking the time to assemble and prepare it, and *then* relaxing and eating it.

Fast food and junk food are ruining our eating habits, wrecking our relationship with food, and undermining one of the best bonding rituals we've got going: eating with each other. It's okay to make food preparation simple and easy, as long as we still preserve the rituals around food preparation and eating that are good for us. Each of us has our own pattern that works best, a personal formula for success when it comes to eating, and it's important to find it and use it, as long as it's healthy and provides adequate nutrition. Again, we're not look-ing for perfection here; we're looking to have a healthy relationship with food, neither a perfect nor a self-denying one. Self-denial is the other side of the coin of overeating, and both indicate an obsessive relationship with food.

But here's another critical point. It's not only *what* we eat but *how* we eat that's important, that impacts how we digest and enjoy our food. Eating as a family is an important bonding ritual. Wandering through the kitchen inhaling good smells goes straight to the oldest part of the brain and soothes. Helping Mom or Dad get dinner on the table bonds families, makes children feel useful, important and part of the group, and teaches kids how to one day take care of themselves and run their own households.

I really think that a lot of problems in our society would clear up naturally if families and friends took the time to prepare wholesome foods, and sit down together and eat them. Even if you can't do it every night, don't worry; a few times a week is enough to do the job, and once or twice is so very much better than nothing. Start wherever you can. Variety is okay if enough time together sets up the pattern. The dinner table is where we learn manners, social skills and camaraderie. Rose Kennedy used the dinner table to train of the most important political families of our day by putting an article of interest on the bulletin board, getting her sons to glance it over and discuss it enthusiastically at the table. One of the reasons we learn social skills at the dinner table is that it's best to stay away from emotionally charged material while we're eating and digesting. Consequently, we learn the art of polite and lively conversation around subjects of the day. This is also a moment each day when parents can keep in touch with their children's lives and find out how their day has gone, and when partners can reconnect after a day apart. It's where we learn the art of living. If it's the family's orientation, it's also one more opportunity for conscious contact with God through a before-dinner prayer.

Play and Enjoy Leisure Activities

Almost every species of animal engages in some form of play. Researchers feel that these are adaptive behaviors that increase their chances of survival. Play performs two important functions for animals, according to Bletcher and Carpenter and Aune. First, it allows them a safe way in which to release aggressions. Second, it gives them practice in behaviors that are typically associated with adulthood. Play seems to perform a similar function with children, allowing them to release their pent-up aggressions, play out their authority issues and get practice at playing adult roles. "You be the mommy, and I'll be the daddy; now you be the teacher, and I'll be your student." Children are constantly slipping in and out of roles, releasing pent-up frustrations, becoming, for a moment, the admonishing authority or the nurturing, all-knowing parent. This gives them a chance to gain some relief from the confines and frustrations of their child roles, and at the same time practice at more mature roles. Children who've just met can appear to be old friends by the end of an afternoon, after the bonding power of play has woven them into each other's worlds.

Adults spend too little time at play according to research, and would benefit greatly from spending more time at it. In the workplace, for example, "adult play helps to alleviate boredom, release tensions, prevent aggression, and create workgroup solidarity," says Norman C. H. Wong of the University of Hawaii. It also facilitates organizational learning, creativity, community-building and group cohesion, and overall, enhances adaptivity, attentiveness to quality and performance.

Play is defined by researchers as an activity that encourages positive emotions and allows people to complete high-order relational goals, such as getting to know each other, learning about each other or engaging in a mutual interest together, at a higher rate than expected. Play is accompanied by smiling and laughter; it should allow participants to control their onset and their offset in the activity. In other words, play is not forced; it encourages autonomy, spontaneity and creativity. Friends or couples who play together report feeling greater intimacy and closeness. And this sense of closeness develops at a faster rate than normal.

Guarding our time for leisure and play is important for our mental health and the mental and emotional health of our relationships. Couples who play together, for example, report having greater intimacy than those who don't. We all need to cut loose and engage in playful, spontaneous activities where we're not caring how we look, sound or are coming across. We abandon the constraints of "normalcy" and take a momentary break from the daily conventions that constrain us. Play is an activity that interrupts those patterns for a brief time so that we can temporarily turn our world on its head. "Curiouser and curiouser," said Alice as she looked through the looking glass and described her new view of the world, as play and imagination transformed it into her "adventures in wonderland." Play can open doors into and out of a safe space, where we can experience ourselves and those around us in innovative and novel ways.

BECOME A *KEEPER OF MEANING*

If you were lucky enough to have a grandmother (or grandfather) who was a *keeper of meaning* or kept the family flame burning, this idea will require little explanation. If you didn't, here's what they do. These special people recognize their very important place in the family system, and sometimes the larger community, and take it very seriously. They *support and love* the generations beneath them, each in their own way. They also *gather the clan* and *maintain family rituals* in a variety of ways, from sharing holidays to Sunday lunches to family vacations. The ones who are successful at this seem to do it with a gentle hand, without pressure, recognizing that people's schedules change, and all gatherings will not look exactly alike. They are our *holders of personal history*. They remember stories about how naughty, young and vulnerable their grandchildren's parents were once upon a time, and they share those stories with their grandchildren. And they nourish and attend to their grandchildren, recognizing that this bene-fits the youngest generation, themselves and the generation in between, that this is the right and good way to be for all concerned. They *teach and mentor,* passing on what they know, whether it's how to turn hospital corners on a bed, make the perfect pot roast, tie flies for fishing, or save and invest capital. They are not afraid to mentor in the art of living and they share their accumulated wisdom, recogniz-ing the power of their own example. They *love for love's sake.* They have the emotional distance and freedom to know that most things work out eventually, and that you might as well enjoy the ride, because that's what life is: the ride. These are the people who become the family lighthouses casting their reassuring glow far into the night. They are often grandparents, and if you're lucky, they are aunts and uncles, too. Or they are special and valued members of a community.

"To grow old successfully," says George Valliant who spearheaded Harvard's Study of Adult Development, the longest study of its kind in the world, "you have to be able to learn from the next generation."

The successful agers in his study all recognized that "biology flows downward." That, to age happily, you need to be connected with the generations beneath you, and not only "hold the fort," but also be open to learning from those younger than you. Whether it's the computer or a new variation on hide-and-seek, part of staying young ourselves is having strong, mutual connections with younger people. Valliant calls this being a "keeper of meaning." Certainly, this is why we're going through a process like the one outlined in this book, so that we can pull meaning and wisdom out of the events of our lives. And what we learn we'll be able to pass along to those we love, both in the words we say and by the examples we set.

In our second half of life, our roles shift. Inevitably, as we lose our parents, we're no longer the children coming home, but the adults creating the home that our children can return to. The demands of our new roles may need some redefining. Valliant also encourages people to *shift from being a human doing to a human being* as they age. He warns against needing to be forever in the "big honcho" role and encourages us to learn to take pleasure in family, friends, a walk on the beach and a long and restful look at the setting sun. Those who cannot comfortably let go the reins of power have a hard time as they grow older and power naturally shifts away from them. They are caught in an old identity and cannot make the transition to a different mode of operating. Perhaps this is one of the reasons that, for generations, women seem to have aged better than men. Our roles traditionally developed the kinds of skills that would be needed as we age. Focus on friends and family, taking pleasure in the simple things of life and being relationship friendly are all skills that women need to effectively raise a family and run a household; they also are the skills needed for successful aging. Perhaps as women shift into power roles in the workplace, we too may experience the loss of authority and difficulty letting go of the reins of power as we age.

When we can forgive those younger than us for taking what used to be our place in the world, we're better able to enjoy them and the rest of our lives. We "adjust our expectations," learning to seek pleasure in what is realistically available to us which, like the animals in the experiments we discussed earlier, allows us to release increased amounts of pleasure chemicals into our bodies; so even though what we have might seem like "less," we can experience it as "more." And when we're in this state of mind, we're more likely to be a pleasant and giving presence to be around, which enhances our relationship experience. When I asked my grandmother what her secret was for living until ninety-four happy and healthy she said, "I'm easy to please, honey, easy to please." She was the one we always wanted to be around. Whether a family holiday, a trip down the river on my sister's boat, a movie or a hamburger at the local deli, Grammie was easy to please. By extension, that meant that, when we were in her presence, so were we, and anything we did seemed like fun.

Though some of these modes of aging may not enter our lives until a decade or two after midlife, others will, and it's well to have a sense of where we're going and what might work best, both *as* and *when* we get there. We may resent getting older less if we can invest in the next generation more. We'll realize that, though we have no choice about growing older and eventually leaving our lives all together, we do have a choice about the legacy we leave. Forgiveness is a legacy worth leaving; it pays itself forward, seeding tolerance and love into the generations that follow, and the very act of planting it nourishes and sustains us.

In part II, we'll explore how to do the work involved in the process of forgiveness, so that we can walk the walk as well as talk the talk.

Either we have hope within us or we don't. It is a dimension of the soul, and it is not essentially dependent on some particular observation of the heart. It transcends the world that is immediately experienced and is anchored somewhere beyond its horizons. Hope in this deep sense is not the same as joy that things are going well, or the willingness to invest in enterprises that are obviously headed for early success, but rather an ability to work for something because it is good, not just because it stands a chance to succeed. Hope is definitely not the same thing as optimism. It is not the conviction that something will turn out well, but the certainty that something makes sense, regardless of how it turns out. It is hope, above all, which gives us the strength to live and continually try new things.

~Vaclav Havel

PART TWO

How to Travel the Path:
Tools and Techniques

We, as a culture, suffer from the lack of forgiveness. Forgiveness as an area of scientific interest is brand-new. I just believe it's such a valuable skill to learn and such a neglected aspect of interpersonal behavior that its absence is chilling and telling culturally.

~Fredrick Luskin
FROM *Research on Forgiveness* by James Robinson

SOME HEALING BASICS

Now we're entering the hands-on part of our book.

Forgiveness is really a verb. It's an action and as such often entails work. It's a skill we can acquire and get consistently better at. In this section, I've attempted to make the learning and doing a bit more user-friendly by providing some tried-and-true exercises that have been popular with my clients over the years. These exercises also develop the ever-useful skills of emotional literacy, which is part of why they are valuable. Generally, people find a process like this interesting, relieving and enjoyable. Even though it's laced with challenging moments, nothing feels better at the end of the day than being true to yourself and contacting your own heart—which is why doing just that has been a subject of theater, literature and spiritual writings for as long as the written word has existed. Healing is best done in groups or shared with a trusted person. [More on that in appendix I where we talk about how to start your own *growth group*.]

JOURNALING, RELAXATION, MEDITATION AND VISUALIZATION

As I've already mentioned, in the early seventies, I became very involved in yoga and meditation. Prior to that, I had been introduced to creative visualization through my interest in theater and personal growth. I found all these disciplines to be deeply healing. Meditation, relaxation and visualization helped me learn how to self-soothe, a developmental task that is critical to master if we are to cope with the inevitable anxieties of life. It's also important to learn as our culture moves faster and faster, so that we don't, in our rushing, attempt to self-soothe with food, drugs, alcohol or other forms of quick-fix mood management which, when done to excess, can cause life complications.

Techniques like visualization can feel almost trance-like, but many people don't realize that self-hypnosis is a natural state; it is an altered state that we frequently go in and out of, like when we go into a trance driving along a highway or watching TV. "Self-hypnosis taps into a natural 'basal ganglia' soothing power source that most people do not even know exists," says Daniel G. Amen. "It is found within you, within your ability to focus your concentration. The basal ganglia are involved with *integrating feelings and movement, shifting and smoothing motor behavior, setting the body's idle speed or anxiety level, modulating motivation, and deriving feelings of pleasure and ecstasy*." People who have been through trauma can become deregulated in the basal ganglia region of the brain. The basal ganglia can become reset to be constantly on the alert. This is not only a phenomenon of war, but also of homes that are characterized by chaos, instability, abuse and/or neglect—all circumstances where those involved learn to be hypervigilant, constantly on the alert for potential trouble. Part of healing from these patterns is to learn to reset the basal ganglia and consciously self-soothe.

We want to make a distinction, however, between self-soothing and using relaxation techniques to not experience or deny genuine feelings of anxiety that need to be processed and understood as we discussed in chapter 4. Our worried feelings may be trying to tell us something, and we don't want to use relaxation techniques to get rid of that voice. What we do want to do is learn to modulate intense feelings that are overwhelming us and keeping us from hearing our inner voices clearly. We want to develop the ability to self-soothe or find a reasonable and calm *set point* within ourselves.

In the program development I've done for Caron Foundation's Center for Self-Development in Wernersville, Pennsylvania, and New York City, and for Freedom Institute's Intensive Outpatient Program in New York City, I incorporate guided imagery, relaxation and meditation. People who have either been addicts themselves, grown up with addiction or both often suffer from some of the symptoms of PTSD. [See chapter 2 and appendix I for a detailed description of these symptoms.]

As I've mentioned, other situations that can trigger the fight, flight or freeze response associated with trauma and cause lasting effects may be an inability to solve a complex or an interpersonal problem at school or work, general anxiety or depression, or physiological issues like body pain, fatigue or chronic infections. Kids with difficult learning disabilities, for example, can experience *cumulative trauma* developed through a constant low level of frustration, anxiety, humiliation and fear of being put on the spot and not knowing the answer. Or someone with chronic body pain that resulted from an accident may develop it from coping with a constant low level of pain. Stress can affect the basal ganglia to a greater or lesser extent, depending on the *severity of the situation, the stage of development when problems occurred and the person's basic genetic disposition.*

Learning techniques of self-soothing can allow people to reset their basal ganglia so that all the functions that fall under its jurisdiction become more regulated. In my own life, thirty years of meditation, guided imagery, relaxation techniques and exercise have convinced me of the importance of bringing these aspects of self under conscious control through regular and deliberate practice.

LIMBIC REGULATION: HOW TO DO A DEEP RELAXATION

Lie down somewhere quiet and comfortable, on your bed or on the floor. Put a small pillow under your head. Uncross your arms and legs, face the ceiling and let your palms fall out in a relaxed position. Allow your feet to relax and fall easily to the sides. Make sure there are as few intruding sounds as possible, but if they exist simply let them be, give them space to exist. Now go to your breath, breathe in and out easily and completely without a pause between inhalation and exhalation and r-e-l-a-x. Allow your thoughts to move on their own through your consciousness, as if you are sitting on a riverbank watching the water flow by. You have no more thought of controlling your thought processes than you would have of controlling the water as it goes along its path. Simply witness your thoughts as they move past your mind's eye, and r-e-l-a-x. Imagine your emotions as running their own growth course. Like observing a flower, let each feeling emerge, bloom fully and watch as the petals of spent emotion fall away. Simply witness. Continue to breathe in and out easily and peacefully as you allow yourself to relax more fully. Mentally go through your body one part at a time and ask your mind to ask your body to *relax*. Relax your forehead, breathe in and out easily and completely without a pause between inhalation and exhalation and r-e-l-a-x. Repeat this process throughout your body, concentrating on the cheeks, eyes, jaw, tongue, neck, shoulders, chest, back, stomach, arms, hands, fingers and fingertips, palms, hips, groin area, thighs, calves, feet and soles of the feet, toes and tips of the toes. Feel a cool wave of relaxation pass through you from your head to your toes. Begin your visualization here [see next exercise] or proceed with the remainder of this relaxation and imagery. As you breathe in or *inhale,* imagine you're breathing in a soft, yellow light that gradually grows inside of you until it fills you completely. On your out-breath or your exhalation, *exhale* any tension or negativity you may be feeling. Repeat this imagery as many times as you wish. Gradually, whenever you feel ready, begin by moving your hands and your feet and slowly come back into the room. Now, move into your day more fully relaxed and aware, or close your eyes and drift off to sleep.

REPATTERNING NEGATIVE
THINKING THROUGH VISUALIZATION

When I was in college, I discovered yoga and meditation and became both a student and a teacher of *hatha yoga.* As I look back, I realize that I was intuitively attracted to what I needed to heal my mind and body from the effects of living with trauma and addiction. Also in college, I came upon guided imagery in theater classes and later in my work with Onsite Workshops in Cumberland Furnace, Tennessee. I've used guided imagery extensively in working with both adults and children, who actually enjoy doing it from a surprisingly young age.

I also learned to use guided imagery myself to repattern what I now know to be a loss of ability to envision a positive future, another legacy of trauma. I developed the habit of nurturing myself through going first into a deep state of relaxation, then visualizing myself operating in situations in my life as I wished to operate, and visualizing situations that I wished to come into my life. At first blush, this can appear to be a sort of attempt at mind control, but, in truth, I had found a way to reeducate my own dysfunctional thinking patterns, trading negative self-concepts for positive ones and dark forecasts for a gloomy future (or simply a future that appeared as no more than a blank screen) for a renewed vision and hope for happiness and all the good that life has to offer.

Guided imagery offers a way to consciously do neural repatterning and let our minds' creative capacities for visualization and imagination do a little synthetic living for us. We can lay down new thinking and feeling patterns that will impact our behavior by imagining ourselves operating as we wish to operate being, as we wish to be, and reeducating knee-jerk reactions and old tapes.

Here's how:

1. Find a comfortable place in which you feel you can sink into a nice, relaxing state.

2. Go to your relaxation breathing and take even, regular, relaxing breaths without pauses between inhalation and exhalation, and r-e-l-a-x. You can use the relaxation techniques described in the previous section, or you can imagine yourself going down an escalator, slowly getting to the bottom where you can start your visualization.

3. Allow yourself to picture a situation or focus on a way of being not necessarily as it is but as you wish it to be. If, for example, you wish to be more comfortable socially, imagine yourself entering and operating in a social situation easily and comfortably. Or if you'd like to be successful in some area of endeavor, imagine yourself as already successful, being in those situations and operating comfortably, *as if* it were real in the here and now.

4. Now, have it, smell it, taste it, feel it, hear it, touch it and let it touch you. Be in this situation as if it were real and happening just this way in the here and now. Engage with all of your senses through the creative picturing of your imagination.

5. Now, release your vision and trust the universe to carry it into its vast, eternal space.

6. After you're finished, slowly begin to move your hands and feet, come back up your escalator or bring your attention back into the room.

7. Repeat this process any time of the day that you feel inclined to

and it is physically safe to do so. (*Not* in a moving car; *yes,* in an airplane or while sitting at the kitchen table or lying on a couch.) It can take as long as ten seconds or ten minutes. And it should feel relaxing, reviving and reeducating.

Enjoy the sense of relaxation and centeredness, and move into your day with pleasure.

THE MANY BENEFITS OF MEDITATION

The place in the brain that has come to be known as the "God spot," or the pituitary gland, begs the question, "Does nature wish for us to have a spiritual, self-reflective way of processing our life experiences?" Those who call this the "God spot" see it as part of a divine plan for human beings. They feel that whoever designed us meant for us to have a spiritual life, that evolution is leading us gradually toward higher consciousness. Sitting in meditation and focusing on the area in the center of the forehead has long been a technique used by saints and sages. But in today's complicated world we are also being challenged to find ways to stay connected to ourselves and our higher purpose. The world is moving faster and so are we. In his book *Megatrends,* John Nesbitt refers to this as the push toward high-tech/high-touch. The more technology alienates us from our human sides, the more we find alternative ways of nourishing them. Meditation over the past two decades has become commonplace. When we see forgiveness as a spontaneous outgrowth of confronting emotional and psychological issues, we can see why meditation and reflection are useful tools in this endeavor.

This simple act in and of itself has several benefits:

• It develops our ability to self-reflect by giving us practice identifying with the part of our mind that watches and witnesses our internal processes.

- It calms our nervous systems, bringing them into balance and soothing the basal ganglia, which allows us to enter and occupy our own bodies. This, of course, leads to greater emotional and psychological calm. As a result, we create fewer problems because we are operating in a more thoughtful, conscious manner.
- It puts us in touch with what is really going on inside us, untangles us from the webs and the dynamics that we're getting caught in, gives us perspective on our lives, and allows us to be less reactive and more proactive in the way we move through our day.
- It integrates thought and feeling. In trauma, our cortex does not necessarily participate fully and effectively in sorting through and storing memories. As unresolved painful memories arise in our minds out of their storage in the "old brain," our cortex can witness them, reflect on them, make sense of them and create new meaning. Because our pituitary gland is stimulated during meditation, our thinking is influenced with a transcendent attitude. This can become a very healing experience.
- It develops a sense of spirituality. We begin to see our lives as journeys of unfolding consciousness. When we see our lives in this way we inevitably come to value our own peace of mind and our unhampered ability to grow spiritually as our top priority. In this prudent light, hanging on to resentments and anger starts to feel self-destructive. We tend to want to work through problems so that we can use our energy to achieve our own inner and outer goals, to enhance our own enjoyment of life. Focusing on the positive becomes a habit of mind.
- Meditation and deep relaxation can become an easy and regular part of our lives. The more we introduce quiet time into our day, the more we grow to value it because its benefits become obvious. We slowly build a reservoir of calm that we can draw from throughout our day.

My suggestion is that we should start wherever we can, whether it's ten minutes first thing in the morning, a half-hour in the late afternoon or twenty-five minutes before bed—better to start somewhere than to wait for the perfect time. We can also do walking meditations, where we mindfully walk to quiet our minds and go within. Or do deep relaxations (that we just learned) during our afternoon slumps. Twenty minutes of a relaxation can yield the benefits of a two-hour nap, and will quiet our minds and put us closer to a meditative state. The time we devote to it will naturally expand as we experience the benefit.

Meditation Made Easy

Meditation is most commonly done sitting in a chair or in the meditation sitting position on the floor. The idea is to lengthen the back or spine so that it's in a gentle S curve, held but comfortable. Again, the breath is regulated as it was in our deep relaxation, breathing in and out easily and completely without a pause between inhalation and exhalation, relaxing the body and bringing the nervous system into balance. Mentally scan your body for any areas of tension or places of holding, and ask your mind to ask your body to release it. Use the same technique of witnessing thoughts and emotions as in the deep relaxation. In sitting meditation, the witnessing experience will usually be more intense than while lying down; the warmth and energy that may run up the spine may release energy that feels stimulating. In sitting, it is not uncommon to experience urges to get up, to move, to fly away mentally. This is precisely why meditation is potentially so healing. We learn to sit through our own internal experience and witness it rather than run from it. As we witness, we see things in a new light. Our own stories pass before our inner eye, and we see them through the lens of where we are today. We have "a-ha" moments: Pieces of the puzzle fall into place, and we make new meaning of what passes before us. We are able to feel parts of us that went on hold or were split off from conscious awareness; we see them differently and then reintegrate them with new understanding and meaning. We heal in the quiet of our own minds and hearts. All of this occurs as we sit in stillness, are mindful of our breath and continue to deepen our meditation.

DON'T FORGET TO BREATHE

Diaphragmatic breathing is central to any relaxation technique. What's the first thing we do when we're scared? Hold our breath, right? Or, we fill up our chest with shallow, nondiaphragmatic breath and hike our shoulders up around our ears. As soon as we hold our breath, the oxygen supply to our brain gets constricted. Simply learning to breathe in an even manner from the diaphragm calms down our nervous systems. It also trains our neural systems to be more relaxed all through the day. One symptom of being scared a lot can be what we call "breath holding." Abused kids can develop this from constantly holding their breath when they feel frightened. This condition can be significantly retrained with practice and awareness.

Alternate-nostril breathing is a technique used by practitioners of yoga and meditation to calm and balance the sympathetic and parasympathetic nervous systems. It involves gently closing one nostril at a time and breathing out of the other for measured, regular breaths. This is done in rounds beginning by breathing through the nostril that's least blocked. (There are many good books on yoga, if you want to learn more about this technique.) As we retrain our breathing patterns slowly and consciously, along with regular relaxation and meditation, we soothe our basal ganglia, repattern our neural networks and create a reservoir of calm that we can draw on throughout our day.

THE POWER OF THE PEN: HOW TO JOURNAL

Though my early childhood was full of support and love, as my father's alcoholism progressed, relationships within our family were put under ever-increasing pressure. Eventually, as is so often the case with alcoholic family systems, we just sort of blew up. My parents divorced, and my father moved away. My two older siblings went off to college and their own lives (carrying great burdens), while my other sister and I were left with our mother. Our family broke in half. All of this happened within a five-year window and was quite traumatic. It made going through normal teenage years difficult and put some of that development on hold. There was, for example, little room to rebel and separate since everything was already falling apart. I became, instead, a little caretaker, always putting other people's needs before my own and trying, at whatever cost to myself, to keep the peace. This is not great for development and autonomy, and really just postpones adolescence for another time in life. Because therapy at that time was rather uncommon (though I came to it soon enough), I found my own way toward healing, mainly through the arts, yoga and meditation, all of which are explored in this section. I found them to be profoundly healing. Psychodrama and writing are both creative-arts therapies.

It was at this time in my life that I discovered the therapeutic value of writing. With no one to talk to about what was going on in my family (not that there weren't caring people around, there were, but in those days no one knew how to talk about emotional pain very well), I learned to use paper as a place to commit my deepest feelings. Writing became a way to work with my emotional pain and loneliness, and I was able to put into words what I was feeling. For me, this transformed feelings of alienation to a deep feeling of in-touchness with truth, with being alive. I experienced that true pain had a purity about it, and that placed me at the center of my own experience.

This translating of emotion into words is very healing. It allows us to label what we're feeling so that we can use our critical thinking to process and understand it. It grows soul. As we journal, our entangled thoughts and emotions unravel before our inner eye, and our minds begin to make sense of the seemingly disparate thoughts and feelings running through them. The knots loosen, and like Theseus in the labyrinth of the Minotaur, we follow threads through the corridors of our psyche, tracing them to their source and then out into the light.

Journaling also elevates the immune system and calms the autonomic system, smoothing out the heartbeat, breathing and perspiration, for example. James Pennebaker has documented this in his book, *Opening Up*, where he uses journaling to help people understand and work with the contents of their inner worlds. Pennebaker paints the picture of journaling as a very active, rather than passive, pursuit in which the body as well as the mind and emotions benefit. In two of the case studies in chapter 5, we used journaling and letter-writing to help us make sense, meaning and order out of emotional and psychological issues, to give a shape to what has been floating around inside of us in a shapeless state. As we freely write our thoughts and feelings on paper, the associative process of our mind goes to work, and things just sort of emerge onto the page, finding their way from muteness into articulation. It's like developing a photograph in a darkroom: The picture slowly emerges through the water. The more completely we can abandon our internal governors and trust the process of writing, the more penetrating our associations and glimpses into our inner world may be. Through journaling, we gain insight and perspective. We see a past problem through the eyes and maturity of today; what may have bewildered us once comes clear as we lay it out in front of newer, wiser eyes.

The basic method is to simply put pen to paper and let your thoughts and feelings pour out freely. Give the editor who lives in your mind a vacation, and let go of worrying about saying things in a coherent or readable way. Simply put pen to paper and trust the process. This is your private space for a full and unedited expression of self. No one need see what you write other than you; this is for your eyes alone unless you choose to share it.

HOW TO WRITE YOUR OWN AFFIRMATION

Affirmation-writing is very personal, for the benefit of the person writing and tailored to the unique needs and wishes of that person. When you write an affirmation, you are:

Reframing: You are taking a situation that might not be working for you and turning that negative into a positive. For example, if you feel anxious about a presentation you may write, "I allow myself to share what I know with others in a relaxed and easy manner. Though I have some fear, I need not let this fear take me over. I rest comfortably in the awareness that I do not have to be perfect in order to be okay." And so on.

Affirming: You are making positive statements about what you believe is possible for you. (I.e. "I can, I will, I allow," and so on.) An affirmation is set in the positive present. "Today I will," or "Today I recognize," or "I am strong enough . . ."

Confronting Your Real Feelings: You are honestly looking at what lies beneath whatever may be blocking you from moving forward, and attempting to find a path through. "Though I may have anxiety in making calls on my own behalf or fears around contacting people for work, today I will allow myself to . . ." And so on.

Shape-Shifting: You are turning something around inside yourself, trusting that a shift in thought and perception, if it is real, has the power to change your life and the way you view the world. Meaningful change begins within and generally involves a shift in perception. Whether the perception is the result of trying a new behavior and seeing that it works or because we "became willing" to "see" something differently, a shift in perception is usually part of a positive move forward.

If you enjoy using quotations, either find one that supports what you're writing or use a quotation as a warm-up to writing your affirmation. If you're writing as a group, you can have a couple of quotation books around to share, or group members can bring a few of their favorite quotations to each meeting and you can share them.

MAKING AMENDS

There is such a thing as a conscience, and most of us have one. When we've hurt another person, we don't feel right within ourselves. We feel shame at our own behavior, we feel twisted inside, we lose our serenity. Continuing to hurt ourselves or others can stem directly from this place within us. We cannot bear the accumulated shame of our own behavior, so we bury our shame under additional acting-out behavior. Addictive behaviors are often attempts at running from our own inner turbulence, misguided attempts at quieting an inner storm. The storm is often about feeling hurt by others or hurting others through our own behavior; the two are intertwined, feeding off each other, fueling each other. Asking for or granting forgiveness offers a way out, a way to make an attempt at restitution, to restore peace and serenity. We've done our part to right a wrong from both sides.

Dr. Ken Hart of the Leeds Forgiveness for Addiction Treatment Study (FATS) says, "Controversy often arises because people fail to understand that forgiveness is always desirable, but attempts at reconciliation may sometimes be ill-advised." Dr. Hart's study is testing two different approaches to forgiveness: *secular* and *spiritual*.

The secular approach aims to speed up the growth of *empathy* and *compassion* so that addicts can better understand the imperfections and flaws of those who have hurt them. In role-play therapy, we do this through what we call role-reversal by giving clients the opportunity to stand in the shoes of another person. Usually, they come to realize that the sense of "badness" they carry around from having interpreted their abuse to mean "something must be wrong with me or I wouldn't be being treated this way" isn't, and probably never was, really true. They were in the wrong place at the wrong time; they got hurt, at least in part, because another person was projecting his or her own unhealed pain onto them. This awareness can be a great burden lifted and allows the hurt person to see her hurt differently and to take it less personally. It can also develop some empathy, as the next question is, "Well, if it wasn't about me in the first place, then what was it about? What was inside the person who hurt me?" This is a step toward real understanding.

The second type of forgiveness tested is *spiritually* based Twelve-Step–oriented forgiveness used by Project MATCH in the United States. In this approach, addicts who have harmed others are encouraged to apologize for their wrongdoing, thereby making attempts at restitution. According to Hart, "Seeking forgiveness through the amends process requires incredible humility; the assistance of a Higher Power (God) helps people to transcend their ego, which normally balks when asked to admit mistakes." He goes on to say, "We think the two treatments can help people in addiction recovery drop the burden of carrying around pain from the past."

These two approaches to forgiveness—gaining empathy if we're the hurt party, and making amends if we're the offending party—are useful cornerstones in our own practical approach to forgiveness. Twelve-Step work has long recognized the need for addicts or those who have perpetrated wrongs to do the Ninth Step: "Made amends to those we had harmed except when to do so would injure them or others."

Alcoholics are generally people who have been deeply hurt by others, and oftentimes, drink or use drugs to deaden their emotional and psychological pain. They are also people who have hurt others deeply through the behavior that has grown out of their addiction. This can also lead them to drink even more, because their shame and remorse at their behavior is so painful to live with that they want to deaden that pain, too. Alcoholics need to forgive themselves and other people so that they can get sober and stay sober.

[AUTHOR'S NOTE: *"Made a list of all persons we had harmed, and became willing to make amends to them all."* This is *Step Eight* of the Twelve Steps that form the cornerstone of Alcoholics Anonymous (AA). The Twelve Steps are also the foundation of other Twelve-Step programs such as Al-Anon, the Twelve-Step program for the family members of addicts, Overeaters Anonymous (OA), Narcotics Anonymous (NA), Sexual Addiction Anonymous (SAA), Gamblers Anonymous (GA), and Debtors Anonymous (DA).

If you wish to do this step as part of your work in part II, you can use the letter writing exercises for asking forgiveness of someone else, granting forgiveness to another person or writing a letter you would like to receive as part of working the step, or any other of the exercises that feel appropriate.]

Stage One: Waking Up

Waking Up

I am carrying something inside of me that is undermining my happiness and stealing my joy. I am sick and tired of holding onto this pain. No matter where it started or who it belongs to, it belongs to me now. It lives inside of me, disturbs my peace of mind and exacts a heavy price; and I am just as sick of my own self-recrimination, of holding something against myself, of hurting my own inner world because I can't let myself or someone who is living in my head and heart off the hook. I am blocked in some way that I don't fully understand, but I'm willing to take a leap of faith into my inner world to look for some answers. I'm slowly coming to the conclusion that whatever grudge or resentment or wound I'm carrying is costing me more than I want to pay. I am waking up, seeing things differently, willing to take a deeper look.

I am willing to begin my journey toward forgiveness.

Self-trust, we know, is the first secret of success.

—Lady Wilde
"Miss Martineau"
Notes on Men, Women and Books

WAKING UP SELF-TEST

Name the forgiveness issue that you're working with and answer the following questions by placing a check in the appropriate box. This is not designed for rating but for elevating your own awareness.

1. How much do you feel this issue is affecting your inner peace today?

❑ Almost not at all   ❑ Very little   ❑ Quite a bit   ❑ Very much

2. How blocked are you from getting in touch with your genuine feelings involved in this issue?

❑ Almost not at all   ❑ Very little   ❑ Quite a bit   ❑ Very much

3. How much fear are you feeling at the thought of honestly addressing your feelings around this issue?

❑ Almost none   ❑ Very little   ❑ Quite a bit   ❑ Very much

4. How much anger or resentment are you feeling associated with this issue?

❑ Almost none   ❑ Very little   ❑ Quite a bit   ❑ Very much

5. How much hurt or sadness are you feeling associated with this issue?

❑ Almost none   ❑ Very little   ❑ Quite a bit   ❑ Very much

6. How much self-recrimination are you feeling around this issue?

❑ Almost none   ❑ Very little   ❑ Quite a bit   ❑ Very much

7. How much guilt or shame do you feel around this issue?

❑ Almost none   ❑ Very little   ❑ Quite a bit   ❑ Very much

8. How much hope do you have that you can work through your feelings surrounding this issue?

❑ Almost none   ❑ Very little   ❑ Quite a bit   ❑ Very much

9. How much energy do you feel is being absorbed by this issue?

❑ Almost none   ❑ Very little   ❑ Quite a bit   ❑ Very much

10. How much do you feel this issue impacts your relationships today?

❑ Almost not at all   ❑ Very little   ❑ Quite a bit   ❑ Very much

11. How much do you feel this issue has impacted your ability to move into future relationships comfortably?

❑ Almost not at all   ❑ Very little   ❑ Quite a bit   ❑ Very much

FORGIVENESS INVENTORY

Answer the following questions on the lines provided or on a separate sheet of paper.

What is the forgiveness issue I'm working with?

_____

_____

_____

_____

Where am I stuck?

_____

_____

_____

_____

What will I gain if I forgive?

_____

_____

_____

_____

What will I need to give up if I forgive?

_____

_____

_____

_____

Why am I afraid to forgive?

_____

_____

_____

_____

What feelings keep coming up when I contemplate forgiving?

_____

_____

_____

_____

What do I feel angry about?

_____

_____

_____

_____

How do I feel hurt?

_____

_____

_____

_____

What, if anything, am I holding against myself?

_____

_____

_____

_____

What, if anything, am I holding against someone else?

_____

_____

_____

_____

What do I think forgiving myself or this person will mean?

_____

_____

_____

_____

What do I want it to mean?

_____

_____

_____

_____

What am I afraid it might mean?

_____

_____

_____

_____

What do I imagine forgiveness can give me that I don't have now?

_____

_____

_____

_____

MIND MAP

Place the issue you're working with in the center circle and write all of the associations you have with it. Put any other situations that get warmed up inside you around this issue on the jutting lines. This is an exercise to bring to consciousness all of the little subplots that get warmed up around a particular issue, to elucidate issues from the past that get triggered or attached to the present. It's best to share this in a safe situation as it may bring up feelings. Don't "cry alone."

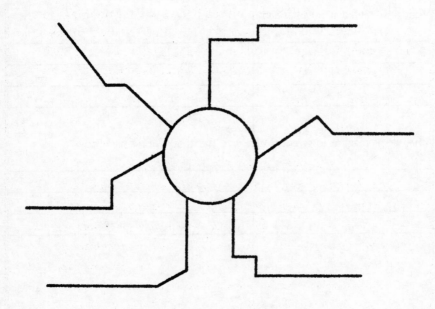

AFFIRMATIONS FOR WAKING UP

Forgiveness

Today, I am willing to take a leap of faith into a process of forgiveness. My willingness to consider forgiveness as an option is an affirmative statement that says that I want more out of life and relationships, that I am engaged and alive. I am willing to feel, to love and be loved.

This implies that I value myself more than I value winning, prevailing or revenge. Forgiveness is the ultimate statement of self-love. If I love myself I don't want to do things to hurt myself. Some things aren't within my control, but forgiveness is. I can't always make sure I don't get hurt, but I can have much to say about how I react to getting hurt.

I learn for myself.

*Ask for divine help in your struggle to forgive.
The God of the Judeo-Christian tradition has an ancient
reputation for compassion and mercy. Try praying FOR your
enemy. Don't just ask for a change in that person's heart or
behavior; really pray FOR him or her. You may find it hard to
find words for such a prayer, but words are not necessary to the
God who knows your mind and heart. Just stand before
God with that person at your side, and let God's love wash
over both of you until it penetrates your heart.*

—Carol Luedering
"Finding a Way to Forgive"
CareNotes

Intimate Relationships

Today, I understand that life is relationship, and relationship is nature's stimulus for growth. I am operating differently today. My intimate relationships call me to stretch and grow where it hurts the most. The people with whom I choose to be intimate are selected by me through a complicated unconscious process that lifts them out of hundreds of possibilities. At some deep level, I look for a person who can, by being a sort of mirror, help me see myself or resolve my deepest childhood wounds, and share my childhood joys and dreams. I choose that person not only to be close to, but also to be my teacher, and that person does the same with me. It is the bond between us and the unconscious knowledge that I am meant to learn from this person that help me through this very painful process of personal growth.

I grow in my intimate relationships.

And throughout all eternity I forgive you,
you forgive me.

—William Blake

My Interaction with My World

I elicit a particular response from the world about how it sees me based on what I'm putting out there. I get a response, then I take in that information, process it well or badly, consciously or unconsciously, and it becomes a part of me. A part of my wiring psychologically, emotionally and spiritually. Then I go back into the world with this ever-forming self and get more responses. Who I am is a product of who I am. Those of us who had great starts in life are lucky, but all of us can do a lot about who we are, and forgiveness is one of those tools that has the power to transform our lives. There's much more to it than meets the eye, more work and more benefit.

I am willing for my life to work out.

Always forgive your enemies—
nothing annoys them so much.

—Oscar Wilde

Our Own Good

Today, I accept that I do not always know what is best for me. There are times when I am completely confused about what to do for myself and those around me. Times when I can't see how my own issues are surfacing and coloring my present. These are the days when I need to pray and to understand that my prayers are heard. I never whisper to God that I am not heard. Prayer is my medium for change and growth. It is with me all the time, and there is no moment when I can't elevate my consciousness and conscious contact through it. It is my way of talking to my higher self and turning over my lower self to the loving, compassionate care of a Higher Power.

I trust in my own good.

I think one should forgive and remember. . . .
If you forgive and forget in the usual sense, you're just driving
what you remember into the subconscious; it stays there and festers.
But to look, even regularly, upon what you remember
and know you've forgiven is achievement.

—Faith Baldwin
The West Wind

Releasing of Perfectionism

Today, I will not demand that my life be perfect in order for me to love it, nor will I demand that all my relationships be perfect for me to value and respect them. If I try to make my life and relationships perfect, I will be constantly engaged in a neurotic battle with my ever-shifting illusions of perfection. There is no such thing as an ideal, and to insist that life be ideal is to miss the forest for the trees. I will not condemn myself to the constant feeling that I have drawn the short straw. Perfection is in the eyes of the beholder—it is subjective. I will not ask the moment to be more than the moment—I will not be conditional in my love of life.

I see perfection in things as they are.

A good garden may have some weeds.

—Thomas Fuller

Fear of Change

Today, I am able to live with my fear that I will not like myself or those close to me if we change. Change is threatening, and healing and growing include change. It doesn't matter to my fearful self if the change is for the better or worse. In fact, change for the better can sometimes be even more threatening. I fear that I will not know how to act or have the tools to be with the "better" without negating or undermining it. I remind myself today, again, that I do not have to grow perfectly. This is not a contest. I will have faith that life wants to to work out, faith in the presence of unseen hands guiding my life.

It's okay that I fear the outcome of change in myself and my relationships.

To lose focus means to lose energy.
The absolutely wrong thing to attempt when we've
lost focus is to rush struggling to pack it all back together again.
Rushing is not the thing to do. Sitting and rocking is the
thing to do. Patience, peace, and rocking renew ideas.
Just holding the idea and the patience to rock it
are what some women might call a luxury.
Wild Woman says it is a necessity.

—Clarissa Pinkola Estes
Women Who Run with the Wolves

Acting As If

There will be times when I do not feel up to things, when there seems to be too big a gap between who I think I am and who I want to be. I believe in being true to myself, in being basically honest. When I first try something new, it may feel as if I am trying on an article of clothing that doesn't quite suit me. But there is nothing wrong with acting "as if." I may need to practice new behaviors in order to become comfortable with them. Sometimes, when I allow myself to act "as if," the old me sort of falls away and makes room for something new. Children do this all the time, trying on different roles and playing with them. There is no reason to commit myself to a limited view of who I am.

I can be who I want to be.

If you haven't forgiven yourself,
how can you forgive others?

—Dolores Huerta
The Progressive

I Am Not Alone

Today, I know that, with God's help, I can do anything I need to do. When I feel alone or shaken up, I can ask for help within myself and know that it is there. Each of us is ultimately alone. Each of us has to learn our own lessons; that is, what we are here to do. We can't learn anyone else's lessons for them, and learning our own is difficult enough. To plow through my own psyche and face the insecurity and wounds that are there is all that I can handle. To try to live other people's lives for them is to separate myself from God because my first access to God is through and within me.

I ask for help in learning what I need to learn.

One on God's side is a majority.

—Wendell Phillips

Surviving meant being born over and over.

—Erica Jong
Fear of Flying

Lesson and Life

I recognize today that I am in charge of my own learning. Life is constantly offering up circumstances that are useful in my personal growth. I can move through the situation, live it out, extract the wisdom that is in it or repeat it over and over again, exhausting myself and learning very little. The deepest and most appropriate things I need to learn in life are generally right in front of me. Life is my guru if I can use it as such. It is rich with subtle learning if I look for it. The real achievement for me today is to learn to be in my own skin, to see truth in all that surrounds me, to know that placing value and judgment is pointless and illusory—all of life is valuable.

My lessons come from my life.

Forgive and forget is a myth.
You may never forget AND you can choose to forgive.
As life goes on and you remember, then is the time to once again
remember that you have already forgiven. Mentally forgive
again if necessary, then move forward. When we allow it,
time can dull the vividness of the memory
of the hurt; the memory will fade.

—Larry Jones

Amends

Today, I am willing for healing to take place in ruptured relationships. I have been doing the best that I can. My acknowledgment that I may have hurt someone else does not diminish me. I have also been hurt, and I extend the same understanding to myself that I do to others. We have all been doing the best that we knew how with the awareness we had to work with. My willingness to make amends speaks to my spiritual growth and desire for honesty. Making amends to others sets things straight with myself. My self-respect is growing to the extent that I am no longer comfortable with unfinished business. I will finish up my side for my own self and allow the rest to be where it is. It is for myself that I forgive; I do not need to control the result.

I am willing to feel clean inside.

Just because you think that hate and non-forgiveness
are justified in a certain case, wake up and realize that you are
still poisoning your own system and you are
doing more damage to yourself.

—Doc Childre

Surely it is much more generous to
forgive and remember, than to forgive and forget.

—Maria Legeworth
"An Essay on the Noble Science of Self-Justification"

WRITE YOUR OWN
AFFIRMATION FOR WAKING UP

[See how to write your own affirmation earlier in part II.]

Stage Two:
Anger and Resentment

Anger and Resentment

I am capable of experiencing and understanding the anger that may be inside of me, knowing that shutting it down, denying it or splitting it out of consciousness does not make it go away—it only hides it. When I hide my anger from myself, I learn nothing from it and it leaks out in less than functional ways. Anger is a natural feeling, one I am willing to face so that I can get past it toward forgiveness. Experiencing my anger doesn't mean I have to act it out or dump it all over my life. Nor does it mean that I give up my right to feel it. I have more options than that. I can tolerate the strength of my angry feelings without acting out or collapsing under their weight. I can be angry *and* forgive. Knowing that I have the strength to experience my own feelings builds confidence and strength within me.

I am capable of experiencing the power of my anger and learning from it.

I am no longer afraid of anger. I find it to be a creative, transforming force; anger is a stage I must go through if I am ever going to get to what lies beyond it.

—Mary Kaye Medinger

from *Walking in Two Worlds* (Kay Vadder Vort, et al.)

ANGER AND RESENTMENT SELF-TEST

These questions deal with anger and resentment.

1. How comfortable are you with your own anger?

❏ Almost not at all   ❏ Very little   ❏ Quite a bit   ❏ Very much

2. How comfortable are you with other people's anger?

❏ Almost not at all   ❏ Very little   ❏ Quite a bit   ❏ Very much

3. How much anger do you feel?

❏ Almost none   ❏ Very little   ❏ Quite a bit   ❏ Very much

4. How much hurt do you feel?

❏ Almost none   ❏ Very little   ❏ Quite a bit   ❏ Very much

5. How flooded with feeling are you?

❏ Almost not at all   ❏ Very little   ❏ Quite a bit   ❏ Very much

6. How angry are you about the fact that you're angry?

❏ Almost not at all   ❏ Very little   ❏ Quite a bit   ❏ Very much

7. How depressed do you feel around your anger?

❏ Almost not at all   ❏ Very little   ❏ Quite a bit   ❏ Very much

8. How overtly aggressive do you become?

❏ Almost not at all   ❏ Very little   ❏ Quite a bit   ❏ Very much

9. How passive–aggressive do you become?

❏ Almost not at all   ❏ Very little   ❏ Quite a bit   ❏ Very much

10. How much does your anger affect your intimate relationships?

❏ Almost not at all   ❏ Very little   ❏ Quite a bit   ❏ Very much

11. How much does your anger affect your career?

❏ Almost not at all   ❏ Very little   ❏ Quite a bit   ❏ Very much

12. How good are you at dealing with your anger in healthy ways?

❑ Almost not at all   ❑ Very little   ❑ Quite a bit   ❑ Very much

13. How much self-recrimination do you feel?

❑ Almost none   ❑ Very little   ❑ Quite a bit   ❑ Very much

14. How comfortable are you with the way you deal with your anger?

❑ Almost not at all   ❑ Very little   ❑ Quite a bit   ❑ Very much

15. How much does anger disrupt your life?

❑ Almost not at all   ❑ Very little   ❑ Quite a bit   ❑ Very much

ANGER JOURNAL

In the space below, write a journal entry allowing your angry feelings to pour out onto the page as freely as you wish. Attach words to your feelings and let them flow.

LETTER-WRITING

Write a letter to someone with whom you have unfinished business, allowing yourself to fully express all your feelings of anger, frustration, resentment and rage. This letter is not to be sent. It is an exercise to help you process your own feelings.

To/Dear _____,

From,

_____

AFFIRMATIONS FOR
ANGER AND RESENTMENT

Owning My Own Anger Responsibly

Today, I am willing to take responsibility for the anger that I carry within me. I am not a bad person because I feel angry. No one wants to think of himself or herself as an angry person, and I am no exception. But when I refuse to acknowledge the anger and resentment that I have stored within me, (1) I turn my back on me and refuse to accept a very important part of myself, and (2) I ask the people close to me to hold my feelings for me, to be the containers of my unconscious or the feelings inside me that I do not wish to see. Because I deny my anger to myself does not mean that it goes away. Today, I am willing to consider that there might be something more to it, that I may be carrying feelings of anger that I need to accept.

I am willing to experience my own anger.

It is easy to fly into a passion—
anybody can do that— but to be angry with the right person
to the right extent at the right time and with the
right object in the right way, that is not easy,
and it is not everyone who can do it.

—Aristotle

Responsibility

Today, I see that I can't release something just because someone tells me that it is the right or nice thing to do. Until I have moved through an internal process of identifying honestly what is going on with me, I can't really let it go. Honesty means that I am willing to be responsible. Whatever negative characteristics may have become a part of me from living with unhealed pain are, unfortunately, mine to deal with now. Projecting and blaming will not get me closer to getting rid of them. If I do not own my feelings, they will own me.

Within my own mind and heart, I am honest.

*I desire you would use all your skill to paint
my picture truly like me; but remark all these roughness,
pimples, warts and everything as you see me,
otherwise I will not pay a farthing for it.*

—Oliver Cromwell (to Peter Lely)

*Let us take men as they are,
not as they ought to be.*

—Franz Schubert

Patience with Myself

Today, I will be patient with myself. When I do not do as well as I wish I would, I will not make that a reason to get down on myself. I will instead recognize that the fastest way to bring myself out of a painful funk is through understanding and being good to myself. I needn't get caught in my own cycle of shame, resentment and blame. If a child is upset, I comfort the child because I understand that is what will make things better. I give myself the same comfort that I would extend to a hurt child knowing that it will help me have the strength to forgive and move on.

I am patient with myself.

So much attention is paid to the aggressive sins,
such as violence and cruelty and greed with all their tragic effects,
that too little attention is paid to the passive sins, such as apathy
and laziness, which in the long run can have a more
devastating effect upon society than the others.

—Eleanor Roosevelt
You Learn by Living

Separation

Today, I see that some of my anger towards my parents or their generation is about my need to separate from them and seek an individual identity. Even if my parents were perfect, it would be natural to want to become my own person. Healthy parents have an easier time allowing this process because they have their own identity and intuitively understand what their children are doing. Less healthy parents take separation as a personal indictment and may tend either to hold on tighter or to reject the relationships altogether. It is difficult to separate under these circumstances because it becomes so threatening. It is difficult to establish an individual identity without fearing either great loss or engulfment.

I see separation for what it is.

We all carry the houses of our youth inside, and our parents, too, grown small enough to fit within our hearts.

—Erica Jong
Fanny: Being the True History of the
Adventures of Fanny Hackabout-Jones

Projection

Today, I understand that when I project my feelings outward and see them as belonging to other people and not to me, I postpone my own self-awareness. The only way I can deal with difficult feelings is first to claim them as my own. Sitting with anxiety, anger, rage and jealousy is not pleasant, but actually experiencing my own feelings is the only way to get through them. I am willing and able to forgive myself. What good does it do me or anyone else if I hang onto self-blame and beat myself up on the inside? I have a right to make mistakes. I am not perfect. There is no such thing as perfect. I am all right the way I am. I can let go.

I own my feelings and am willing to experience them.

Self-forgiveness brings your mental and emotional energy systems back into balance. That's all. No big deal. It's not necessarily religious or spiritual, it's just good ol' street sense—the missing link in intelligence that scientists are looking for. Once you practice forgiving and releasing yourself, you'll realize the benefits soon in the way you feel overall.

—Doc Childre
The HeartMath Solution

Blaming Others

Today, I understand that dumping blame on someone else does not relieve pain or make my life better. If I reach out to others by attacking and blaming them, how can I expect them to hear anything that I say? If I want to be heard, I need to risk being seen—not as I wish to be seen but as I am. I ask too much of someone else when I say obnoxious things and yet insist on being heard. If I really want someone to understand me, I need to risk being vulnerable and letting my feelings show. Pointing a finger at someone else will only make them want to point a finger at me. It is hard to feel vulnerable, but with practice, it will become easier. I will be left with more of my real self if I don't tear at the self of someone else.

I take this small step toward great growth.

Forgiveness is the only way to break the cycle of blame— and pain—in a relationship. . . . It does not settle all questions of blame and justice and fairness. . . . But it does allow relationships to start over. In that way, said Solzhenitsyn, we differ from all animals. It is not our capacity to think that makes us different, but our capacity to repent, and to forgive.

—Philip Yancey
"The Unnatural Act"
Christianity Today

A Healthy Heart

Today, I will pray for help in forgiveness. My prayers have power in unseen realms. Research has borne out over and over again that prayer can be as effective a healer as medication. I will rely on the deep truth of the power of the unseen; invisible hands will guide my prayer. There is a peace within me that surpasses all understanding. Today, I will cultivate that peace by taking time to go within. The world within me is as real as anything I see. It sustains and nurtures me. It is of more value to me than I can imagine. I need this part of me to be alive and well. I need a healthy heart.

I take time to go within.

Humanity is never so beautiful as when
praying for forgiveness, or else
forgiving another.

—Jean Paul Richter

Anger and Blame

Today, I accept my feelings of anger and blame without beating myself up for them. Feelings aren't facts; they are meant to inform me of what is going on inside me. When I constantly judge myself for what I feel, I make my difficult emotions much more complicated, and they last ten times as long. There is nothing inherently wrong with any feelings—so what if I am angry and feel like getting mad? Accepting this allows the feeling to pass through me. Fighting it keeps me tangled up inside with no way out. Judging myself doesn't help anyone, least of all me. Frightening feelings are just frightening feelings. I do not have to overreact to them.

My own feelings need not toss me in every direction.

We are well advised to keep on nodding terms with the people we used to be, whether we find them attractive company or not. Otherwise they run up unannounced and surprise us, come hammering on the mind's door at 4:00 A.M. of a bad night and demand to know who deserted them, who betrayed them, who is going to make amends.

—Joan Didion
"On Keeping a Notebook"
Slouching Towards Bethlehem

The Witness

Today, I will become aware of that part of me that is separate and observes all that I say, do, think and feel. I have a witness within me that can become a very useful part of my life. Watching my behavior with a little bit of objectivity will help me to see myself as I really am. I will look with a compassionate eye. Just as I know it is not right to hurt others intentionally, it is equally not right to hurt myself. I recognize the godlike nature within me and others—we are all a part of the same Higher Power. By allowing my mind to watch itself with no thought of controlling or participating, I can learn a great deal about the way I work.

I am an uncritical observer of my own inner workings.

You need only claim the events of your life to make yourself yours. When you truly possess all you have been and done, which may take some time, you are fierce with reality.

—Florida Scott-Maxwell
The Measure of My Days

WRITE YOUR OWN AFFIRMATION
FOR ANGER AND RESENTMENT

Stage Three:
Hurt and Sadness

Hurt and Sadness

I am capable of tolerating emotional pain and coming out the other end whole and intact, with more of me, and a deeper awareness of and connection to my authentic self. There is information waiting to be mined inside my pain, parts of me that are being held in silence that long to speak, places within me that want to be felt and understood. Though my sorrow may make me feel like I am falling apart, I know I will not. I trust in myself and a power greater than me to hold me through my pain. I will get through these feelings; I can survive them. The yearning inside of me for what I may have lost, or for what never got a chance to happen, is natural and a part of the grief process. If I am willing to feel it, I will get past it; if I shut it down, minimize it or rewrite it into some cover-up story, I am only hurting myself in the long run. I need to feel what I am forgiving if I'm going to forgive it; whether it's myself I'm forgiving or another person.

I can tolerate the strength of my own pain.

*Oh! Grief is fantastic . . . as light, it fills all things
and, like light, it gives its own colors to all.*

—Mary Shelley
The Last Man

GRIEF SELF-TEST

This self-test deals with experiences related to both anger and sadness.

1. How much unresolved emotion do you feel surrounding this loss?

❑ Almost none   ❑ Very little   ❑ Quite a bit   ❑ Very much

2. How blocked are you from getting in touch with your genuine feelings involved in this issue?

❑ Almost not at all   ❑ Very little   ❑ Quite a bit   ❑ Very much

3. How disrupted in your daily routines do you feel?

❑ Almost not at all   ❑ Very little   ❑ Quite a bit   ❑ Very much

4. How much depression do you feel?

❑ Almost none   ❑ Very little   ❑ Quite a bit   ❑ Very much

5. How much yearning do you feel?

❑ Almost none   ❑ Very little   ❑ Quite a bit   ❑ Very much

6. How much sadness do you feel?

❑ Almost none   ❑ Very little   ❑ Quite a bit   ❑ Very much

7. How much anger do you feel?

❑ Almost none   ❑ Very little   ❑ Quite a bit   ❑ Very much

8. How much ghosting (continued psychic presence) of the lost person, situation or part of self do you feel?

❑ Almost none   ❑ Very little   ❑ Quite a bit   ❑ Very much

9. How much fear of the future do you feel?

❑ Almost none   ❑ Very little   ❑ Quite a bit   ❑ Very much

10. How much trouble are you having organizing yourself?

❑ Almost none   ❑ Very little   ❑ Quite a bit   ❑ Very much

11. How interested in your life do you feel?

❑ Almost not at all   ❑ Very little   ❑ Quite a bit   ❑ Very much

12. How much old, unresolved grief is being activated and remembered as a result of this current issue?

❑ Almost none   ❑ Very little   ❑ Quite a bit   ❑ Very much

13. How tired do you feel?

❑ Almost not at all   ❑ Very little   ❑ Quite a bit   ❑ Very much

14. How much hope do you feel about your life and the future?

❑ Almost none   ❑ Very little   ❑ Quite a bit   ❑ Very much

15. How much regret do you feel?

❑ Almost none   ❑ Very little   ❑ Quite a bit   ❑ Very much

16. How much shame or embarrassment do you feel?

❑ Almost none   ❑ Very little   ❑ Quite a bit   ❑ Very much

IF YOUR HEART HAD A VOICE

Reverse roles with your hurting heart and write a journal entry as your heart in the space below. Then reverse roles back to yourself.

I am _____ heart and I . . .

_____

_____

_____

_____

_____

_____

_____

_____

_____

_____

_____

_____

_____

_____

JOURNAL ENTRY

Write one or more journal entries allowing your thoughts and feelings to unravel onto the page. Let yourself express your hurt and sadness over the issue you're working with.

_____

_____

_____

_____

_____

_____

_____

_____

_____

_____

_____

_____

_____

_____

_____

_____

_____

A LETTER OF FORGIVENESS TO YOURSELF

In the space below, write a letter to yourself allowing yourself to freely express the feelings you've been holding onto in relationship to yourself. Whatever you may have been holding onto, you can let go of here.

Dear _____,

_____

_____

_____

_____

_____

_____

_____

_____

_____

_____

Love,

_____

AFFIRMATIONS FOR HURT AND SADNESS

Entering the Darkness

Today, I will allow myself to enter into the dark and searing painful experiences of my past, and cry it all out. If I can bring emotional literacy and forgiveness into the "occupied territory" of my inner world, I can give myself the freedom I desire. I have a world within me that is deep and peaceful. The grief that I carry hidden in silence finds its way to the surface of my life in a thousand little ways. There is no longer any safety for me in hiding. My security comes from full awareness and acceptance of who I am. Until I understand my grief and allow myself to know it, I will not be free of its grip.

I am strong enough to grieve.

Let mourning stop when one's grief is fully expressed.

—Confucius

Prayer and Miracles

Today, I will pray for a miracle in a situation that seems too much for me to handle or understand. There are times when I just don't have what it takes to work out a situation. I'm too loaded up with fears and anxieties. What could it hurt to pray for a little divine guidance or intervention? At the very least, it will help ease my burden; and at best, it will aid in a genuine shift in perception that might truly help my situation. When I feel stuck and as if I have explored every option and am still nowhere, I will pray for a miracle.

I allow my consciousness to reach out into the unknown and ask for help.

A miracle is a shift in perception
and prayer is the medium of miracles.

—from *A Course in Miracles*

Freeing Me

Today, I understand that in forgiving someone else I free myself. I held back on forgiveness because it seemed too kind an act for those who had hurt me. Why should I make them feel good? Why should I let them off the hook? I understand now that forgiving someone else and letting go—when I am truly ready—dissolves the resentment that is stored within me. I will not jump to forgiveness too quickly, forcing myself to do what I am not sincerely able to do. I will not forgive because it is the right thing to do. I will fully feel and acknowledge all that blocks me, and I will give myself the time I need to do this. When I do forgive, it will be to set myself free, to let go of the past and move on.

I forgive to free myself.

In the long run, it's not a question of whether they deserve to be forgiven. You're not forgiving them for their sake. You're doing it for yourself. For your own health and well-being, forgiveness is simply the most energy-efficient option. It frees you from the incredibly toxic, debilitating drain of holding a grudge. Don't let these people live rent-free in your head. If they hurt you before, why let them keep doing it year after year in your mind? It's not worth it but it takes heart effort to stop it. You can muster that heart power to forgive them as a way of looking out for yourself. It's one thing you can be totally selfish about.

—Doc Childre and Howard Martin
The HeartMath Solution

Suffering

Today, I will not hide my pain and suffering from myself or from my Higher Power. When I bring my most honest and pure self to the fore and understand my essential powerlessness over situations, when I am truly willing to turn over this angst to a power greater than myself, something changes. I let go and create space for a shift in perception. I experience a quiet awakening in my life, and forces that did not have room to enter are coming in to heal me. It is in letting go that I have a chance of achieving what I desire in my life. Holding on pushes away what I want, while releasing lets it all have enough breathing room so it can stay alive.

I open my heart to my Higher Power.

Being unwanted, unloved, uncared for,
forgotten by everybody; I think that is a much greater hunger,
a much greater poverty than the person who has
nothing to eat. . . . We must find each other.

—Mother Teresa

Truth

Today, I accept that without truth there is nothing. Truth is the soil out of which sustenance grows and nourishment comes, so that we can move in healthy directions. Lies have no food value and starve my spirit; but truth, though it can hurt, has a way of hoeing and tilling the soil so that some new growth can occur. Even though knowing the truth may seem unnecessary somewhere inside, I know it anyway. Bringing truth out into the open gives me a chance to lift the veil of secrecy that has made a wound feel like a dark hole. It allows angst to transform and break into a thousand little somethings that each contain usable and illuminating information that can again nurture health and life.

I am willing to live with truth.

*Truth is the strong compost in which beauty
may sometimes germinate.*

—Christopher Morley

*A sharp knife cuts the quickest
and hurts the least.*

—Katharine Hepburn
quoted in *Look* magazine

Healing

Sometimes, healing doesn't feel good. Sometimes, it involves deep pain. Facing and feeling my own sadness hurts, though forgiveness is in that very pain. The effect of healing is gentle, freeing and wonderful, but the road leading to it can be hellish. Now, I understand what the Psalms mean by "valley of the shadow of death." They were referring to a spiritual enlightenment involving a death and a rebirth. In order to be born into enlightenment, it is necessary that I face and clear out the dark and scary parts of myself. I need all of me for a life of spiritual freedom.

Today, I know that I was never alone along the way, and that I need never feel alone again.

The incoherence that results from holding onto resentments and unforgiving attitudes keeps you from being aligned with your true self. It can block you from your next level of quality life experience. Metaphorically, it's the curtain standing between the room you're living in now and a new room, much larger and full of beautiful objects. The act of forgiveness removes the curtain. Clearing up your old accounts can free up so much energy that you jump right into a whole new house. Forgiving releases you from the punishment of a self-made prison where you are both the inmate and the jailer.

—Doc Childre and Howard Martin
The HeartMath Solution

Ego Death

When I begin to experience real love, I go through an ego death. On my road to spiritual freedom, which is nothing more than learning to love, I go through what has long been called a dark night of the soul. This is a death of the ego, not in the Freudian sense, but in the way ego is defined in Eastern philosophy. I have a small "I" and a large "I." Part of my path toward expansion into my larger external self, which is of God and Love, is a death of my smaller self, which sees the world as here only to feed my needs. Really it is through the recognition of giving and receiving and of loving that we become full. In forgiving myself for being human, I release my spirit.

I allow and understand my ego death.

It is through giving that we receive, and it is through dying that we are born to eternal life.

—St. Francis of Assisi

WRITE YOUR OWN AFFIRMATION
FOR HURT AND SADNESS

Stage Four:
Acceptance, Integration
and Letting Go

Acceptance, Integration and Letting Go

I feel parts of myself coming back to me. I realize that I didn't need to be so frightened about going within and exploring my inner life. All I found was more of me and that turned out to be okay. In fact, I feel freer and stronger for having accepted feelings and thoughts that I may have been blocking—processing them and integrating them into my inner world with greater understanding and insight. I can make new meaning of the circumstances of my life, I can see things differently, viewing the "same landscape through different eyes," as Marcel Proust says. Somewhere in all of this I seem to have let go of a significant portion of the hurt and rancor that I was holding in my heart and mind. I feel freer, less burdened; released of something I hardly knew I was carrying until it was gone. That edgy feeling I used to have that something disquieting could pop up from inside me and throw me off balance has lessened, and in its place is a new-found confidence that I can tolerate my own powerful feelings without being knocked over; I can think and feel at the same time, put words to emotions and describe my inner experience. I feel more whole.

Integration is a quiet feeling of self-mastery, an inner freedom and confidence.

If I can let you go as trees let go
Lose what I lose to keep what I can keep
The strong root still alive under the snow
Love will endure—if I can let you go.

—May Sarton
"The Autumn Sonnets"
A Durable Fire

WRITE A LETTER YOU
WOULD LIKE TO RECEIVE

In the space below, write a letter to yourself that you would like to receive. It can be a letter of apology, a letter asking for your forgiveness, a letter expressing love or whatever you know you'd like to hear from that person, or from a part of yourself (e.g., your child self or your self from another time in your life).

Dear _____,

From,

_____

ROLE-REVERSAL JOURNALING

Mentally reverse roles with someone you're dealing with and write a journal entry as that person. The idea is to stand in that person's shoes for a moment and see through his or her eyes. Remember, think and write as he or she would. Then reverse roles and come back to being yourself.

I am _____ and I feel . . .

_____

_____

_____

_____

_____

_____

_____

_____

_____

_____

_____

_____

I am _____ and I feel . . .

_____

_____

_____

_____

_____

_____

_____

_____

_____

_____

_____

_____

_____

_____

_____

_____

WRITE A JOURNAL ENTRY AS YOURSELF

In the space below, write a journal entry expressing how you feel after doing the past two exercises, and where you are in your process.

WRITE A LETTER ASKING FOR SOMEONE'S FORGIVENESS

In the space below, write a letter in which you ask for another person's forgiveness. It is natural to carry appropriate, or even irrational, feelings of guilt along with a wish for forgiveness. Allow yourself to ask for that forgiveness now.

Dear _____,

_____

_____

_____

_____

_____

_____

_____

_____

_____

_____

_____

_____

From,

_____

AFFIRMATIONS FOR ACCEPTANCE, INTEGRATION AND LETTING GO

Inner Belief

I believe in this world; it is the place that I have been born into. I love the breeze and the grass, the sky and the water. I have an intimate exchange with nature—like a lover. I feel held and nourished by it. I believe in people; they are the species to which I belong. I recognize that, underneath our superficial differences, we all want and need the same things. I believe that truth and goodness will prevail. I have experienced and seen more healing than I thought would ever happen. I feel good with small gains. I see deep meaning in quiet things, and I am moved by a power that I cannot explain but that I sense inside and out. Today, I feel good.

I believe in life.

*Forgiveness is the answer to the child's dream
of a miracle by which what is broken is made whole again,
what is soiled is again made clean.*

—Dag Hammarskjöld

Personal Truth

Today, I know that no one from my past needs to see things the way I do for me to get better and move on. Trying to convince others of what I have learned through my own journey can be an exercise in futility and delay my progress. First of all, each of us has our own truth that is unique unto itself. Second of all, each of us is at a different level of understanding and acceptance of who and where we are in life. Each member in my family had different experiences. That I thought we somehow matched up was an illusion. We each experienced our childhoods in our own way and have a right to our own perceptions. I do not have to get anyone to see it my way in order for me to feel comfortable. My truth is my truth, theirs is theirs.

I honor my own experiences and personal truth, as well as those of others.

The language of truth is too simple
for inexperienced ears.

—Frances Wright
A Few Days in Athens

Learning

Today, I do not accept other people's truth as my truth. Even if what they believe seems better or more obvious, I need to give myself credit for feeling and seeing what I feel and see. Learning is meaningful to me as it relates to or is understood within the workings of my own mind. Without something in me making it relevant, learning is very disconnected. I am the learner behind the information; I am the seer behind the seen. I learn by direct experience.

I learn to trust the perceptions that I gain from my own observation of life.

The day the child realizes that all adults
are imperfect, he becomes an adolescent; the day he
forgives them, he becomes an adult; the day
he forgives himself, he becomes wise.

—Alden Nowlan

Life is either a daring adventure or nothing.
To keep our faces toward change and behave like free spirits
in the presence of fate is strength undefeatable.

—Helen Keller
Let Us Have Faith

Higher Power Within Me

Today, I recognize that a Higher Power lives and breathes inside me, through me, as me. I used to think that God was the chairperson of somebody else's board, and I spent my time in search of another person's version of a Higher Power. But really, there is no searching—it is more like an acceptance. That is the well-kept secret: that God lives not in the heavens or inside special buildings, but within my very self. My direct access to myself is my direct access to my Higher Power, and my estrangement from myself is my estrangement from my Higher Power. We are co-creators, hand-in-glove, a team. Today, I see allowing God into my life as an act of surrender, acceptance and love.

I love my Higher Power, and my Higher Power loves me— we are one.

You've always had the power to return home right there in your shoes, you just had to learn it for yourself.

—L. Frank Baum
The Wizard of Oz

Inner Hearing, Inner Sight

Today, I will trust my own heart. The clear message that whispers within me has more to tell me than a thousand voices. I have a guide within me who knows what is best for me. There is a part of me that sees the whole picture and knows how it all fits together. My inner voice may come in the form of a strong sense, a pull from within, a gut feeling or a quiet knowing. However my inner voice comes to me, I will learn to pay attention. In my heart I know what is going on. Though I am conditioned by the world to look constantly outside myself for meaning, today I recognize that it is deeply important for me to hear what I am saying from within.

I will trust my inner voice.

I could be whatever I wanted to be
if I trusted that music, that song, that vibration
of God that was <u>inside</u> of me.

—Shirley MacLaine
It's All in the Playing

I know
the soft wind will blow me home.

—Yü Hsüan-chi
"Living in the Summer Mountains"
The Orchid Boat

Being with Life

Today, I allow myself just to be with life. Somehow, it doesn't have to prove anything to me or give me any more than I already have to be okay. The lessons I have learned through working through all that blocks my forgiveness have taught me that I can face my most difficult feelings and still come home to a place of love and acceptance. Life is always renewing itself; nothing lasts, good or bad, and that is just the way it is. It is enough today to enjoy my coffee, to take a walk, to appreciate the people in my life. I can rest in a quiet sort of understanding that this is what it's all about; all the searching turned up such an ordinary but beautiful thing.

I am enraptured with the ordinary.

We are all, it seems, saving ourselves for the Senior Prom.
But many of us forget that somewhere along
the line we must learn to dance.

—Alan Harrington

Forgiveness is still and quietly does nothing.
It offends no aspect of reality, nor seeks to twist it to
appearances it likes. It merely looks, and waits, and judges not.
He who would not forgive must judge, for he must justify his
failure to forgive. But he who would forgive himself
must learn to welcome truth exactly as it is.

—from A Course in Miracles

Healing Society

Today, I will light one candle, and that candle is myself. I will keep my own flame burning. I turn my sight to light and love and goodness. For today, there is no need to be discouraged. So what if I see and identify all the ills of society and diagnose it as sick—what good will that do me or anyone else? I heal society by healing myself. Just as life is lived one day at a time, the world will heal one person at a time. Each time I think a positive, loving thought, it goes into the ether and vibrates. This is nothing particularly mystical; I have but to sit near someone and look at her face to feel how her thoughts affect me. I take ownership of my own inner workings and their effect on myself and others.

I do my part to heal the world.

Forgiveness is giving up the resentment to which you are entitled and offering to the person who hurt you friendlier attitudes to which they are not entitled.

—Robert Enright

Leaving Abuse Behind

Today, I see my life as my life. If I do not take care of it, make plans and dream dreams, who will? I am not second in my own heart—there has to be a place on this Earth where I come first, so that the little child inside me feels loved and held. I will come first with me. In the same way that I will protect my children from harm, I will protect myself. In a way, forgiveness allows me to do just that. If I forgive, the prize that I get is often inner peace. I seem to be releasing another person, but in doing so, I also release the toxic feelings inside me as I go over and over their offenses in my mind. It's just not worth sacrificing my inner tranquillity to hang onto a negative feeling about them. And in letting go, I also forgive myself—because I am worth it. I deserve inner peace.

I can live a calm and pleasant life.

I've learned that when you have an argument
with your spouse, the first one who says,
"I'm sorry I hurt your feelings; please forgive me,"
is the winner.

—from *Live and Learn and Pass It On*

Being in the Moment

Today, I see that the only real point of power is in the present, which is to say that life cannot be lived backward or forward, but only in the context of today. If I truly let myself have this moment and all that it contains, I will be in quiet possession of great eternal wealth. All that is, is in this moment where all the waters meet and all the wisdom of the ages lies; it is the now that calls me to it with open arms. I work out my past, not because it is right or good or proper, but because it allows me to be in fuller possession of my present. By releasing and returning to me those parts of me that remain prisoner in my own psychic and emotional jail, I can have access to the now.

I allow myself this moment.

*Real generosity toward the future lies
in giving all to the present.*

—Albert Camus

Learning from Life

There are no "buts" today. I am what I am, others are what they are, life is what it is. I will not parenthesize my growth with a "but," or hold back my forward-moving spirit with second-guesses. For today, I am living with things as they are. I am exactly where I am meant to be, learning what I need to learn. All I need do is move through situations with willingness to learn and openness to feel. When feelings are brought up, I can accept them as what is happening within me—no need to resist and analyze them. Transformation will happen in the moving through and the acceptance of them. I trust that my life is unfolding in such a way that what I need to learn will be before me. I am willing to learn.

I see the "table prepared."

*There are no little things. "Little things,"
so-called, are the hinges of the universe.*

—Fanny Fern
Ginger-Snaps

*To keep a lamp burning we have to
keep putting oil in it.*

—Mother Teresa

The Mystery

Today, I accept that part of myself that will never be satisfied, and I comfort and tame it. There is a place in me that knows it will never necessarily solve the eternal questions of life: Who am I and where do I come from, and where do I go when I die? At times, I can get depressed about that and feel that there's no real point to life. But I am beginning to feel that to accept and love this side of myself is what also gives life beauty and meaning. Perhaps meaning is not knowing and understanding, but an acceptance of mystery, an embracing of the unknown. After all, it is that mystery that gives even the most ordinary circumstance an eternal sort of glow—a sense of depth, a feeling that there is more.

I accept that I will never fully understand—I embrace the mystery.

The soul is restless and furious;
it wants to tear itself apart and cure itself of being human.

—Ugo Betti

A Return to Living

Today, I keep my house clean and let go of the rest— some of the ways that I wish to live will not be readily understood by others. I will keep my own scorecard clean and not worry about the results, readily forgiving myself for my mistakes and showing others forgiveness for theirs. I will act in a way that makes it easier for me to live with myself— that keeps my own conscience clear. Other people's negative projections of me no longer run me. I am the one who makes the decisions about who I want to be. I need not defend and explain myself again and again. I need not ask permission to be who I am. I allow myself to be happy in my own skin today. I think well of myself, no matter what others think of me.

I create my own self.

To be really great in little things,
to be truly noble and heroic in the insipid details
of everyday life, is a virtue so rare as
to be worthy of canonization.

—Harriet Beecher Stowe

One of the secrets of a happy life is
continuous small treats.

—Iris Murdoch
The Sea, the Sea

Letting Go

Letting go of the past and moving on is a tall order; it requires a kind of releasing that I still find difficult to do. My past will always be in the shadows of my memory to haunt me if I do not recognize it as a part of me. If I pretend it's not important, grit my teeth and force myself to numb myself, I have missed the point of this process. On the other hand, if I am unwilling to let go no matter how many times I have worked through certain issues, I am also not allowing myself to be fully healthy and return to life. The part of my healing that is a flowing through the stored pain from the past is a decisive, forward-moving action.

I understand that part of my process of healing is letting go and moving on.

Treasure the shadow. . . .
There are no shadows save from substance cast.

—Edith M. Thomas
"Mirage"
The Dancers

There is a time, when passing through light,
that you walk in your own shadow.

—Keri Hulme
The Bone People

WRITE YOUR OWN AFFIRMATION
FOR ACCEPTANCE

WRITE YOUR OWN AFFIRMATION
FOR INTEGRATION

WRITE YOUR OWN AFFIRMATION
FOR LETTING GO

Stage Five:
Reorganization and Reinvestment

Reorganization and Reinvestment

I have been through a journey of forgiveness. I've faced my anger and hurt and brought order and clarity to my inner world. I've accepted the things I cannot change and changed the things that I could. Because I've shown the courage to face my inner demons and look them in the eye, I feel stronger and more competent. Forgiveness of myself and others has offered me a way out of pain and confusion, and now I find I have a renewed interest in life. I see things differently. I feel liberated from something that was tying up my energy. And I recognize and accept my own humanity, and the humanity of others. I am ready and willing to reinvest in the ideal of love. I want to find worthy projects and passions, and put my energy toward them. I have something to give to the world, and the world has something to give to me. I am right where I am supposed to be and I've met the challenges of my life. I am ready to live.

I invest my energy with care and gusto.

Forgiveness is a rebirth of hope, a reorganization of thought, and a reconstruction of dreams. Once forgiving begins, dreams can be rebuilt. When forgiving is complete, meaning has been extracted from the worst of experiences and used to create a new set of moral rules and a new interpretation of life's events.

—Beverly Flanigan
Forgiving the Unforgivable: Overcoming the Legacy of Intimate Wounds

FORGIVENESS SELF-TEST

Take this test again after working through all the exercises in part II. Name the forgiveness issue that you're working with, and answer the following questions by placing a check in the appropriate box.

1. How much do you feel this issue is affecting your inner peace today?

❑ Almost not at all   ❑ Very little   ❑ Quite a bit   ❑ Very much

2. How blocked are you from getting in touch with your genuine feelings involved in this issue?

❑ Almost not at all   ❑ Very little   ❑ Quite a bit   ❑ Very much

3. How much fear are you feeling at the thought of honestly addressing your feelings around this issue?

❑ Almost none   ❑ Very little   ❑ Quite a bit   ❑ Very much

4. How much anger or resentment are you feeling associated with this issue?

❑ Almost none   ❑ Very little   ❑ Quite a bit   ❑ Very much

5. How much hurt or sadness are you feeling associated with this issue?

❑ Almost none   ❑ Very little   ❑ Quite a bit   ❑ Very much

6. How much self-recrimination are you feeling around this issue?

❑ Almost none   ❑ Very little   ❑ Quite a bit   ❑ Very much

7. How much guilt or shame do you feel around this issue?

❑ Almost none   ❑ Very little   ❑ Quite a bit   ❑ Very much

8. How much hope do you have that you can work through your feelings surrounding this issue?

❑ Almost none   ❑ Very little   ❑ Quite a bit   ❑ Very much

9. How much energy do you feel is being absorbed by this issue?

❑ Almost none   ❑ Very little   ❑ Quite a bit   ❑ Very much

10. How much do you feel this issue impacts your relationships today?

❑ Almost not at all   ❑ Very little   ❑ Quite a bit   ❑ Very much

11. How much do you feel this issue has impacted your ability to move into future relationships comfortably?

❑ Almost not at all   ❑ Very little   ❑ Quite a bit   ❑ Very much

WRITE A LETTER GRANTING FORGIVENESS TO SOMEONE WHO HAS HURT YOU

In the space below, write a letter granting someone who has hurt you the gift of forgiveness. Speak freely and fully about all of your feelings relating to the hurt and why you've decided to consider forgiveness.

Dear _____,

From,

_____

VISUALIZING MY FUTURE AS I WISH IT TO BE

Follow the steps for doing a creative visualization [from earlier in part II]. After you have fully visualized your life or a particular situation as you wish it to be, write in the space below six things or situations you would like to see manifest or happen in your life. Visualize them, then release that vision for brief moments throughout the day.

1. _____

_____

_____

_____

2. _____

_____

_____

_____

3. _____

_____

_____

_____

4. _____

_____

_____

_____

_____

_____

5. _____

_____

_____

_____

_____

_____

6. _____

_____

_____

_____

_____

_____

LETTER TO GOD

In the space below, write down this life circumstance as you wish to or pray to experience it.

Leave this space in the middle blank so that God will have room to work.

In the space below write down things in this circumstance as they are.

AFFIRMATIONS FOR
REORGANIZATION AND REINVESTMENT

The Creative Power of My Thoughts

Today, I recognize that I tend to produce in my life what I feel is true for myself. Thoughts have a creative power of their own. If I look closely, I can see my thoughts come to life. I create the possibility of what I would like by first experiencing it in my mind. I will visualize what I would like to have in my life in my mind's eye. I will accept what I see in my inner eye as being there for me, and I will fully participate in my vision as if it were mine. I will be specific about what I see, smell, feel, and I will accept my inner vision as fully as possible. I will enjoy my vision, then let it go and move on in my day, releasing it with no thought of controlling it further. I will let it happen, if it is right for me, in God's time.

All good things are possible for me.

If one advances confidently in the direction of his dreams,
and endeavors to live the life which he has imagined,
he will meet with a success unexpected
in common hours.

—Henry David Thoreau

Standing in Self

Today, I own the truth of my journey. If I am to stand centered and strong within my life and self, I will need to plant a garden within my own soul. A garden for me to nurture and to nurture me. A haven of beauty. I will find my own voice and sing my song because if I don't sing it, it will not be sung. It is all I have, and it is enough. I do not need to prove anything to anyone anymore. I have come home—to me. The truth is, I was here all along, only I forgot to look for myself. Instead, I searched for me in other people's meaning and became lost in their stories. I am not lost today. I know that there is nowhere to look for me but within myself, and no one to lead me there but me.

Thank you, life, for letting me see this.

To err is human; to forgive, divine.

—Alexander Pope

Friendship

Today, I make choices about my company and friends. Whom I choose to spend time with is very important to me, and the relationships that I begin I wish to respect and nurture. A handful of dear friends is far more meaningful to me than lots of acquaintances. I choose to share myself where I feel a return of good feeling. I want both to have a friend and to be a friend. One of the unusual gifts of growing up in a dysfunctional household was that I learned the value of friendship because I had to turn to my friends to meet very deep needs. I am grateful for my friends, and for what I learned and felt from them.

I value friendship.

She is a friend of my mind.
She gather me, man. The pieces I am,
she gather them and give them back
to me in all the right order.

—Toni Morrison
Beloved

I Am Whole

Today, I see that my life is up to me. How I choose to live, what I will accomplish, how I conduct my intimate relationships, how I treat myself, all are in my own hands. I am no longer afraid that pain and anxiety will return me to a state of helplessness and vulnerability. Let it come; I am ready to meet it head-on. I am strong in the awareness that I can live as I choose to live. I have been willing to walk a path of inner transformation that, though difficult, has built a strength in me and a knowledge that I can survive my most painful feelings. I do not need to be afraid of my life if I am not afraid of myself. I have met and tamed the monsters that live inside me. I am comfortable in my own skin.

I am free to be who I am.

Forgiveness is an act of the imagination.
It dares you to imagine a better future, one that is based
on the blessed possibility that your hurt will not be the final word
on the matter. It challenges you to give up your destructive
thoughts about the situation and to believe in the possibility of a
better future. It builds confidence that you can
survive the pain and grow from it.

—Larry James
from *CelebrateLove.com*

Inside My Mind

Today, I am grateful to feel alive and to recognize that life is a spiritual journey. All my life circumstances are spiritual challenges, if I choose to look at them that way. Getting free of my own overattachment to people, places, things and ideas, mistaking them for me, releases my spirit. Once my spirit is released, it can travel and experience the real beauty of life. Life surrounds me; it is inside, outside and everywhere. If I am free and still inside, life is there. If I am not ruminating and filling my mind with unnecessary pre-occupations—life is there, spirit is there—waiting to be seen and felt.

I allow my mind its freedom.

There is one spectacle grander than the sea,
that is the sky; there is one spectacle grander than the sky,
that is the interior of the soul.

—Victor Hugo

Dreaming Dreams

Today, I will dream dreams. There is nothing wrong with having a couple of dreams for myself if they are realistic and don't remove me from life too much. To work toward a dream can be a constructive use of my talents and energies. It can give me a positive focus. If my dreams are wild and I am not willing to do the work necessary to realize them, they will only frustrate me and lower my self-esteem. If, however, I am able to dream what makes sense for me and work to put it within my reach, it can be a real process of growth and challenge. My energy and enthusiasm can help me move through blocks, and my commitment can show me that love and effort can be their own reward.

I can stretch myself.

Dreams are . . . illustrations from the book
your soul is writing about you.

—Marsha Norman
The Fortune Teller

Having Fun

Today, I will have fun. What's the point of all the work I do striving toward releasing self-destructive patterns if my life doesn't become lighter and happier? Even though I am working through deep issues, there is no reason why I can't have some enjoyment in the process. Fun is when I relax and let things happen—when I can laugh at myself and other people—when I don't take everything in life so seriously. It is when I can enjoy a seemingly meaningless conversation just for its own sake. Fun is when it doesn't have to be all my way—when the heavy load is removed, when my meter is turned off and I just goof around in the moment. Fun is something I don't have enough of for a number of silly reasons. Today I see that there is no reason not to enjoy myself.

I can let go and have fun.

On with the dance, let joy be unconfined is my motto,
whether there's any dance to dance
or any joy to unconfine.

—Mark Twain

Spiritual Transformation

Today, I see that to change my life I have to change myself. Nothing less than a spiritual transformation will allow me to experience my current life as an alive, serene and whole person. When I say that I would like world peace, first I will understand that without inner peace there will be no world peace. One of the ways in which I can serve the cause of humanity is to be, within myself, a genuinely spiritual person—respecting all sects and creeds, but standing on my own as a conduit of higher truth, recognizing that each person has equal access to that knowledge. I will look for truth today within myself rather than outside. I will not wait for peace to be handed to me as some sort of prize for good behavior but will do the inner work needed to achieve it.

I seek truth within myself.

No matter how big or soft or warm your bed is,
you still have to get out of it.

—Grace Slick

Becoming Real

Today, I let go and become real. I know that by holding on too tightly, I squeeze the life out of myself and those around me. This journey has taught me to value being authentic above being something or someone. Forgiveness is a process of facing and removing those obstacles that have been in the way on my road back to myself. It has been my willingness to risk and trust that I can tolerate the intensity of my own emotions, which has transformed darkness to light, emotional illiteracy to literacy. Now it is time for me to live each day as it comes and share some of what I have received. I feel more open to life and confident about my ability to hold onto myself, even when I am in intimate connection. I can find that balance between holding on too hard and giving too much away.

I am open to life and all it holds.

To remain whole, be twisted!
To become straight, let yourself be bent.
To become full, be hollow.
Be tattered, that you may be renewed.

—Lao-tzu

Hesitation

Today, I will walk the walk and talk the talk. It will not be good for me, ultimately, to half commit myself. In a way, the particular path that I take is less significant than that I take a path. It doesn't help to second-guess myself and my experience. Commitment to a path is really commitment to myself. I am allowing myself to take a clear direction, one in which I can actualize my talents on a day-to-day basis, one that will allow me to build a foundation and a structure in which I can live. I will have a passion in life, a passion that takes me beyond myself, a passion to love, nourish, be led and challenged by. I will follow it, and it will follow me.

I deserve a passion in my life.

He became an infidel hesitating between two mosques.

—Islamic Saying

WRITE YOUR OWN AFFIRMATION
FOR REORGANIZATION AND REINVESTMENT

Conclusion: Healed, Whole and Handling Life

When you get into a tight place and it feels as if everything is going against you till you think you cannot hold on a minute longer, never give up then, for that is just the time and the place that the tide will turn.

~EDNA ST. VINCENT MILLAY

NINE QUALITIES OF FORGIVERS

Forgivers tend to experience a sense of mastery over their own difficult emotions.

They tend to feel in charge of and responsible for their own joy.

They tend to have an optimistic, rather than a pessimistic, view of life.

They tend to value intimacy and connection more than being right or seeking revenge.

They tend to have passion for living, and enthusiastically put their energy into interests that are meaningful to them or those they care about.

They tend to feel connected to their families and their communities.

They tend to be altruistic and to have a heightened sense of compassion for others.

They tend to prioritize and enjoy their relationships and feel nourished by them.

They tend to see life as a gift.

GROWING SOUL:
WISDOM VERSUS DESPAIR

Having walked through this forgiveness process stage by stage, we may have discovered that in forgiving someone else, we have expanded our own souls. We may have seen that in embracing pain, we actually get through it more quickly and economically than when we avoid it. Our own humanity and the humanity of other people may feel less threatening to us now that we have been willing to stand and face our own inner world. We may feel a renewed sense of strength and mastery as we learn we can survive even our most painful feelings. And we may understand the profound importance of forgiving ourselves and how that allows us to live comfortably with intimacy and lead a happy life.

When we've truly forgiven ourselves, it naturally extends outward (if our forgiveness is more than lip service). How can we hold someone else to a standard that we're not holding ourselves to? We're no longer robbing ourselves of joy. We see life as a gift that we have for a limited amount of time, and we wish to do well by it, to do our part to get it to work. We value and enjoy our relationships. We understand the difference between isolation, and being alone and *with* ourselves. We respect humility in ourselves and others, and see arrogance for what it is: a defense against feeling scared or small, or an inability to tolerate feeling ordinary. We value intimacy with ourselves and others, and do the necessary work to maintain it. We recognize the importance of stable, nourishing relationships to our overall sense of well-being.

Wisdom is often bought with the currency of pain. It is the product of looking deeply into life, not necessarily as we wish it were but as it is. It's the gold that's left when we sift through the sand and debris of life's inevitable pain. Though that bit of gold may feel small as we hold it in our hand, it is ours alone—earned with our own sweat and toil, and no one can take it from us. It has purchasing power in the world and can be traded for whatever we need to live well and comfortably. It can be used to improve our living conditions. We have power over the quality of our lives. Though we may not always be able to tailor each situation to our desires, we can tailor how we live with what we have.

Using the alchemy of forgiveness to light a path in working through issues that undermine our joy and inner peace is one way to cultivate wisdom. Perhaps despair is what we feel when we can't, for whatever reason, find our way through pain or anger or disappointment and disillusionment toward some kind of understanding and relief. When we lose hope or faith in life and relationships.

Midlife, because of the directions that our own bodies are taking us, offers us another opportunity to reassess, to live more consciously and to elevate consciousness. We can use midlife to draw that gentle line in the sand, to consider how we want to live in the second half of our lives. Using the wisdom we have accumulated so far, we have an opportunity to make the most of this gift called life.

Pop psychology, I fear, has created the myth of the perfect relationship. But no one is perfect. No relationship is free of issues. It's not the fact that we have issues, but what we do with the issues we have that may make the difference in the quality of our relationships. When we try to get our relationships to be perfect, it's a losing battle. Part of making psychology available to the masses through the self-help movement has contributed to marvelous personal growth. The other part has probably contributed to a lot of people feeling like they shouldn't allow themselves to feel satisfied with what they have, that they're "selling themselves short" or weak for not wanting to have it all, not achieving that ultimate intimacy or self-awareness or perfect life. But having it all is just not necessarily having it all. Dudley Moore taught us a hilarious lesson in being careful about what we wish for in his film, *Bedazzled*. He made a Faustian contract with the devil, trading his soul for the power to have any wish that he wanted granted. But no matter how hard he tried to get his life and relationships to be perfect, there was always some funny twist to whatever he got when his request was finally met. When he wished to be together always with his beloved, for example, the wish was granted, but she was a nun and he was a monk. Something always went wrong.

An old wise person told me long ago to "learn to see perfection in what is." The very state of wanting things to be different is an unhappy one. And it keeps us from enjoying what we have and seeing clearly enough to make the subtle but significant changes that will likely improve it. The sweeping changes that we imagine will bring us happiness often bring as much pain along with them. Then we have two choices: to admit we overshot and back up and feel our disappointment honestly, or to block it because admitting it is just too painful, so we become only half-alive in our hearts. "Love what you have," says Meryl Streep so movingly in the film *One True Thing* (the screen adaptation of Anna Quindlen's book of the same name). *Love what you have.* And forgive, because otherwise, you'll lose what you have. If we want to have relationships in our lives we'll have to learn the art of forgiveness and use it often because nothing is perfect. In fact, if we have relationships in our lives, we're already using it. This doesn't mean we should tolerate abuse or be a patsy or stay in a relationship that's all wrong; it means that we recognize that nothing and no one is perfect, including us. We can make mistakes and forgive ourselves, and we can allow others to make mistakes and forgive them. D. W. Winnecot, the British psychoanalyst, had a beautiful phrase for a mother who is able to usher her children into adulthood successfully. He called her "the good-enough mother." Not perfect, not flawless, not sensational, but *good enough* to meet a child's basic needs so that she can develop into a *healthy-enough* adult. I extend this concept to other relationships. "The *good-enough* relationship" is one that meets what Abraham Maslow would call "basic trust." It allows us to live in a *stable-enough* world with fundamental needs for connection and security met well-enough; not perfectly, but *well-enough.* The myth of perfection teaches members of our society to constantly be on the run, looking for the proverbial "more." But we may, in our unbridled passion and persistence in thinking that "bigger is better," destroy ourselves from within. Because some-times—in fact, a lot of the time—"less is more."

And all our needs cannot necessarily be satisfied by people. "Man cannot live by bread alone," says the Bible. Some of our thirst is another kind of thirst, some of our hunger is another kind of hunger.

SPIRITUAL HUNGER

Some hunger is so deep that it can only be satisfied spiritually. Therapy cannot satisfy this hunger because people can't satisfy it. When we try to find an answer to why we feel hungry at an exclusively psychological level, when the only place we look for answers is in what we did or didn't get from those close to us, we bump up against the wall of therapy's natural limits. Certainly, we will need to resolve those emotional and psychological issues that are in the way of our ability to have trust and faith in life and relationships. But somewhere along the line, spiritual evolution will always involve a leap of faith, into the unknown, into the unseen. In fact, it can be as a result of running up against the limits of therapy that we seek a spiritual solution. Having explored every other avenue in our search for answers, we despair at having nowhere else to go. Then comes the leap into what can feel like a walk through the shadowy depths and confusion of darkness, but is ultimately a path toward the light. It is often just this dark passage that we will want to avoid. But until we feel the power of our own hunger and need, we tend not to open our souls to be fed. Just as water can-not enter a full vessel, God cannot fill a full container. If we are con-stantly staving off our spiritual hunger with the junk food of this world, we will always wind up feeling undernourished.

God's love and forgiveness are free, always waiting for us to open our hearts to them, alive in both the religious and the quantum physi-cal sense. Scientists and mystics agree that we live in an alive universe. Regardless of whether we choose to call this life force God, Universal Mind, Higher Power, or protons and neutrons, it is there nonetheless, breathing vitality into all that we see and all that we are, demonstrating its state of aliveness. Keats describes our human search: "Beauty is truth, and truth beauty, that's all we know on earth and all we need to know." T. S. Eliot sees the delicate balance we need to achieve in order to open our hearts to grace and surrender: "Teach me to care and not to care, teach me to be still." "Does anyone ever appreciate life while they live it?" asks Emily in Thornton Wilder's *Our Town*. "Saints and poets maybe, they do some," replies the stage manager.

Grace and surrender are always a part of spiritual awakening, it seems to me. So is humility. How many times I have heard it shared in the Twelve-Step program: "I came to these rooms on my knees." A humble heart cuts away at the tangled underbrush that clouds our vision so that we can finally see. But it isn't easy to get there. That's why so many of us only become humble when we feel we have little left to lose or have run out of other alternatives. Life will hurt sometimes—there's no way around that—but as a member of my group said recently, "I'd rather hurt than be numb." She would rather take the risk of feeling than live with an illusion of safety because she has tasted something better; she knows what it feels like to have her heart be alive.

SILVER LININGS

Much of the evidence discussed in this book suggests that attitude plays a crucial role in how our lives do or do not feel good to us. The way we "see" the events of our lives has much to do with how we experience our quality of life. Norman Vincent Peale thought that when we go to heaven we'll be asked one question and one question only: "What did you do with what you were given?"

Finding the lessons contained within adverse experience, seeing life as a constant process of growth in which we are meant to perceive ever deeper layers of meaning and experience, can make the difference between lives well lived and a life merely lived through.

Actively looking for the silver linings contained within difficult life experiences is a way of reframing the situations of our lives so that they contribute to our sense of the good of life. Reframing also allows us to transcend the ordinary boundaries of thought and emotion surrounding a circumstance, and see it within the larger framework or in the context of the "big picture." It teaches us to use daily situations as stepping-stones for personal growth. When we operate from this mind-set, that feeling of being out of control or the victim of circumstances transforms. We see ourselves, instead, as people in control of our own response to life. We write our own story, our own interpretation of life, instead of it being written for us. This profound sense of authorship opens the door to inner riches and is the most powerful antidote to meaninglessness there is. "The mass of men lead lives of quiet desperation," said Thoreau. But there is no reason to. There is always deeper meaning to be found if we work with it until it works.

When my son Alex was five years old, a car hit him. I had just had an operation for a cancer condition three months earlier (surgical menopause) and was anxiously awaiting summer when Marina and Alex could be done with school, and run and play and swim to their hearts' content, and I could pay attention to them without being preoccupied by my own recovery. But then a car threw a new problem in front of us. Having cancer, however, was much easier than seeing my then little boy hurt and in pain. His zone of safety had been forever penetrated; at five he now knew that bad things can happen and they could happen to him. He knew pain, and all the fear and anxiety that go along with it. It was a bitter pill to swallow. But he was the bravest little boy, uncomplaining and courageous. He was present with his pain and expressed it, but brought such courage to each day. He was in a full-leg cast for six weeks and a half-leg cast for another six (the entire summer). In his full cast, he learned to fish. To this day, he loves fishing. At five, he could fish for five or six hours straight and feel that no time had passed when it was time to go home. He went into deep states of mind in order to cope; this was obvious by the look of serenity that frequently came over his little face. In his half-cast, he could outrun any kid at the lake, do flips off the diving board and jump on the trampoline.

One day, Alex and I were driving in the car on an errand, when he began to bring up something that was bothering him.

He said, "Mom, no, never mind."

I said, "No, what is it, Alex?"

"It's not important," he replied.

"What is it, honey? It might be important," I said.

Then he said something I'll never forget: "It's important if you die or something, or maybe have an accident or cancer, but the rest isn't really important."

I was stunned that Alex was able to do this kind of thinking at six years old (he'd had a birthday since the accident). All I could say was, "Well, if you understand that, Ali, you'll always be able to live a happy life."

He wasn't dismissing what was bothering him; we went on to talk about it. He just had it in perspective as "not that important," compared to what *can* happen. That was his silver lining. He learned something that has never left him to this day. Last weekend he graduated from college, tall, handsome and wonderful. He has always had this ability to place the events of his life into a philosophical framework, to see all sides. And I am sure that this quality has only just begun to serve him.

When I was a kid, I used to watch *Auntie Mame* with my mother and sisters whenever it was at a movie theater or on TV. We loved it. The zaniness of it, the permission to enjoy life. We were Greeks, believers of enjoying life with every bone in our bodies, living in a work-ethic world. Not that we don't believe in work; we work hard. But wherever possible during work, if we can exaggerate a small pleasure, or stretch out a pleasant moment, or get an extra laugh, we're culturally trained to do it. We love people and we respect the mystery of life, because we're taught that life and family (along with numerous adopted surrogate relatives) are what's really important. These were great lessons on living and they've never failed me. To love people is to love life; to respect family is to respect yourself and God; to stand in awe of the mystery of God is a sure ticket to a front-row seat in the theater of life.

Every family has its own story to tell about forgiveness, understanding and love. My editor, Lisa Drucker, mentioned that she heard Maya Angelou interviewed on the *Today* show, talking about the profound value of courage and love: ". . . probably the most important lesson is to know that you have been loved." She understood this on a gut level.

Lisa then went on to tell me that she has long considered her greatest blessing in life to be her parents' love for her, and their raising her to feel completely secure of their love, that it was abiding no matter what, absolutely unconditional. If her parents were angry about or hurt by something she'd done—or she was by something either or both of them had done—the feeling applied only to the action, not to their fundamental feelings about each other. Lisa said she carries her parents' love for her and hers for them into the world every day, and always will, even when her parents are gone.

Lisa attributes her parents' ability to raise her this way to their own upbringing at the end of the Depression and during World War II. They grew up with the understanding that nothing matters more—or is more sustaining—than love. In fact, Lisa said that her grandmother always said, "Money and things are only things. Today, they're yours; tomorrow, someone else's." Her parents took this to heart. Even during the turbulent days following September 11, as a family, they weathered the maelstrom of feelings by relying on their long-held belief that love is all that really matters.

Knowing you are completely accepted and loved gives you a sense of safety that nothing else can, and it also leads to the ability to forgive yourself and others. When you start from feelings of safety and love, forgiveness feels natural. Imagine being loved that way, and forgive yourself as a way to begin the journey of acceptance and healing.

THE GIFT THAT KEEPS ON GIVING

Life is a gift.

We learned a lot on September 11. Churches, synagogues and mosques had record-high attendance in the days that followed the attack on the World Trade Center. In front of our eyes, so many lives were taken away with no warning. Finished. Their time here on Earth brought to a sudden close. Then waiting for the other shoe to drop: hypervigilance. And an awakening of spiritual hunger, a deep need to find meaning not only in death, but also in life. In my workshops and groups during the days that followed, reactions ran the gamut. Despair, sadness, helplessness and rage. And a newfound commitment. To life. A renewed appreciation of the beauty of living, and the responsibilities that go along with a great gift. And recognizing the paradox that we are simultaneously masters of our own fate and part of a grander plan. How to find sanity in this delicate balance is, as much as anything, an act of surrender: not the kind of surrender that is another form of giving up, but the kind that allows us to relax and let go so that we are ready for right action whenever necessary. The kind that recognizes that we aren't in charge of everything, the kind that trusts in something larger than ourselves.

And then came the collapse of the seventh-largest Fortune 500 corporation. Another apocalyptic moment. Another reexamination of our values. Then the scandals: disheartening greed juxtaposed with such recent heroism.

Have we created lifestyles that can't be lived? Become rich only to be spiritually poor? As the old saying goes, "No one on their deathbed says, 'I wish I'd spent more time at the office.'" It doesn't take an expert to figure out that living life too fast means that we lose our ability to taste it, to enjoy it, to value what we already have. Our ability to walk into a day and receive the gifts that are sewn into its invisible lining requires us to be in a state of openness, to be receptive, to be aware. A willingness to be grateful for what we have.

Our families are undergoing dramatic shifts and changes, and I often worry that, in our pain at all the potential alienation that can accompany change, we'll lose touch with the family's profound importance as the foundation of our lives and the cornerstone of our society. The workplace has become the place we go to get our needs met—our need for intimacy, and a sense of worth and belonging. And then we rush through the rest of our lives as if they weren't that important. What we need is balance. Perhaps as women, in our exuberance at being finally allowed entry into what had for centuries been a male bastion—the workplace—we've joined in undervaluing the profound importance of the roles we *have* played throughout the centuries. The roles of mother and keeper of the hearth. *There is no role more important.* With three decades added to our life spans in the second half of the last century, we really do have time to have it all, especially if we don't have to have it all in the same decade. I think we're the lucky ones: Now, we can do anything. We can work, be mothers and wives, *and* have our own identities. It's not easy to balance it all, but it's not impossible either, if we keep our values straight. Men, too, are beginning to experience the home and childbearing in a new, more intimate way. As we enter the workplace, they can and should enter the home. And it's our generation that has begun this painful and exhilarating redefining of roles. Good for us.

The events of September 11 have also taught us all a lot about trauma, our personal and cultural values, and forgiveness. They have been a wake-up call, getting us to take a deeper look, to reexamine what we hold dear.

Living in New York City was like being in a laboratory for trauma research, and as a researcher in this area, I paid attention. As soon as I heard news of the attacks I began to call my husband at his office and our daughter at work. Our son was at college in a relatively calm locale, thank God. I couldn't get a line out. Time seemed elongated as I methodically kept dialing the phone. Each time anxiety tried to grip my throat, I told myself not to borrow trouble, things were okay. Eventually, I was able to get through to my daughter's workplace. Her boss told me, "Marina's fine. She's meeting her father at Grand Central, and they're walking home together." Her compassionate voice will always stay with me. Then came more standing still, time stretched out into something I could almost see and sense as unattached to reality. I don't know how long I sat in that chair waiting before it occurred to me to look out the window. What I saw was another unusual sight. Row after row of people walking the eight miles out of downtown Manhattan. Mostly in stunned silence. This went on all day, as people headed north and away from Ground Zero. Streams of people in orderly, eerie syncopation, walking in a strange vigil toward safety. Stunned and somber. Shutdown and numb. We all were, thank goodness, or we would have been running around like chickens with our heads cut off. It all seemed very unreal. All this shock and disbelief belong to the initial set of responses to trauma.

When Brandt, Marina, and a friend of hers from work got home, we all sat together in a sort of stupor. No feelings yet. Later when we could afford them, not now when they would get in the way of our ability to do what needed to be done first. My next set of memories is from when we went out to get something to eat and look around. Literally everyone on the Upper West Side was wandering around in a daze. People were walking through traffic lights, the streets were silent and the disorientation was palpable. We felt disoriented like Dorothy in *The Wizard of Oz*, who doesn't know quite where she is after her house whirled around in the sky and landed somewhere else. The familiar was suddenly unfamiliar. The difference for us was that we were trying to get our bearings in a world that looked the same but felt different. Downtown, where Marina's friends were, it had been another story. Not only was the familiar suddenly unfamiliar, it was also horrible. An apocalyptic nightmare. Chaos reigned as people feared for their lives, leapt from buildings and ran in every direction seeking safety, only to find new debris falling through the air, holding briefcases or newspapers over their heads to shield themselves.

Everyone who could leave town did leave town. The next day we went to the country for an overnight. It was gorgeous. This beautiful blue sky and green grass felt so different from the inner darkness we were all carrying. The world around us and our experiences of the day before were peculiarly out of sync, that feeling of watching life instead of being in it was everywhere. Again, like Dorothy walking out of a black-and-white world into one of Technicolor. Strange. What did it all mean? Would we ever feel safe again? Still no subtle feelings, only fear, muscle tension, anxiety.

It felt so good, though, to be out of the city. We felt human again, and hopeful. But the next day, we needed to go back. Because both my husband and I are therapists, this was no time to be gone. So back to town. More muscle tension. The smell from Ground Zero came all the way up to 125th Street. The next day, I was scheduled to do one of my monthly workshops for Caron Foundation, so I began to put material on trauma on paper so that I could help clients process this strange set of events. It was in the writing down and organizing of my thoughts on paper that I began to feel better myself. I wrote an article entitled, "Triumphing over an Unseen Enemy," which made its way into several publications that explained the types of human reactions to trauma [see excerpts in appendix II].

We have witnessed our country going through many stages toward forgiveness around the events of September 11. Ultimately, what people came to recognize was that we had to confront terrorism courageously and openly, do what was necessary to root it out of our world, and then forgive and rebuild on what would ultimately bring peace. That terrorism had to go, but forgiveness had to follow so that we could all have a world that wasn't going to blow up around us. Relationships aren't all that different. The lessons of forgiveness are as old as the Bible. It is forgiveness that has the power to make what has been broken whole again. It spans the hearts of humans throughout history giving us hope that wounds can heal and hearts can mend. As

Anne Frank said in the midst of suffering through one of history's darkest hours: "I still believe that people are really good at heart." And as St. Exupéry put it in *The Little Prince:* "It is only with the heart that one can see rightly, what is essential is invisible to the eye." As long as we can keep our hearts alive, we will know what to do and how to act.

Forgiveness is a way to keep our hearts alive.

◆

The weak can never forgive. Forgiveness is the attribute of the strong.

~**Mahatma Gandhi**

AFFIRMATIONS TO LIVE BY

Love

Today, I accept that love is not a sentiment but an energy. When I see love in a sentimental context, I wait for the situation to appear before I allow myself to experience the feeling. The energy of love is always available to me. I can consciously allow it to pass through me and surround me. I can wrap myself in an experience of love and send it out to others. I can call on this energy in times of need and use it to heal myself physically, mentally and spiritually. When I think and feel love, I connect with those energies around me—I allow myself to be with a loving universe. What I feel inside is my business. Why not give love a try in the privacy of my own mind and heart?

I attract the energy of love.

Love heals. . . . Love is the most powerful known stimulant to the immune system.

—Bernie Siegel, M.D.

Meditation

Today, I recognize the source of light and wisdom that is within me. When I look outside myself to learn about what is actually inside, I need to exercise great discernment because some of what I see fits and some does not. There is a fountain within me that is ever full and waiting to be discovered. When I can rest quietly in this inner place, I experience a sense of fullness, and my desire to go outside diminishes and gives way to a preference for undisturbed peace. Solitude takes on a different meaning when I can contact that quiet within. Life softens, and external things become less important. I look for this place within me on a daily basis.

I search within.

When you have shut your doors and
darkened your room, remember, never to say
that you are alone, but God is within,
and your genius is within.

—Epictetus

Wholeness

Today, I recognize my essential wholeness. While I see myself as deficient and look to others to complete me, I condemn myself to a life of reactivity. In this mode, I can only spend my days trying to bend myself into the shape that I feel will make me lovable to others; and if they love me, I will feel both momentarily full and terrified that the feeling will go away. I will see them as in charge of my feeling loved, and I will go about using massive control maneuvers and manipulations to keep my supply on tap. If they do not love me, I may feel belittled and furious at having compromised myself to no avail. The only solution is to seek wholeness within.

I look within for love.

*I cannot and will not cut my conscience
to fit this year's fashions.*

—Lillian Hellman

Inner Newness

I am new inside today. I feel pink and tender, as if young tissue were growing within. I have been willing to take an ultimate risk by looking at the state of my life and insides, not as I wish they were, but as they actually are. I have experienced an inner death. I have walked through spaces inside my mind and heart that felt life-threatening, and I have felt the terror of full honesty. What I did not expect was this sense of birth and newness. Somehow, life feels full of possibility for new and different experiences. I thought that I would be stuck in anger and blame forever, but I see today that I did not need to feel so down on myself for feeling those feelings. They are just a part of the process.

I accept my feelings, whether I like them or not.

Growth is the only evidence of life.

—John Henry Newman

Faith in a Providential God

Today, I know that there is nothing to be afraid of because my Higher Power and the energy of love underpin all that is. At the very core of me is not darkness and fear, but light and love. Maybe I am afraid to admit to the extent of my hatred, because I am afraid to admit to the extent of my love. When I allow myself to be at the source of love and to recognize it as a fundamental mystery of creation, I sense that no matter what happens I will be all right; I am where I am meant to be.

I allow love to be the basis of my life.

You must love all that God has created,
both his entire world and each single tiny sand grain of it.
Love each tiny leaf, each beam of sunshine. You must love
the animals, love every plant. If you love all things, you will also
attain the divine mystery that is in all things. For then your
ability to perceive the truth will grow every day, and your
mind will open itself to an all-embracing love.

—Fyodor Dostoyevski

Simplifying My Life

It is time for me to simplify. More activity, money, trips, lessons, and so on are not the answer. That hole inside me that I am trying to fill is not satisfied in this manner; over-feeding it only increases its capacity—starving it makes it shut down. When I can simplify and regulate my life so that I can really experience it as it is happening, I will have enough. I will experience my own spontaneity and creativity in the course of living my day.

I will simplify my life.

Creativity is a gift.
It doesn't come through if the air is cluttered.

—John Lennon

The Wisdom of Forgiveness

We forgive, if we are wise, not for the other person, but for ourselves. We forgive, not to erase a wrong, but to relieve the residue of the wrong that is alive within us. We forgive because it is less painful than holding on to resentment. We forgive because without it we condemn ourselves to repeating endlessly the very trauma or situation that hurt us. We forgive because ultimately it is the smartest action to take on our own behalf. We forgive because it restores us to a sense of inner balance.

I have the wisdom to forgive for my own peace of mind.

Wisdom is harder to do than to know.

—Yula Moses
in John Langston Gwaltney's *Drylongso*

Appendix I

Forgiveness is the economy of the heart. . . . Forgiveness saves expense of anger, the cost of hatred, the waste of spirits.

~HANNAH MORE
CHRISTIANITY: A PRACTICAL PRINCIPLE

My suggestion is that women can play a very important role in establishing peace. Instead of being carried away by science they should follow the path of nonviolence because women by nature are endowed with the quality of forgiveness. Women will never succeed in aping men in everything, nor can they develop the gift nature has bestowed on them by doing so. They should neither allow their family members to have, nor should they themselves have any connection with anything relating to war. God has endowed women with hearts overflowing with love. They should utilize the gift properly. That power is all the more effective because it is mute. I hold that God has sent women as messengers of the gospel of nonviolence.

~MAHATMA GANDHI

FORGIVENESS AND KIDS

A study in *USA Today* from the 1980s reported that most parents spend less than seven minutes a week talking with their kids. Another study conducted by Michael Resnick of the University of Minnesota found that limbic bonding was a stronger factor in predicting teen pregnancies, substance abuse, violence or suicidal behaviors than more traditional markers like single-parent families or insufficient resources of time and money. Teens who reported feeling loved and cared about got into significantly fewer problematic behaviors than their counterparts who did not. Seven minutes a week, according to Dr. Daniel Amen, is not enough time to create a sustaining limbic bond with your child. Amen actually gives a four-point prescription for developing healthy limbic bonds with our children, which are, as the research reveals, their greatest immunity against problems.

1. "Spend twenty minutes a day with your child doing something that he or she would like to do." He advises that you protect that time by telling the child that you feel time together is important and you really wish to be with him or her.
2. "During this time there are to be no parental commands, no questions, and no directions." This is the time to establish an intimacy that feels mutual and sustaining.
3. "Notice as many positive behaviors as you can." Noticing positive behavior is much more effective in shaping behavior than emphasizing the negative.
4. "Do much more listening than talking."

The limbic bonds that we create in and with our children are the blueprints that they will be working off of for the rest of their lives. The patterns they carry will influence who they choose to spend time with, marry or be in relationship with, as well as how they relate to themselves and their world.

When my first child was born, I got some wise advice that I decided to follow scrupulously. The advice was to tell my children that I wouldn't get mad at them if they did something wrong, as long as they told me the truth. The idea was to train them to tell the truth, and to understand that this would have a far-reaching effect upon their own habits of mind as they grew up. I stuck to this advice.

So one day when Alex was about seven, he and his buddy, Keith, came into my room with a sheepish look. Alex said, "Mom, I have something to tell you that's a little mistake." I braced myself for what was sure to follow. "Well," he began, "Keith and I were playing ball and by 'accident' I had the ball in my hand, and by 'an accident' it fell out, and by 'accident' the ball fell into the window and well, by 'accident' the window was closed, and the ball kind of hit and sort of fell through it and made a little hole, not a very big one." (Oh, gee that's a relief.) Then he looked at me with his winsome little face and said, "I didn't mean to do it, Mom, it was an accident." (Clearly established by now.) Trying to suppress both a smile and some annoyance at the thought of a broken basement window, I said, "I'm glad you told me the truth, Alex." He walked out of the room, put his arm around his friend and said, "See, I told you she wouldn't get mad." I felt at that moment very grateful for the advice I'd been given and proud of myself for following it carefully enough so that Alex felt that he didn't need to hide from me. I understood that there could well be things much more significant in his life that might occur, and I wanted him to feel he could tell me the truth, no matter what. That, of course, proved true. A broken window is such a small price to pay, and it paved the way for honesty around far more significant matters. Alex understood that he would be forgiven his indiscretions, and so he felt he could free to tell the truth about them. This kept his conscience clear. He didn't have to keep secrets from his parents in order to preserve family harmony. He didn't have to carry his burdens alone in his own heart; he could get them off his chest and feel peaceful. Today, he is a wonderful young man with a highly developed sense of right and wrong, and a very big heart.

A different example comes to mind with Marina. When she was around two or so, she dropped and broke something. As I was about to fuss in some way, I watched as she got annoyed with herself. This tiny tot put her puffy little hands to her puffy little child cheeks and said, "Oh, Marina, Marina, Marina. Oh, no, look what I did." She was harder on herself than I would ever have dreamt of being on her and I understood immediately that, rather than discipline her, I would need to help her not be so hard on herself. She was the sort of child I almost encouraged to be naughty once in a while. She was just born with such powerful internal monitors that I felt she needed to internalize some softer, it's-no-big-deal kind of voice. She needed to learn to forgive herself. Now she teaches me that when I get too hard on myself. She, too, has a subtle, mature, highly developed and personalized morality.

Naturally, there were as many incidences where Marina needed forgiveness for mistakes, or Alex needed to be less hard on and more forgiving toward himself, but these two examples are ones that have stuck with me over time. Raising children in an atmosphere of forgiveness really allows them to develop a fuller and more personal sense of morality, because they aren't constantly warding off a sense of guilt or resentment that twists up their insides. They learn to see the world as a friendly place, and they learn that mistakes are part of life, part of taking risks and moving forward. Ask any successful person and they'll tell you that part of succeeding is being able to tolerate failure without either crumbling or giving up. It's hard to live through failure if you see it as unforgivable and feel you either have to avoid it or hide it from others.

Being forgiving didn't mean that our kids got away with murder. Rather it opened the door for long discussions of how a wrong might be righted, what might be done differently the next time, and what attitudes they might incorporate so they wouldn't feel so bad that it immobilized them. An attitude of forgiveness, I hope, lightened their emotional load. More than once over the years, our kids came to us with situations from their lives, or with friends who needed help but didn't know where to turn. And I really think they have learned to tell the truth to themselves because they've learned over and over again from personal experience that the truth is where you need to start to effectively work out any problem.

~

A Child of Happiness always seems like an old soul living in a new body, and her face is very serious until she smiles, and then the sunlight lights up the world. . . . Children of Happiness look always not quite the same as other children. They have strong, straight legs and walk with purpose. They laugh as do all children, and they play as do all children, they talk child talk as do all children, but they are different, they are blessed, they are special, they are sacred.

~Anne Cameron
Daughters of Copper Women

A DEVELOPMENTAL APPROACH TO TEACHING FORGIVENESS TO KIDS

Emotional literacy (the ability to accurately label, articulate and process our emotions) requires that we have access to our authentic feelings. When we don't forgive, we're probably not confronting our full range of emotions. This doesn't mean that forgiving in a superficial way means that we've worked through what's eating us. Only that we need to be willing to live with our own truth to have emotional literacy, even if that truth is that we're not ready, for whatever reason, to forgive.

Building the skills involved with emotional literacy is a lifetime task that begins at birth. In the following paragraphs, I'll attempt to outline a developmental approach to building skills of forgiveness and emotional literacy.

INFANT TO AGE TWO

In this period, the child develops relational skills, language skills, social skills, fine- and gross-motor skills. She absorbs information through all of her senses. She learns, mostly from her primary caregivers, what the world is about. This is where, as Erik Erikson says, children learn "trust versus mistrust."

The baby is learning: "Is my world a safe and loving place or, cry as I might, will my needs never feel adequately met? Am I understood by those closest to me? Can they understand what I'm trying to say to them, feel along with me, join me in my tiny, flailing efforts to communicate with them, or are they emotionally distant, unable to discern who I am? Am I left in my own world of pain or pleasure, or do soft sounds and loving arms surround me when I'm hungry, aching or want to share my pleasure at being alive? What is it like to be alive and feel my way into this world?"

I divided relational and social skills here because by using the term "relational skills," I'm trying to communicate something subtler and more profound than we sometimes see social skills as being. I'm talking about the brain and biological wiring that takes place during our early development that actually wires the child for further personal and relational development—that time in the life of the child where the baby feels one with mother (or father), where nature and nurture meet, and each tiny interaction in their world lays down the internal wiring for further development. Neurobiologists now understand that our biology, far from being fixed at birth, is a cooperative process in which the child's internal wiring is set up through her interactions in her early relational world. She then uses this new knowledge to interact at a more complex level, to elicit a new response and to form, in turn, more wiring, a broader template. And so it goes. Far from being a static world that babies enter into with fixed personalities, this model represents a fluid, dynamic picture of development.

Understanding development in this way makes it easy to see how a basis for forgiveness is set up from our earliest experience. Are we forgiven for urinating and defecating all over our parents' world, for being helpless and demanding, for needing constantly to be attended to in every possible way and for exhausting those around us to the point of distraction? Or are we made to feel that our needs and wishes are too overwhelming to be met? D. W. Winnecott, whom we've already discussed, talks about the *good-enough* mother, who addresses herself to the overwhelming task of mothering in a manner that is *good enough;* not perfect (none of us are), but good enough to create in our tiny infants the sense of basic trust that Abraham Maslow refers to as a fundamental human need. All children need to learn to tolerate frustration, to learn to wait a bit for this or that need to be met. The art of mothering lies in finding the right balance between over- and under-responding; the right balance so that our children grow up seeing the world as basically a good place that they can enjoy, participate in and belong to. A world in which they can meet their needs in reasonable ways, a world that is both challenging and supportive. A place within which they can become who they are becoming.

AGE TWO AND A HALF TO AGE SIX

By this age, the child is up and around, interacting fully with her environment and testing it for veracity, dependability and excitement. She has a sense of herself, and her parents have a sense of her. Her language development is well established, and her emotional personality is significantly begun.

Around this age a subtle shift begins to take place between caretaking and companionship. These little ones love to be included in everything that is going on in the family. They want to feel important and long to be Mommy's Little Helper. It is a stage that Erikson refers to as industry versus dependence. Allowing them to feel useful and industrious by breaking down small tasks into a manageable size feels wonderful to these little children. They can help prepare meals, put away groceries, make decisions about their day and feel like a vital part of family life. Marina had a little grocery cart that we took with us to the grocery store. She followed me around (or I followed her around) and picked out some things she thought she or we might like to have from the grocery shelves that were at her level. Over time this also became a great reading exercise, as she was motivated to understand what was in the product to see if it was healthy.

Development of emotional literacy remains a dynamic interactive process between the child and her ever-expanding world. Her primary interactions are still with family, and the content and quality of her interactions and those she witnesses in her relational environment will set the foundation for how she interprets and understands the world. We pay considerable attention, time and money these days to early education. Mathematical concepts and letters of the alphabet are constantly in front of us, and few among us fail to recognize the importance of this period for early learning. But emotional literacy is a concept only beginning to be understood. It, too, can be taught, and much emotional learning is taking place simultaneously with other kinds of learning.

As for the learning of forgiveness, what better time? This could be seen as an especially important time to set a good foundation for self-forgiveness. Small children are constantly straining the nerves of those around them, pushing our limits and challenging the most peace-loving among us to keep our cool. So first of all, as parents, we'll need to forgive ourselves for our feelings of incompetence and overwhelm. This is a period when the child is making sense and meaning of the interactions and events of her world with the powers of reasoning available to her at this stage of her development. Children whose little transgressions are forgiven are likely to internalize this as a pattern for how to treat themselves. Children who are dealt with harshly learn to scold themselves mercilessly. Again, the key is balance: enough accountability and reality so children come to understand that glasses really do break, and people have genuine feelings that get hurt, over-taxed and pleasured. Too much indulgence and the child does not develop enough sense of reality to tolerate the slings and arrows that she will inevitably encounter in making her way through the world; too little indulgence and she learns to raise defensive walls to shut out the world, put on a false face and keep her true feelings hidden, even from herself.

Children can be very needy at this stage. They begin to realize that they are separate people from their parents, which is both exciting and terrifying. They idolize the parents who have the power to grant their wishes for anything from an ice-cream cone to a peaceful evening, who can turn their world upside down and inside out if they choose to, and upon whom they are still totally dependent. Their neediness makes them tremendously vulnerable to both our love and our scorn, both of which they take wholly to heart. They learn big lessons at this stage about whether it is safe to need, love and depend on other people, and whether mistakes and imperfections are tolerable and forgivable.

AGE SEVEN TO AGE ELEVEN

These are commonly called "the latency years," when children are considered calmer and more educable than they are either previously or during adolescence. The task of teaching emotional literacy at this time might be compared to diagramming a sentence. By now, children have their basic emotional vocabulary in place, and if they've grown up in a relatively healthy environment, they have the right word attached to its appropriate, corresponding feeling. The sense the small child makes of experience is heavily tinted with what psychologists call "magical thinking" (thinking that is not necessarily reality-based; thinking, that is, through the eyes of a child). There is still magical thinking present in the minds of latency-age children, but they learn more about the world and reality each year. They are learning to make basic sense of their emotional life. While the younger child may say "I am mad," in a general sort of way (that is, the feeling seems pervasive and not too specific), the latency-age child is learning to break down her emotional experience in a more specific manner. She is developing some emotional order. "I am mad at my mother because she won't let me watch TV" might be an example of what she would say. Or "My feelings are hurt because I wasn't invited to Susie's birthday party, and I'm mad at her." Or "I'm happy because I got the part I wanted in the play. I'll have fun at rehearsals. Everyone wanted the part, so I feel special." Learning to break feelings down into understandable components at this age can help to sustain internal order when adolescence hits.

Here, too, the child is learning lessons on forgiveness. Are my feelings acceptable to my parents, my teachers and my friends? Which feelings get me in trouble, and which ones get me stroked? Which please and which annoy those in my world? Am I forgiven for not getting it right all the time, or when I miscalculate am I in trouble? Can I be my authentic self and sill be loved and accepted by my family or my school world, or do I need to put on a false self in order to gain support and acceptance? As parents, we need to forgive ourselves for not knowing the right answer to all their questions and to learn to say, "I don't know, but maybe we can find out together."

Lessons learned at this stage, though they may seem quiet, have resonance throughout life. I have heard parents say over and over that kids are "so resilient" when they're young. But I beg to differ. I think that what parents interpret as resilience is oftentimes the latency-age child's ability to "fall asleep and wake up better in the morning." Or parents read silence to mean that their children are not bothered by something. But this ability to wipe the emotional slate clean can also cover up anxiety or upset that may be building beneath the surface. Though this is a relatively placid period of development, children are sponges soaking up the values, expectations and moral parameters of their environments. This is an age where children can continue not only to rely on natural resilience, but also to actively build it by talking about what is going through their minds in a simple, uncomplicated manner. They can learn how to work with their emotional world simply by experiencing it in a safe and natural way. They can explore and define the boundaries of their inner terrain. Their parents can help by being *good-enough* listeners, and by respecting the burgeoning autonomy of the children and their growing need to move into their own, individuated world while remaining securely connected to family; by forgiving their children's wish to be themselves, not just the manifestation of the parents' wishes and dreams.

AGE TWELVE TO AGE SEVENTEEN

Now come the famous adolescent years: turmoil, power struggles and relationship crises, the years that strain even the calmest parent–child relationships. One of the most important things to understand about these years is that though your children seem to be totally disinterested in everything you say, they still need their parents to remain visible and stable, so that they have something to push against. We are still their compass in the world, a lighthouse they steer their course toward or away from, a fixed point. Parents often misinterpret adolescents' wishes to separate, individuate and self-define as a rejection of them. DON'T TAKE IT PERSONALLY. If you do, you will behave in ways that only complicate the relationship and their emotional learning. Forgive them for wanting to push you away and become their own person. And forgive yourself for your mixed emotions of wanting to let go and hang on all at once.

At this age, young people have the ability to think in abstract ways. That is, they can hold more than one concrete concept in their minds at once. They can see what is around them and imagine a life that could be or is to come. Forgiveness at this age is so important. You may feel you don't know your own child some days but, rest assured, they often feel the same way about themselves. They need to understand that we will allow them to *separate and stay connected to us,* that we will not punish them for their wish not to be us, that we will forgive them for wanting lives and identities separate from the ones we've given them.

AGE EIGHTEEN TO AGE TWENTY-FIVE

This is when you have to forgive your children for growing up and leaving you, and forgive yourself for wanting to push them away and hang onto them for dear life simultaneously. After all your hard work and devotion, they have the audacity to want to have their own lives. Suddenly, they seem to develop amnesia about who has been taking care of them all these years; that is, until their college bills or rent come due. It's hard to balance how near and how far to be, hard to get the distance right; impossible, in fact. So we have to forgive ourselves for getting it consistently wrong, and forgive them for constantly letting us know that we've gotten it wrong . . . again.

Young adults have a huge task ahead of them and moving into their own, separate lives can be both exhilarating and terrifying. The developmental task of creating their own separate lives and saying goodbye to childhood looms in front of them. They are in mourning for their childhood, letting it go but without a consolidated adult identity. This can be a rocky phase in the lives of young people. They will need our forgiveness for not doing it perfectly, and we'll need theirs. And we each will have to forgive ourselves accordingly. This is a period during which home becomes a safe harbor that children can sail from and back to; we keep our lighthouse burning, so that they can find their way to shore.

∽

The hearts of small children are delicate organs. A cruel beginning in this world can twist them into curious shapes.

∽Carson McCullers
The Ballad of the Sad Café

HOW TO START A GROWTH SUPPORT GROUP OF YOUR OWN

Starting your own self-help growth group can offer women an opportunity to get together and share in meaningful ways, and can pull them out of their normal routines and provide some time for self-reflection. This book can be a good starting point. Women are relationship-oriented and understand how to support each other intuitively. A growth group can help you to carve out some time in your month to focus on your own life, and also experience the support and caring of other women. It's important that the group follows ground rules so that advice and cross-talk are avoided, and cohesion and respect are maintained. This type of group is not a substitute for therapy and shouldn't be used as such. Once a month is probably a reasonable goal, but each group can decide for themselves how often to meet.

KEEP A SIMPLE FORMAT

Choose a section of the book each month that the group wishes to focus on, and everyone, of course, should read it. Spend as many sessions working with a section as the group decides is right for them. Ask each group member to come prepared with a particular few paragraphs from the book that they would like to discuss, an affirmation that spoke to them or something they've written that they would like to share.

Invite each group member to read their piece and tell the group why they chose it. Limit this to four or five minutes per person. Next, open the floor for sharing whatever comes up from the readers' own lives around the subject of this reading, then allow group members to identify and share. [Follow ground rules for sharing at the end of appendix I.] Repeat this process as many times as you wish. The group may choose to spend the whole meeting on one idea or stage, or work with more than one. The format can vary to accommodate the needs of the group.

Affirmation-Writing

If the group wishes to, about two-thirds of the way through the get-together, group members can write their own affirmations. [See "Writing Your Own Affirmation" in part II.]

If you use affirmation-writing, then, as a closing activity for the group, invite each person to read her own affirmation. After reading, let each person come up with one or two small or large actions that they can take toward personal growth. It may be an internal action such as, "I will be less critical of myself this month," or "I'll be less negative in my attitude"; or an external one like, "I'll plan a pleasure activity every week," or "I'll set aside quiet time each day." If you don't write affirmations, you can still make an affirmative statement, and discuss one or two actions toward personal growth as a closing activity.

After each person has read her affirmation and made her affirmative statement, allow time for socializing. Now is the time to share a cup of tea or dessert. (Some groups may wish to start with a potluck dinner and save dessert for after the meeting, while others may find it easier to keep it to a dessert-only evening. The group can decide on types of food, e.g., comfort, healthy, spa, ethnic, etc.) In any case, it's important to leave a little time to relax and regroup before returning to your regular routines.

You can begin the next meeting with a quick "check-in" about how your month has gone if you like. Select a "timer," and limit the check-in to two or three minutes, whatever time the group agrees upon. Then move along and do the regular format.

Don't hesitate to make this an intergenerational group if that works out naturally. Any composition is fine, but there is no need to keep it to only one age.

GROUND RULES FOR GROWTH GROUPS

- **Respect for each member.** Each member is responsible for her own growth, and needs to feel safe and comfortable sharing openly and honestly without fearing attack or criticism.
- **Stay away from advice or criticism.** If anyone in the group gives too much advice or criticism, gently remind her that this is not part of the ground rules.
- **Do not allow any one member to dominate the time.** It's a good idea to time the sharing so that everyone gets a fair turn, and to time other talking so that no one person dominates the time.
- **Avoid cross-talk.** Allow each person to share fully without interruption or unnecessary feedback. The purpose is to share, listen and identify with others, not to impose a particular point of view on anyone. No response to sharing is required.
- **No mood-altering beverages or chemicals.** Even smoking and eating can take you out of the moment, and may best be kept for the beginning or the end of your meeting. Simple beverages are fine.
- **Be punctual.** It's hard on group cohesion when people come in late and interrupt the flow of the sharing. Come on time and leave on time.
- **Have fun.** This group should feel like self-care, a place to share and grow and enjoy community with others. It's not therapy and should in no way feel intimidating.
- **This is *not* therapy.** For difficult issues, seek the help of a professional.

For information on meditation tapes, workshops, chats and consulting, log on to: *www.tiandayton.com.*

Appendix II

SYMPTOMS OF PTSD
(VAN DER KOLK 1994, DAYTON 2000)

1. **Learned Helplessness:** A person loses the feeling that she can affect or change what's going on, and this becomes a quality of personality.
2. **Depression:** Unexpressed and unfelt emotion may contribute to flat internal world—or agitated/anxious depression. Anger, rage and sadness that remain unfelt, unexpressed or unprocessed in a way that leads to no resolution.
3. **Emotional Constriction:** Emotional numbness and/or shutdown as a defense against overwhelming pain and threat. Restricted range of affect or authentic expression of emotion.
4. **Distorted Reasoning:** Convoluted attempts to make sense of chaotic, confusing, frightening or painful experience that feels senseless.
5. **Loss of Trust and Faith:** Because of deep ruptures in primary, dependency relationships and breakdown of an orderly world.
6. **Hypervigilance:** Anxiety, waiting for the other shoe to drop—constantly scanning environment and relationships for signs of potential danger or repeated rupture.

7. **Traumatic Bonding:** Unhealthy bonding style resulting from power imbalance in relationships and lack of other sources of support at the time trauma(s) occurred and subsequently.

8. **Loss of Ability to Take in Support:** Due to fear of trusting and depending upon relationships and PTSD's numbness and emotional shutdown.

9. **Loss of Ability to Modulate Emotion:** Go from zero to ten and ten to zero without intermediate stages, black-and-white thinking, feeling and behavior, no shades of gray as a result of trauma's numbing versus high-affect responses.

10. **Easily Triggered:** Stimuli reminiscent of trauma, e.g., yelling, loud noises, criticism, gunfire or subtle stimuli (such as vocal changes or eye movements) trigger person into shutting down, acting out or intense emotional states. Or subtle stimuli such as changes in eye expression or feeling humiliated, for example.

11. **High-Risk Behaviors:** Speeding, sexual acting out, spending, fighting or other behaviors done in a way that puts one at risk. Misguided attempts to jump-start numb inner world or act out pain from an intense pain-filled inner world.

12. **Disorganized Inner World:** Disorganized object constancy and/or sense of relatedness. Fused feelings (e.g., anger and sex).

13. **Survival Guilt:** From witnessing abuse and trauma and surviving, from "getting out" of a particular family system.

14. **Development of Rigid Psychological Defenses:** Dissociation, denial, splitting, repression, minimization, intellectualization, projection, idealization, for some examples or developing rather impenetrable "character armor."

15. **Cycles of Reenactment:** Unconscious repetition of pain-filled dynamics, the continual recreation of dysfunctional dynamics from the past.

16. **Somatic Disturbances:** The body gets traumatized as well as the mind and heart and stores trauma in its tissues and musculature.

17. **Desire to Self Medicate:** Attempts to quiet and control turbulent,

troubled inner world through the use of drugs and alcohol or behavioral addictions.

From *Trauma and Addiction* (©2000 Tian Dayton, Ph.D)

TRIUMPHING OVER AN UNSEEN ENEMY

[AUTHOR'S NOTE: The following contains excerpts from my original article. See *tiandayton.com* for complete article.]

TYPICAL REACTIONS

You may experience any number of the following reactions as a response to disasters like September 11 and be well within a normal range. You might say these are normal responses to an abnormal situation. Some may persist over time, but they should lessen as things around the situation stabilize.

INITIAL RESPONSES

Disbelief: Events don't make sense within context of normal life; life feels surreal, like a movie

Numbness: A trauma response that allows us to function through times of danger

Disorientation or confusion: Things aren't working in their normal way

Somatic disturbances: Nausea, headaches, heart racing, sweating, vomiting, muscle tension or soreness

Feelings of helplessness alternating with anger or rage

Unusual fear with an increased sense of vulnerability

Dissociation: The mind goes somewhere else; doesn't feel in sync with emotions

Clarity: A heightened sense of awareness

Ongoing Responses

Sleep disturbances: Trouble falling or staying asleep; nightmares

A shaken sense of trust and faith

Flashbacks: Snatches of memory, often frightening, that flash across the mind

Hypervigilance: Waiting for the other shoe to drop; edgy, jumpy, reactive

Free-floating anxiety: Anxiety that is not easily connected to specific events in the present

Restimulation of previous painful emotions and memories

Survival guilt: Guilt about being the one who "got away"

Continued somatic effects: Muscle tension or soreness, unusual tiredness, head- or backaches, stomach problems

Difficulty modulating emotional reactions; swinging from shutdown to high intensity, no shades of gray

Depression with feelings of **despair**

Desire to engage in **high-risk behaviors**

Impaired ability to **conceptualize a positive future**

Desire to self-medicate with drugs, alcohol, food, sex, spending, etc.

Fear for personal safety

Denial and minimization

Your Personal Response to Trauma

Everyone's reaction and ongoing responses to traumatic events vary. Factors that influence how a person reacts include:

History of prior traumatization or loss, such as death, divorce or addiction

Age or developmental level: How old was the person at the time of the traumatic event(s)?

Preexisting personality: How sensitive is the person? How resilient?

Severity of the stressor: How significant was the trauma? How many senses were involved.

Genetic predisposition: What is the person's physical makeup?

Access to support surrounding the actual events and general support system: Was the person able to talk about the event(s) and process the emotions, or did he or she have to go it alone and tough it out?

Bibliography

Amen, Daniel G. *Change Your Brain, Change Your Life.* New York: Three Rivers Press, 1998.

Baill, Cori. "Menopause Management: How to Tame Your Raging Hormones," *Speaking of Women's Health,* August 10, 2002.

Bard, Arthur S., and Mitchell G. Bard. *Understanding The Brain.* Alpha, A Pearson Education Company, 2002.

Beasley, D. "Fight versus Flight." *ABC News Internet Ventures,* 2000.

Childre, Doc. *Forgiveness—A Real Stress Buster.* HeartMath LLC, 2001.

Conway, Jim and Sally. "Women at Midlife: Finding Your Identity." *Midlife Dimensions* 2000.

Covington, Stephanie. *Helping Women Recover Curriculum: A Program for Treating Addiction.* Center City, MN: Hazelden, 1997.

Damasio, Antonio. *Descartes' Error: Emotions, Reason and the Human Brain.* New York: Avon Books, 1995.

————. *The Feeling of What Happens.* New York: Harcourt, Inc., 1999.

Dossey, Larry. *Be Careful What You Pray For . . . You Just Might Get It.* San Francisco: Harper San Francisco, 1997.

————. *Healing Words.* San Francisco: Harper San Francisco, 1993.

Dowrick, Stephanie. *Forgiveness and Other Acts of Love . . .* New York: Viking, 1997.

Enright, Robert. *Forgiveness Is a Choice*. Washington, D.C.: International Forgiveness Institute, APA Books, 2000.

————. *Helping Clients Forgive*. Washington, D.C.: International Forgiveness Institute, APA Books, 2000.

FocusOn MensHealth.com. various articles

Geary, David C. *Male, Female: The Evolution of Human Sex Differences*. Washington, D.C.: APA Books, 1998.

Gellaty, Angus, and Oscar Zarate. *Mind and Brain*. United Kingdom: Icon Books, 1998.

Goldman, Robert M., with Ronald Klatz and Lisa Berger. *Brain Fitness*. New York: Doubleday, 1998.

Goode, Erica. "Treatment Can Ease Lingering Trauma of Sept. 11." *The New York Times,* November 20, 2001.

Guindon, Mary H. "Feminist Therapy: What's It All About?" *Selfhelp Magazine,* 2002.

Gurwitch, Robin H. "Reactions and Guidelines For Children Following Trauma/ Disaster." *Psychology in Daily Life.*

Hand, Elizabeth. "Science and Fantasy." *The Washington Post,* October 29, 1995.

Howard, Pierce J. *The Owner's Manual for the Brain*. Atlanta: Bard Press, 2000.

Johnston, Victor S. *Why We Feel: The Science of Human Emotions*. New York: Perseus Books, 1999.

Kaku, Michio. *Hyperspace: A Scientific Odyssey Through Parallel Universes, Time Warps and the Tenth Dimension*. New York: Anchor, 1995.

Karen, Robert. *The Forgiving Self*. New York: Doubleday, 2001.

Kotulak, Ronald. *Inside the Brain*. Andrews McMeel Publishing, 1996.

LeDoux, Joseph. *The Synaptic Self*. New York: Viking Penguin Group, 2002.

Lerner, Harriet. *Anger Dos and Don'ts*. Topeka, Kans.: Menninger Foundation.

Lewis, Thomas, Fari Fmini and Richard Lannon. *A General Theory of Love*. New York: Vintage Books, A Division of Random House, Inc., 2000.

Luskin, Frederic. "The Art and Science of Forgiveness." *Stanford Medicine* 16, 4 (summer 1999).

————. "Forgiveness." *Healing Currents Magazine,* Sept.–Oct., 1996.

————. "The Study of Forgiveness with Victims and Offenders." A Campaign for Forgiveness Research, 1999–2001.

Lyness, Karen S. "Study Dispels Perception That Women Leave Jobs More than Men Do." *Monitor on Psychology* 33 (April 4, 2002).

"Magic Stream, What Makes People the Happiest? It's Not Money or Popularity." *Freud Online.* (*http://fly.hiwaay.net/~garson/selfesteem0301.htm.*)

Northrup, Christiane. *The Wisdom of Menopause: Creating Physical and Emotional Health During the Change.* New York: Doubleday, 2001.

————. "The Mother of All Wake-Up Calls." *Today,* April 1, 2002.

Ornish, Dean. *Love & Survival.* New York: Harper Perennial, 1998.

Ornstein, Robert, and Charles Shencionis. *The Healing Brain: A Scientific Reader.* New York: Guilford Press, 1999.

Partenheimer, David. "Breast Cancer Patients Who Actively Express Their Emotions Do Better Emotionally and Physically, Says New Study." APA Press Release, October 22, 2000.

Peeke, Pamela. "What Menopause May Mean to You." *Today,* April 2, 2002.

Pennebaker, James W. *Opening Up: The Healing Power of Expressing Emotions.* New York: Guilford Press, 1997.

Pert, Candace B. *Molecules of Emotion: Why You Feel the Way You Feel.* New York: Simon & Schuster, 1999.

"Project Rachel Helps Women Find Forgiveness After Abortion." *Salt Lake Tribune,* May 15, 1999.

Rosenthal, Norman E. *The Emotional Revolution.* Secaucus, N.J.: Citadel Press/Kensington Publishing, 2002.

Russell, Peter. *The Brain Book.* New York: Plume, 1979.

Showalter, Douglas K. "Forgive and Remember!" *A Sermon of Forgiving.* 1996.

Smith, Deborah. "Major National Studies of Women's Health Are Providing New Insights." *Monitor on Psychology* 33 (May 5, 2002).

Stanton, Annette L. "Psychotherapy May Be as Useful as Drugs in Treating Depression, Study Suggests." *APA Monitor Online* 30 (September 8, 1999).

Swanson, Naomi G. "Women Face Higher Risk at Work than Men." *Monitor on Psychology* 31 (September 8, 2000).

Thoresen, Carl E. *Spirituality and Health: Is There a Relationship?* 1999.

Vaillant, George E. *Aging Well.* New York: Little, Brown and Company, 2002.

Van der Kolk, Bessel. *Psychological Trauma.* Washington, D.C.: American Psychiatric Press, Inc., 1987.

Walsch, Neale Donald. *Forgiveness—The Greatest Healer of All.* Hillsboro, Oreg.: Beyond Words Publishing, 1999.

Wright, Rusty. "Forgiveness Can Be Good for Your Health." Probe Ministries, 2000.

Zohar, Danah. *Quantum Self: Human Nature and Consciousness Defined by the New Physics.* New York: HarperTrade, 1991.

————. *SQ: Connecting with Our Spiritual Intelligence.* San Francisco: Bloomsbury USA, 2001.

About the Author

Tian Dayton, Ph.D., T.E.P., is a therapist in private practice in New York City. In addition to her doctoral degree in clinical psychology, she holds a master's degree in educational psychology and two Montessori teaching certifications. Dr. Dayton is certified as a trainer by the American Society for Group Psychotherapy and Psychodrama (ASGPP), of which she is a fellow. She is also a winner of the ASGPP's Scholor's award and cofounder of The American Society for Experiential Therapy (ASET). She was on the faculty of the Drama Therapy Program at New York University for eight years, and is currently Director of Program Development at the Caron Foundation's Center for Self-Development and program consultant for Freedom Institute's Intensive Outpatient Program.

Dr. Dayton has been a sought-after speaker and presenter of psychodrama over the past two decades at many conferences nationwide. She has made numerous radio and TV appearances, including: MSNBC, *Montel*, *Geraldo*, *Ricki Lake*, America's Health Network, NPR and *Gary Null*. She is the author of numerous articles and twelve books, including: *Trauma and Addiction*; *Heartwounds*; *The Quiet Voice of Soul*; *The Drama Within*; Doubleday's pick of the month, *The Soul's Companion*; the recovery bestseller, *Daily*

Affirmations for Forgiving and Moving On (which is a companion to *The Magic of Forgiveness*); and *It's My Life: A Power Book for Teens,* also a bestseller. She was the editorial consultant for the award-winning film *The Process,* which features her work in psychodrama (*www.TheProcess.info*).

For further information, visit *www.tiandayton.com.*